T5-ARZ-407

Success and Failure in Monetary Reform

Success and Failure in Monetary Reform

Monetary commitment and the role of institutions

Andreas Freytag,

University of Cologne, Germany

Edward Elgar

Cheltenham, UK • Northhampton, MA, USA

Published by
Edward Elgar Publishing Limited
Glensanda House
Montpellier Parade
Cheltenham
Glos GL50 1UA
UK

Edward Elgar Publishing, Inc.
136 West Street
Suite 202
Northampton
Massachusetts 01060
USA

A catalogue record for this book
is available from the British Library

Library of Congress Cataloguing in Publication Data

Freytag, Andreas
JK Success and failure in monetary reform : monetary commitment and the role of institutions / Andreas Freytag
p.cm
Includes bibliographical references and index.
1. Monetary policy. I. Title

HG230.3 F746 2002
339.5'3–dc21

2002022080

ISBN 1 84064 817 1

Printed and bound in Great Britain by MPG Books Ltd, Bodmin, Cornwall

Contents

List of Tables and Figures

1. Tables

2. Figures

List of Abbreviations

AC	Reserve country
BLUE	Best linear unbiased estimator
BONEX	Dollar denominated Argentine government bonds
CB	Central bank
CBI	Central bank independence
CBS	Currency board system
CC	Committing country
CEO	Chief executive officer
CFA	French Franc Zone
CPI	Consumer price inflation
DEG	Deutsche Investitions- und Entwicklungsgesellschaft
ECB	European Central Bank
EMS	European Monetary System
EMU	European Monetary Union
ER	Exchange rate
ESAF	Enhanced structural adjustment facilities
ESCB	European System of Central Banks
EU	European Union
G7	Group of seven
G8	Group of eight
GDP	Gross domestic product
GNP	Gross national product
IMF	International Monetary Fund
IO(s)	International organisation(s)
JEP	Journal of Economic Perspectives
M0, M1, M2	Different monetary aggregates
ND	Normal distribution
NPB	National Bank of Poland
OECD	Organisation for Economic Co-operation and Development
OLS	Ordinary least squares
PPP	Purchasing power parity
R^2, R^2adj	Coefficient of determination
SVR	Sachverständigenrat zur Begutachtung der gesamtwirtschaflichen Entwicklung, Council of Economic Experts
USA	United States of America
UK	United Kingdom

List of Symbols and Variables

1. Symbols

φ	Adjustment parameter
α	Change in demand for real money
β	Parameter
ϕ	Cost function of inflation
ε	Error term
π	Inflation rate
δ	Weight given to seigniorage by policymakers
σ^2	Variance
*	Superscript for optimal or objective values
bd	Budget deficit
C	Commitment
CA	Current account
E	Expectation operator
^{e}	Superscript for expected values
EX	Exports
exp	Exponential function
FB	Fiscal balance
FOI	Financial opposition to inflation
G	Group in the Index of Economic Freedom
g	Growth rate
GL, GLS	Subscript for the index of Gwartney and Lawson (1997) and Gwartney, Lawson and Samida (2000), respectively
H	Number of years with inflation higher than 100 per cent p.a.
I	Set of information
IF	Institutional setting
IF_i	Institutional factor
IM	Imports
$INDEX$	Dummy for indexation
j	Country subscript
k	Cost function of expected inflation
L	Demand for real money
ln	Natural logarithm
M	Monetary base
m	Money growth rate
max	Maximise

n	Number of observations
N	Actual employment
N_n	Natural employment
P	Price level
R	Revenue
REPIN	Dummy for repressed inflation
REPRIS	Dummy for political reprisal
S	Seigniorage
s	Time, also used as subscript
SIET	Successful irregular executive transfer
SHOCK	Dummy for external shocks
t	Moment of monetary reform
u	Subscript for unweighted
UIET	Unsuccessful irregular executive transfer
v	Velocity of circulation
$w1$, $w2$, $w3$	Subscript for weighted, different weights
Y	National income
Z	Policymakers' objective function

2. Variables (used in Chapter 6)*

BAL	Proxy for growth differentials
C	Index of commitment
ACPI, *WCPI*	Proxy for post-reform inflation
EF,	Proxy for economic freedom, based on Gwartney and Lawson (1997)
EF2000	Proxy for economic freedom, based on Gwartney, Lawson and Samida (2000)
FS	Fiscal stability
LM	Labour market flexibility
OP	Openness
POI	Public opposition to inflation
PostBW	Dummy for the post Bretton Woods era
PS	Political stability
RC	Properties of the reserve currency
SEIGN	Seigniorage

* The different specifications of all variables can be found in Appendix 2.

Foreword

Monetary policy has always affected people's life to a great extent. Inflation is costly and socially unjust; it reduces economic welfare and increases distrust in markets. On the same token, it has always been very attractive to government as a means to raise public funds or reduce public debt and to spur economic activities. When the costs of inflation become unbearable for the population, governments reformed the monetary framework. In some countries, one can observe regular cycles of hyperinflation and reform.

I have been interested in the political economy of policy reform since I was a second-year undergraduate student in economics. After my first readings in political economy/public choice, I became curious why some reforms work and others do not. Whereas there is a widespread knowledge about how to explain poor economic policy using public choice, the literature on the political economy of economic policy reform does not fill libraries. There is, however, a wide and rich literature on normative aspects of reforms, including timing and sequencing of single reform steps. Thus, this book is the attempt to merge these normative strands with the positive public choice analysis.

Somewhat related to my interest in policy reform is another motivation for working on this topic: I felt increasingly uncomfortable with the literature on proper monetary frameworks. The debate concentrated almost on regimes rather than on situations. The discussion went along the following lines: do fixed or flexible exchange rates guarantee stability? Is a currency board better suited to foster macroeconomic stabilisation than an independent central bank plus a soft peg? Not enough attention has been paid to the circumstances in which a country is in when the decision on monetary frameworks is due. I found this situation rather unsatisfactory, so I decided to think about the relations between monetary policy and the institutional setting or – as it is called in the German ORDO tradition – economic order. Fortunately, since I started the project, it has turned out that I am not the only one who wants to know more about these relations. The literature on institutional aspects of monetary policy is increasing.

While I finished this study, I have benefited very much from enormous help by a number of friends and colleagues. First, I would like to mention the stimulating atmosphere at the Institut für Wirtschaftspolitik an der Universität zu Köln. I am particularly grateful to Juergen B. Donges, who not only supervised the whole project, but who also made extremely valuable comments on all parts and at all stages of the project. I could learn very much from his incredible feeling for policy relevance. I also thank my colleagues Pia Weiss and Stefan Mai who went through the manuscript carefully several times. Last but not least, it was a pleasure to discuss the project with Hans Willgerodt, whose encyclopaedic knowledge about monetary policy in the 20th century proved extremely helpful.

I am also indebted to John Wood with whom I spent much time at the University of Cambridge during the winter of 1997/98 and who since then has always been willing to read parts of the project and to discuss single issues extensively. To share his knowledge in the history of central banking enabled me to improve my judgement on monetary policy. During my stay in Cambridge, I had the opportunity to discuss the issue widely in particular I would like to emphasise Willem H. Buiter, whose comments clarified a number of questions. I also received many helpful comments and criticisms from Thomas Mayer and many – partly unknown – colleagues in seminars and conferences, held in Germany as well as abroad.

An earlier version of the book has been accepted by the Faculty for Economics and Social Science of the University of Cologne as Habilitationsschrift. In addition, it is my pleasure to thank Edward Elgar and his staff. As usual, the collaboration with them was excellent. Finally, I gratefully acknowledge financial aid by the Otto Wolff-Stifung. Without this generous support, I would have been unable to successfully carry out such an endeavour.

December 2001 Andreas Freytag

1. Introduction

I. THE PROBLEM

The 20th century witnessed many periods of high and chronic inflation, sometimes even hyperinflation, and numerous attempts to counteract these. We have identified more than 70 monetary reforms world-wide since World War I. The post-war history of monetary policy can be roughly divided into four phases. The 1920s and 1930s were characterised by economic instability. Until 1924, the main problem was high inflation, particularly in Europe. This changed remarkably afterwards when inflation rates were low, partly even negative, and the world was hit by the depression. Part of the statistically low inflation was due to repressed prices. World War II added to the problems. Directly after the war, inflation rates in many of the countries involved were once again very high. The second phase began with the establishment of the Bretton Woods system. In its era, there was in general a reasonably high stability world-wide; only very few examples of high inflation can be found. 1973 marked the end of this phase when the Bretton Woods system was abandoned. The following two decades were characterised by severe monetary crises, in particular in the developing countries. In some Latin American countries, hyperinflation occurred, while others, like Israel, had to deal with chronic inflation for many years. In addition, industrialised countries also suffered from annual inflation rates which were higher than usual. As for the fourth phase, the 1990s can be defined as a decade of disinflation. Not only industrialised countries, but also parts of the developing world have been very successful in this respect. To give a few examples, many countries in transition, for instance the Czech Republic, Slovakia, Hungary and Poland, as well as some Latin American economies, e.g. Brazil and Argentina, have managed to reduce inflation remarkably. Generally speaking, the consciousness for monetary stability and – even more important – for its threats has increased across the world. Some observers even think of the 'New Economy' to come with high real growth rates and low inflation rates.

This certainly seems too optimistic. In a paper money standard, inflation cannot be regarded as being definitely eradicated. This critical judgement is based on the cause of inflation which today is identified as being a monetary phenomenon. Money growth exceeding growth of GDP (plus the decrease in the velocity of circulation) is responsible for a rising price level. In general, the causes of excessive money growth are deficiencies in other policy fields. Mainly fiscal problems and labour market distortions contribute to the pressure on monetary policymakers to raise the money supply as a means to eliminate these difficulties. Monetary policymakers do not operate in isolation from other politicians, bureaucrats and interest groups. On the contrary, they have to bear permanent pressure to increase money supply and thereby support the government in fulfilling its tasks. The major problem arising from this constellation is the problem of credibility. If the public believes that monetary policy will be used for other objectives than price stability and, thus, a positive inflation rate is likely, aggregate individual behaviour will be inconsistent with price stability. From the central banker's point of view, there is a choice among two evils. If the monetary authority remained austere, unemployment or fiscal deficits would be the consequence, raising pressure to increase money supply. If the authority conceded, its monetary policy would be incredible. A vicious circle could result from the lack of credibility.

Thus, inflation on the whole is a political economy problem. If it is true that it is not '...an exaggeration to say that history is largely a history of inflation, and usually inflation engineered by governments and for the gain of governments – ...' (von Hayek 1990, p. 34), it cannot be ruled out that the future has similarly dark prospects on offer. In other words, it is highly plausible that inflation will remain a problem in the future. Even today, there are some countries which suffer from rising inflation, among them European countries. In some it might become necessary to reform the monetary regime in due course.

Therefore, it makes sense to analyse monetary reforms theoretically and empirically. The results of this research will be the base for a discussion of policy options for those countries where the actual monetary regime proves insufficient to combat inflationary pressures. Consequently, this study deals with the question of why monetary reforms sometimes do succeed and sometimes do not. Obviously in the latter cases, the credibility of the new monetary regime is not sufficient. So, formulated precisely: which are the determinants that make a monetary reform credible?

II. A NEW APPROACH TO ANALYSE MONETARY REFORM

a) State of the art

Credibility of monetary policy has been in the focus of the economic literature for more than two decades since Kydland and Prescott (1977) published their pathbreaking article. Due to the importance of credibility, an exact and generally accepted definition of credibility would be useful, but cannot be found. A good approximation is to define a monetary policy announcement as being credible if the public's beliefs about future monetary policy are in line with the announced policy. Under the assumption that the public forms rational expectations, it will be able to assess a monetary policy announcement. An originally optimal monetary policy then may turn out to be suboptimal after a while, if the announcement differs from the believed future course of monetary policy. Dynamic inconsistency occurs which has been analysed widely. The unanimous result of the respective literature is that commitment to rules rather than discretion allows for credible monetary policy.

The question concerning the determinants of a monetary reform's credibility raised at the end of the foregoing subsection has not yet been answered satisfactorily. This is due to some characteristics of the literature on credibility and commitment. In general, a regime switch is not its focus. This causes two shortcomings with respect to the problem of this study: (1) concepts of monetary commitment existing in the literature are not comprehensive enough. Often, some decisive features of commitment are ignored. (2) the institutional constraints to credibility of monetary commitment are mainly neglected. (3) But even if the analysis explicitly deals with a monetary reform, the regime switch is in general not analysed comprehensively. Only single aspects of the problem are examined.

Ad (1): in macroeconomic analyses only limited credit is given to the complex nature of commitment. Repeatedly, it is interpreted as the commitment to an inflation rate, e.g. zero inflation. However, commitment is correctly interpreted as a rule, more precisely a monetary regime (Brennan and Buchanan 1981). This rule should be as comprehensive and transparent as possible to allow the public to evaluate future monetary policy. It also should contain details about the exchange rate policy and convertibility restriction. Even indicators of central bank independence do not fulfil this requirement for they do not include the external monetary relations which often go beyond the responsibility of central banks. This leads to the fundamental question of who commits to the monetary regime; a number of important contributions focus narrowly on commitments of central bankers (e.g. Rogoff 1985; Vickers 1986 Walsh 1995). It seems plausible that this focus only relocates the underlying principal-agent problems (McCallum 1997).

Ad (2): countries differ in many institutional respects, e.g. concerning their political system, their fiscal policies or the organisation of their labour market. Because of the political nature of inflation, a thorough analysis has to take into account the interdependencies of the monetary regime and institutional aspects. In other words: elements of the economic order are closely interrelated. Many studies on monetary commitment neglect these institutional constraints to the credibility and success of monetary commitment.

Ad (3): even the literature on monetary reforms and stabilisation programmes often concentrates on single aspects. Most studies separate the analysis into economic policy areas. For instance exchange rate policy, monetary policy and trade policy are dealt with in single chapters or sections (e.g. Little et al. 1993). There is no theory about why some monetary reforms fail and others do not, considering the interdependence of the monetary regime and other institutions. A monetary reform which is pursued without observance of institutional features in the country can only by chance be successful.[1]

These omissions might have consequences for the quality of a monetary regime in a reform attempt. In particular, two dangers resulting from these shortcomings have to be mentioned. First, it cannot be excluded that proposals for monetary reform are based on textbook versions of monetary regimes which are compared with existing and – necessarily – imperfect monetary regimes (Kenen 1994, pp. 2f). If these textbook versions are applied to the imperfect world, there is no guarantee that the success of the reform is achieved automatically. Second, if differences between countries are overlooked, reform proposals may come 'off the peg'. Again, the monetary reform might fail because it is not adjusted to the situation in the respective country. This danger is especially great if monetary reformers follow the advice of those advisers favouring a certain monetary regime. The latter may be tempted to search for countries where their favourite regime can be applied.

Apart from the fact that the failure of a monetary regime implemented via a reform is costly for the respective country, there is a reputational loss for this policy rule in case of failure. It may well be the case that the monetary regime implemented through the reform and which eventually failed fits in

---

1 This does not affect the generally accepted necessity to control the money growth to make the reform work (see Chapter 2, section II).

general. The reason for the failure may be the fact that due to the above-mentioned weaknesses the implementation of the monetary regime has not been careful enough. But even if the reform proposal is not implemented, but only repeatedly advocated, monetary systems can suffer enormous discredit. First-best proposals and superficial advice cause principally good proposals to be politically difficult to enforce.

An example underlining this topic is the handling of the so-called 'Washington Consensus'. This contains ten elements of economic order proven to be welfare-enhancing and compatible with a free and open society.[2] For many policy advisers including the so-called Washington institutions (IMF and World Bank), it is desirable to reform economic policy along the lines of this blueprint. The Washington Consensus can be interpreted as a normative manual for policy reformers. Their remaining task is to search for the necessary majority to push through the reform.

Although the Consensus seems economically reasonable, it has often been questioned and the proponents have been criticised and accused of simplifying the nature of the problem of economic order, especially in developing countries. To propose the Washington Consensus as a remedy for all countries with economic problems, without carefully taking the institutional setting into consideration, can politically discredit the meaningful proposal as such and weaken the position of reformers who generally agree with the elements of the Consensus.

b) Aims and scope of the study

The existing literature obviously does not fully explore the economics of monetary reforms. Interconnections are overlooked since matters are treated separately. To fill this gap is the primary objective of the study. The determinants of credibility of monetary reforms are to be examined. It has to be analysed why reform attempts with similar concepts have created very different results or why countries with extremely different monetary regimes after comparable monetary problems reach corresponding inflation rates. For this purpose, we first have to develop a comprehensive concept of commitment – as a monetary regime including rules for domestic monetary policy as well as external financial relations.[3] In a subsequent part, the role of institutions for the success of a monetary reform has to be analysed carefully. The institutions – formal or informal, created or spontaneously evolved – affecting credibility have to be identified and operationalised. The theoretical

---

2 For a list of elements and their description see Williamson (1994, pp. 26–28).

3 To make clear the comprehensiveness, throughout the study we use the term 'monetary reform' instead of 'currency reform' which occasionally is used alternatively. The term 'monetary reform' indicates a regime switch whereas the latter term seems to be narrower, restricted to the introduction of a new currency.

analysis should lead to unambiguous hypotheses which can be assessed empirically. An empirical test of the theoretical findings will also be the subject of the study. At the end of the process, there should be a clear statement on the determinants of credibility and success of monetary reforms.

The findings of the theoretical and empirical analysis are employed to answer the question, which type of monetary regime is most likely to make a monetary reform a success given the institutional setting in a potential reform country? To be of use for the design of monetary policy after a period of low stability, the study has to generate policy options for countries with monetary problems which avoid the two dangers mentioned above. Following this reasoning, policy recommendations have to be differentiated in that they are not simple textbook versions of monetary regimes. Moreover, they have to be carefully adjusted to the underlying problems that induce the government to rely on money growth for other policy areas and thus cause inflation, as well as to institutional features in the country willing to reform. That does not exclude that monetary reforms are accompanied by reforms of other elements of economic order, e.g. fiscal reform. Whereas the institutional setting is regarded as being exogenous in the theoretical and empirical analysis, it is seen as being interdependent with monetary policy in the policy-oriented enquiry. In addition, the study is made against the background of policymaking in democratic societies. Although the economic causes of inflation do not differ between democratic and undemocratic societies, it has to be analysed in a democratic surrounding. Thus, it has to be considered that reform options also have to be implemented in such a political setting.[4]

Given the broad scope of the subject 'monetary reform', one has to restrict the research topic without cutting off important issues. The subject is strictly limited to the analytical and policy-oriented objectives mentioned above. Thus, we do not want to discuss the origins of inflation in greater detail than necessary to understand reform. In addition, at least as regards the theoretical analysis no attempt is made to understand what has induced the government to change the monetary regime. It is assumed that it is willing and determined to pursue a monetary reform that stops inflation. Only in the part of the study where policy options are discussed, this topic has to be raised when dealing with the enforcement of reform proposals. Buchanan (1983) divides the analysis of monetary policy and reform into three stages: first, alternative policy measures under a given regime are discussed. This is the subject of monetary economics, especially monetary theory. Second, the necessity of a regime switch is analysed. Third, the question is discussed,

4 Inflation can also occur in undemocratic societies. The positive analysis is also valid for such regimes. However, implementation problems differ from democratic societies and will not be subject of the study.

which regime among the given set of alternatives is more desirable? We neglect the first stage, regard the discussion on the second stage as settled in that the need for a regime switch is not doubted any longer, and concentrate almost completely on the third stage. Despite this restriction, the issue covered by the study is extensive. This has implications for the methodological stance of the study.

c) The ORDO approach as methodological foundation

The ORDO approach of the Freiburg School of Law and Economics emphasises the importance of rules in economic policy. An economic order is a set of rules agreed on by the citizens in consensus. Thus, there is a distinction between the rules of the game and the game itself. The main principle is co-ordination through markets as opposed to sub-ordination through a hierarchically centralised system. Each economic order consists of components such as the monetary regime, the foreign trade regime, the labour market regime etc. Ideally, each economic policy field is left to a specialised agency. Following this view, one agency, be it a central bank or a currency board or the like, is exclusively responsible for monetary policy. There are no other duties for this agency. The logic behind this restriction is to avoid trade-offs between two policy objectives as confirmed by Tinbergen (1952).

In addition, the components of economic order strongly depend on each other with monetary policy being regarded as a very important one (Eucken 1955). For example, volatile inflation resulting from a bad monetary policy has an impact on the labour market. Relative prices do no longer reflect scarcities. As a consequence, wages may also no longer reflect scarcities and full employment may be missed, even if the labour market regime in principle is compatible with full employment. One implication of the interdependence of parts of the economic order is that a monetary reformer is forced to take into account the other components of economic order. In other words, following the ORDO approach, institutions are important for the design of a monetary reform. Thus, this approach is exactly suited to be the methodological foundation of the study.

The normative objective of ORDO is to search for an appropriate economic order (choice of rules). This has two advantageous consequences for our purpose: first, the neglect of institutions is overcome. They can be incorporated into the analysis as constraints for monetary policy. Second, a high priority is given to economic policy. In this sense, it is a constructivist approach as the institutional constraints are deliberately created and have a mainly formal character. To complete the picture, one has to add in those institutions that evolve spontaneously and those that are informal rather than formal.[5] One weakness of the ORDO school is that the attempt to be more realistic may create a lack of formal elegance and theoretical rigour. This is particularly important for empirical work since econometric models need to be based on theoretical models.

This weakness can be overcome with the help of macroeconomics which has modelled monetary policy and commitment very well. The analysis is mainly based on neo-classical techniques. Having said this, the macroeconomic results are very precise and can be easily assessed if the assumptions are made clear. Therefore, a macroeconomic model is developed as theoretical ground for the econometric analysis. The model has to capture the main findings of the theoretical analysis, i.e. it should operate with a comprehensive concept of commitment and institutional constraints to monetary reform. Following this reasoning, the quality of the macroeconomic model depends on the richness of the institutional analysis with the ORDO approach.

Consequently, we regard the two approaches as being complementary rather than substitutional. It makes sense to combine them. As for the results in a positive and normative respect, similar conclusions can be derived from both perspectives. It is acknowledged that high inflation is caused by excessive money supply which has its roots in failures in other policy fields and pressures from vested interests. This is a political economy issue. As for the policy conclusions, monetary commitment is a crucial device to make a monetary reform credible and thus to stabilise an economy, in particular after a period of high and volatile inflation. As it will become clear throughout the study, thinking in the tradition of ORDO is best suited to tackle the problem at hand. It forces to add institutions into the analysis and to focus on policy relevance. To understand the nature of monetary reforms demands an acknowledgement of economic order, albeit with neo-classical underpinning.

III. PLAN OF THE STUDY

The study consists of nine chapters, including the introduction. The theoretical foundations are laid in Chapters 2 through 4. In *Chapter 2*, we investigate why the concept of credibility is so important in monetary policy and how credibility can be enhanced through a commitment to a new monetary regime after severe inflation. The chapter starts with a theoretical and empirical review of the economic costs of inflation leading to the

5 It has to be emphasised that the ORDO school also takes notice of informal and spontaneous institutions. See Vanberg (1998, p. 174).

question of why inflation occurs. High inflation is caused by money growth which is rooted in deficiencies in other policy areas – the topic of Chapter 2, section II. In particular, the difficulties to raise revenues induces governments to increase the money supply. Instead of solving fiscal problems, inflation creates future inflationary expectations. A monetary reform has a chance to break these expectations, if it is credible. The role of commitment to enhance credibility is discussed in the third section. It begins with some remarks on the assignment problem reiterating the – mainly technical – relevance of Tinbergen's law. It is then shown theoretically that monetary commitment changes the calculus of government in that it makes inflation politically costly. Commitment is related to the overall economic order which makes it necessary to clarify hitherto underexposed questions on the upholder of commitment and on the compatibility of commitment and democracy. In the fourth section, a first empirical appraisal of these –rather general – theoretical considerations is given by presenting an overview on the empirical literature on the causal relation between commitment and macroeconomic performance. It turns out that the commonly used concept of central bank independence (CBI) is only a weak approximation of commitment. Consequently, in the final section, a comprehensive index of legal commitment is developed.

Chapter 3 is dedicated to a detailed analysis of institutional constraints to commitment. After a short introduction the institutional factors affecting the success of monetary commitment are discussed. These institutional factors are political stability, fiscal stability, labour market flexibility, openness of the country, in particular to trade, the public attitude to inflation and some properties of a reserve currency. As an alternative to the thus defined institutional setting, the concept of economic freedom is introduced. Some preliminary conclusions complete the chapter.

In *Chapter 4*, the findings of the preceding chapters are integrated to form a positive theory of monetary reform. In the first section, we define monetary reforms before different monetary regimes are introduced as prototypes for a monetary reform. Three principal systems can be distinguished: a central bank system, a currency board system and the denationalisation of money. Second, each prototype is assigned to a range of the degree of commitment. The considerations are then formalised in a model to calculate the relation between the degree of legal commitment, the institutional setting in the country and the resulting level of post-reform inflation. This model is based on a standard macroeconomic approach. The chapter concludes with the discussion of an ex-ante proxy for credibility as a means to assess whether or not a planned monetary reform will have a positive impact on the expectations of the public prior to the reform. This proxy reflects the necessity of the monetary commitment to be compatible with the institutional setting.

The theoretical considerations are subject to empirical assessment in Chapters 5 through 7. This part of the study commences with an overview on monetary reforms in the 20th century in *Chapter 5*. Some common features and peculiarities are discussed briefly. In this chapter, we also introduce monetary reforms which seem appropriate for the econometric analysis and for case studies.

In *Chapter 6*, the theoretical findings are assessed econometrically. First, the model developed in chapter 4 is transformed into an econometric model. Second, the best suiting specifications of the variables for commitment and institutional factors – which are developed in the *Appendices* – are chosen. Third, a cross-sectional ordinary least square (OLS) estimation of the model is pursued. The results do not allow us to reject the theoretical considerations. Monetary commitment as well as institutional constraints are determinants of success and failure of monetary reforms. In addition, the ex-ante proxy for credibility contributes to an explanation of success and failure of monetary reforms. Other variables such as the need for seigniorage and a dummy for the post-Bretton Woods era also add to the explanation. In the fourth section, the results are discussed in detail. Finally, the potential for policy simulation is checked.

Not least because of the diversity of the econometric sample, it is necessary to back the statistical evidence by case studies. This is done in *Chapter 7*. On the whole, 12 monetary reforms are investigated. In the first section, they are categorised into complete successes, moderate successes and failures. In subsequent sections, the importance of monetary commitment, institutional factors and additional determinants of success are discussed, quoting evidence from one or more of the cases. It turns out that the institutional factors do not contribute equally to the fate of a monetary reform. In addition, they have varying importance in different countries. Lessons from the empirical part including both the econometric analysis and case studies are drawn.

In *Chapter 8*, policy options are discussed. The chapter starts with an analysis of how to implement a monetary reform in political reality. Special emphasis is put on the role of economic advisers and on external support. Second, special lessons for a successful monetary reform derived from the preceding parts are summarised. Third, candidates for reform are identified. The dark prospects of sub-Saharan Africa are discussed briefly in this section. In the fourth section, policy simulations for five countries, namely Russia, Venezuela, Ecuador, Argentina and Poland are carried out. Both in the public discussion and the academic literature, reform proposals for these countries were recently made. These proposals are analysed against the background of the theoretical and empirical findings in two subsequent sections.

The study ends with a summary and conclusions in *Chapter 9.*

2. Inflation, Credibility and Monetary Commitment

I. THE ECONOMIC COSTS OF INFLATION

This study is about monetary reform after inflation. Since normally reforms are made after periods of severe inflation we restrict our analysis to annual inflation rates of 10 per cent or more. It is worth while to distinguish two typical patterns of the course of inflation: chronic inflation and hyperinflation (Végh 1995, p. 38). Chronic inflation persists for years with medium to high, at any rate volatile annual inflation rates. The annual rates vary between 10 per cent and several hundreds, per cent (Végh 1995; Fischer 1981). The normative judgement of a 10 per cent inflation depends on the perspective one has. To reach 10 per cent inflation per year within two or three years after the start of a disinflation programme, is certainly a success. To be stuck with 10 per cent over 15 or more years after the reform can no longer be called a success. Moreover, whereas in the first instance costs spring from disinflation, in the latter case there are costs of inflation (see below).

Hyperinflation is at odds with chronic inflation. Following Cagan (1956) we define hyperinflation as inflation rates of equal to or more than 50 per cent per month. Normally, hyperinflation does not last as long as chronic inflation for the cost of it in the short run is much higher than in cases of chronic inflation (especially when wages, taxes etc. are indexed). Hyperinflations are characterised by decreasing real balances, increasing dollarisation, an enormous public budget deficit, partly caused by the hyperinflation itself (Oliveira–Tanzi effect), an undervaluation of the domestic currency on the foreign exchange markets and a bad reputation of the government (Bernholz 1995, pp. 263–270). These properties also make hyperinflation very costly.

a) Theoretical considerations

Inflation is never without costs, no matter which level it reaches; economic costs are not restricted to chronic inflation and hyperinflation.[1] Even if it is fully anticipated, there are costs: first, there is an excess burden (Bailey 1956); second, the holdings of money are not optimal; third, there are menu costs; and fourth, if marginal tax rates are progressive the real tax burden rises. Inflation causes particularly high costs if it is chronic or in case of hyperinflation. In this case, it can only be imperfectly anticipated. The most important costs are associated with inefficient allocation of factors and distortions in the use of resources and with the distribution of wealth and income. In the following, we briefly remind the reader of the costs associated with inflation.

1. The informational content of prices is reduced or destroyed by inflation. An increase in prices cannot be traced back unambiguously to changing scarcities. The reason could also be inflation. Prices no longer function as signals indicating new entrepreneurial chances. Resources will not be allocated to their best use.
2. In addition, information about scarcities becomes obsolete faster than in times of stability. Economic agents then have to use resources to obtain the correct information which is costly (De Gregorio 1992; Murphy, Shleifer and Vishny 1990).
3. The real interest rate can become negative if the inflation rate has been underestimated at the time when a contract on a credit has been signed or a bond has been purchased. Money loses its function as a storage of value. This has negative distributive consequences. The borrower gains at the expense of the lender.
4. However, if the inflation rate has been overestimated, the real interest rate is rather high. Then, the distributive effect is exactly opposite: the lender gains at the expense of the borrower. Fisher (1924, pp. 6–9), therefore, argues that deflation is as undesirable as inflation. He goes even further by making the point that after hyperinflation no efforts should be made to bring the prices down to a pre-inflation level. The distributive effects are too arbitrary.
5. As a consequence of (3) and (4), this experience will cause people to avoid investment at home (see Keynes 1924). They either purchase durable goods or they invest abroad. Inflation can cause capital flight. In the long run, intertemporal markets will lose their importance and

[1] For a comprehensive analysis see e.g. Glaß (1996, pp. 14–26), IMF ((a), October 1996, pp. 116–125), Bofinger, Reischle and Schächter (1996, pp. 76–96) and Laidler and Parkin (1975, pp. 786–794).

eventually will be abandoned completely. This will deter foreign direct investment. Lower real investment will reduce employment and growth. Both will *ceteris paribus* be lower than in case of long-term monetary stability.

6. High and volatile inflation also diminish savings. If individuals cannot ensure that they keep the real value of capital plus an adequate rate of return for holding savings, they will spend their income on consumption. This also has negative consequences on growth and employment (see (5)).
7. It is even unclear whether the public budget can be improved when the government monetises its deficits. On the one hand, bonds held by the central bank and the public devalue regularly. The real value of the bonds is lower at the time of repayment than at the time of issuing. The government gains from this devaluing. On the other hand, inflation reduces real tax revenues since the tax payment can be delayed. However, if marginal tax rates are progressive with respect to nominal income or capital and tax deductions are limited to a nominal value, the real value of tax revenues increases. To sum up, the net effect on the real public budget is a priori not clear. Only if the government is able to force the public to buy its bonds, it will certainly gain from inflation tax. Moreover, nominal seigniorage is higher if the government systematically varies the inflation rate (Johnson 1977). There is an incentive for the government to be dishonest.
8. The pattern of consumption is not constant when inflation is extremely volatile. If this period persists, firms are unable to predict the potential turnover (in terms of volumes). Their success becomes very arbitrary and does not depend on properties like product quality and entrepreneurial abilities.
9. Finally, inflation reduces the social consensus within a society if certain groups systematically lose whereas others win. For instance, wage negotiations become more controversial since future inflation rate is not predicable.[2] It will only be obvious a posteriori whether the real income has risen or fallen. Either employees or employers will be discontent with the result: if real wages have fallen, unions will put in another demand for higher salaries; in the second case, people will be dismissed. At any rate, the social climate suffers from inflation.

Naturally, these costs are the lowest if the inflation rate is moderate and constantly high over a long period. People then are able to successfully adjust to inflation by indexing their contracts or by concentrating on the conclusion

---

[2] It is never exactly predicable, but the mean variation of the prediction reaches a considerable value in case of high and volatile inflation rates.

of short-term contracts. Similarly, costs of inflation are highest if inflation rates are very high and volatile. In other words: the higher the costs of inflation, the less people are able to anticipate them.

b) Some empirical evidence

In this subsection, we briefly assess empirically how inflation affects other macroeconomic variables such as employment, growth and investment. The evidence is relatively unambiguous as regards inflation and economic growth. Countries with high inflation grow slower than countries with stable price levels. Estimating a sample of over 100 countries from 1960 to 1990, Barro (1995) comes to the conclusion that this negative correlation is particularly high when inflation rates are higher than 10 per cent. The negative effect of inflation on growth has a seemingly low magnitude: an increase in average inflation by ten percentage points leads to a loss of growth by approximately 0.2 to 0.3 per cent. However, in the long run the loss in gross domestic product (GDP) is remarkable. He also shows that investment is negatively correlated with inflation. Similar results are estimated by De Gregorio (1992), Grimes (1991) and Fry, Goodhart and Almeida (1996, pp. 13–26) who analyse the correlation of inflation and growth for Latin America and The Bank of England Group, respectively. Again the results are more convincing for countries with high inflation rates. Nevertheless, Grimes (1991) as well as Ghosh and Phillips (1998) show that even very low inflation rates are very likely to reduce economic growth rates. Lucas (1996, pp. 668f), on the other hand, reports a lack in relationship between economic growth and inflation. He also concludes that inflation and unemployment are not associated. At least, there is no evidence for the negatively sloped long-run Phillips curve (see section III).

We also find that other theoretical considerations can be confirmed by the history of hyperinflations. During the German hyperinflation 1922/23,[3] the government had enormous difficulties to collect enough taxes to cover the costs. The tax policy was changed: the relative importance of direct taxes diminished whereas indirect taxes gained importance, especially by shifting the tax base from volumes to values. It could also be observed that banks did not want to take on small banking accounts. Savings, therefore, declined sharply. Not only did consumption increase relatively, but also the pattern of consumption was permanently changing. This made it difficult for the state agency for statistics to figure out the correct inflation rate. Finally, unemployment increased during the last month of hyperinflation to about 25 per cent. Moreover, it seems that a special group, namely the members of unions, was especially hit by unemployment. Furthermore, the distributive

[3] For this paragraph see Kiehling (2000).

effects were regarded as being extremely unjust: a few people gained at the expense of the majority. The last two points indicate that inflation enhances social tensions.

II. THE NEED FOR CREDIBILITY (AFTER A PERIOD OF HIGH INFLATION)

a) The monetary character of inflation

There can be no doubt that inflation is a monetary phenomenon. The theoretical argument for the monetary character of inflation is given by the quantity theory of money.[4] Money is a veil that is used to value and trade real stocks and flows in the economy. Their scarcity cannot be overcome by monetary expansion. Therefore, money determines the price level (*P*), at least in the long run. The quantity equation is the formalisation of this argument:

$$M \cdot v = Y \cdot P \text{, or in the dynamic form}^{5} \quad (2.1)$$
$$gM + gv = gY + gP \quad (2.2)$$

This is the basis of monetary policy regardless of the monetary regime. Prudent monetary policymakers, thus, take into account the quantity equation when pursuing monetary policy. They are only requested to increase the stock of money (*M*) to the same extent as national income (*Y*) deducting the increase in the velocity of circulation (*v*) which in turn is the inverse of the demand for money (*L*). Higher monetary expansion leads to a higher aggregate demand on the markets for goods and services which *ceteris paribus* meets a constant supply. Therefore, the price level inevitably rises.[6] The empirical picture is unambiguous. In a simple correlation between average annual monetary growth rates and average annual inflation from 1960 to 1990 for 110 countries, McCandless and Weber (1995) show that nearly all points lie on the 45-degree line with a very high correlation,

4 For a survey on the quantity theory of money see Friedman (1987). See also the survey in Laidler and Parkin (1975).

5 In the following, *g* stands for growth rates.

6 Only under Keynesian assumptions, i.e. fixed prices, inflation can be prevented and economic activity will be stimulated (Vane and Thompson, 1992, chapter 2 and pp. 77–80).

regardless whether M0, M1 or M2 has been chosen as the proper monetary aggregate. This leads Lucas (1996, p. 668) to the conclusion that „...the prediction that prices respond proportionally to changes in money in the long run,..., has received ample – I would say decisive – confirmation, in data from many times and places.“.[7] Other explanations for inflation, such as varying exchange rates, price for oil or other commodities and an output gap (IMF (a), October 1996, pp. 114f), seem plausible only at first glance. If, and only if, after the occurrence of a shock described there the central bank accommodates the need for more money, an inflationary process starts. Otherwise, there only will be real effects after real shocks. The effects of these shocks may be cushioned by flexible prices.

So, why can inflation happen, given its negative economic consequences? The dynamic form of the quantity theory seems to be rather simple, given the transmission mechanism is wellknown and given there are no forecast errors. As for the transmission mechanism, it is not very wellknown (Tietmeyer and Willeke 1996, pp. 44f). Moreover, the policymaker has to estimate the future development of both Y and v. The monetary growth rate will be based on these forecasts. Sometimes, it may seem necessary to allow for a minimum of inflation, since there could be sticky prices; due to psychological reasons, it seems to be easier to raise prices than to lower them. In this case, there will be a small rate of inflation making structural changes easier. Anyway, these problems do not cause severe and long-lasting inflation.

In addition, we have to take into account that forecasts can be erroneous. On the one hand, the monetary authorities may overestimate the growth rate of national income or underestimate the change in velocity of circulation. Then, monetary expansion is too high. The price level rises faster than planned (normally with a time-lag). On the other hand, the policymaker may underestimate national income growth or overestimate the change in velocity. In this case, the price level has to fall. If prices are sticky, the economy will face a recession. But forecast errors are not systematic. This can be expressed in equation (2.3):

$$m = g^e Y + g^e P - g^e v + \varepsilon \qquad (2.3),$$

where ε is the error term with $\varepsilon \sim \text{ND}(0, \sigma_\varepsilon^2)$; *ND* stands for normal distribution, g^e denotes growth rates, expected by the government. However, forecast errors can only be responsible for small rates of inflation. Moreover, inflation cannot become chronic. Policymakers who create inflation through a

[7] Needless to say that Lucas has changes in money beyond growth of the production potential in mind.

wrong estimation of future national income or velocity of circulation eventually will learn and try to improve their performance. Thus, it is completely impossible to trace back severe inflation, let alone hyperinflation, to forecast errors.

b) A political economy explanation of inflation

Thus, there must be different reasons for inflation. Whereas until in the early 1970s, macroeconomic theory used to model policymakers as being benevolent dictators who try to maximise an aggregate welfare function, this has changed since then. Monetary policymakers are seen as individuals with personal interests (Persson and Tabellini 1990). These interests are incorporated in an objective function of the following general form:

$$Z = f(\underset{-}{\pi}, \underset{+}{N}, \underset{+}{S}, \underset{+}{CA}, \ldots) \qquad (2.4).$$

Z denotes the utility of the policymaker, π, the rate of inflation, N stands for employment, S for seigniorage and CA denotes the balance of the current account. The policymaker is assumed to maximise Z with respect to π.[8] Thus, it can be taken for granted that, in most cases, inflation is created deliberately by governments who use monetary policy to achieve other than monetary objectives which are a part of Z. Obviously, the policymakers lack policy instruments or face distortions so that these objectives cannot be met without the help of monetary policy. The prevalent political motives for inflation are the employment motive, the balance-of-payments motive and the revenue motive (Cukierman 1992, chapters 3 through 5; Newlyn 1962, pp. 148–166).[9]

The employment motive

In this context, the government makes use of the alleged money illusion of the public, meaning it does not recognise the surprise inflation at once. The supply of labour then will rise and employment will increase. A short-run Phillips relation exists which can be expressed in equation (2.5):

$$N - N_n = \varphi(m - m^e) \text{ where } \varphi > 0 \qquad (2.5).$$

---

8 The arguments in the objective function can be interpreted as proxies for the utility of the policymaker in charge. Her/his personal utility may also depend on being in office or on the preferences of her/his constituencies (Alesina and Tabellini 1988). Yet, choosing the arguments in (2.4) provides for the advantage that they are observable.

9 This is a very general political economy discussion of monetary policy. For a more detailed analysis see the papers in Mayer (1990), especially the contribution by Hetzel (1990).

The difference between natural employment (N_n) and actual employment (N) is equivalent to the monetary expansion where φ denotes the adjustment parameter for the deviation of money growth (m) from the expected money growth (m^e). Especially before a general election, it sometimes seems attractive to use monetary expansion to create a political business cycle.[10] To put it differently, policymakers act as if they believe in the money illusion of the public (Mueller 1989, p. 286). McCallum (1997) suggests that much of the inflation from the 1960s through the 1980s can be explained by the widespread belief among politicians in the negatively sloped Phillips curve.

Inflation on grounds of the employment motive of policymakers can lead to more employment only via two channels. One is adaptive expectations, that is the public forms its expectation only by considering the past. If the government raises inflation every year, the public never will be able to anticipate the inflation rate of the following year properly. Thus, employment will remain above its natural level N_n. However, the adaptive expectation hypothesis only has limited explanatory power. It presumes that individuals are not able and/or willing to learn from past experience. Assuming rational expectations (see below), instead, leads to the second channel of inflation. The policymaker has private information about the economic environment and/or about his own attitude and properties which the public does not have. In this case, it may be possible to betray the public, at least in the short run.[11] Theoretical analyses and empirical observation suggest that monetary policy is an inappropriate means to raise employment permanently. The long-run Phillips curve is not negatively sloped (e.g. Friedman 1987, pp. 25f and Broaddus 1995).

The balance-of-payments motive

Sometimes, it seems politically appealing to increase the inflation rate when the current account is in persistent deficit. The government uses monetary expansion as a device to reduce the current account deficit.[12] In a flexible exchange rate regime, inflation causes the domestic currency to devalute (in nominal terms) compared to foreign currencies. Provided a normal reaction of trade flows, i.e. the Marshall–Lerner condition holds,[13] the

---

10 See Belke (1996, pp. 7-157) for a comprehensive survey. See also Jankowski (2000) for a recent overview.

11 For a survey on this strand of literature see Alesina and Tabellini (1988, pp. 543 permanently 546).

12 Sometimes, however, economic policy seems to be directed to run huge and persistent deficits in order to be subject to international help. See Willgerodt (1978, p. 215) for an example.

13 Theoretically, the Marshall–Lerner condition requires a balanced current account before the depreciation. See Krugman and Obstfeld (1994, pp. 476 permanently 478).

devaluation is designed to stimulate exports and to repress imports. It is impossible for a trial, which improves the current account, will finally end up in a hyperinflation. It can, however, contribute to chronic inflation.

While the monetary expansion will cause inflation, the effect on the current account depends on the reaction of capital flows on the depreciation. This is because the current account mirrors the capital account and the development of a country's official reserves (Böhm-Bawerk 1914; Meyer 1938). Put differently, the balance of payments is the result of intertemporal decisionmaking of internationally acting domestic and foreign savers and investors. If capital flows do not alter after the depreciation, the subsequent surge in demand for exports and the decreasing demand for imports will finally – at least partly – reverse the depreciation. Rather than taking notice of the intertemporal character of the balance of payments, in politics depreciation (and protectionism) are suggested and pursued in order to reduce a current account deficit.[14] Accordingly, those countries that tried to improve on their current account via inflation completely failed.[15]

The revenue motive

The central reason for policymakers to increase the money supply is their inability to balance the public sector's budget. Especially in countries with hyperinflation, there is a high and persistent fiscal deficit, in other words the urgent need for seigniorage which has largely contributed to inflation. The problems concerning a balanced budget regularly occur for four reasons: too many public enterprises, high-risk premia on capital markets, an excessive welfare state and an inefficient tax system. At the same time, the government is unable or unwilling to cut expenditure elsewhere. The first reason is that governments have taken responsibilities which from an economic point of view are mainly private obligations. For instance, the state often runs a variety of enterprises. Especially carriers like electricity, transport and telecommunication firms have been or still are state-run in many countries. Although there is no economic reason why these enterprises should automatically produce losses in a competitive environment, as a monopolist they normally have done so, among others since the state has tried to realise social objectives via price policies. Moreover, they have not been forced to work efficiently, i.e. X-inefficiency occurred. In former socialist countries,

---

14 In the contemporary academic literature on the balance of payments, the intertemporal approach is widely accepted as being the relevant theoretical model to explain balances in the current account. For a discussion of different approaches to the balance of payments and especially the intertemporal approach as well as for a critical survey of the literature see Dluhosch, Freytag and Krüger (1996).

15 Israel in 1984/85 is an example. Inflation went up to a triple-digit level, but the current account did not substantially improve. See Cukierman (1992, pp. 83f) for a description.

there are still a number of other state-run enterprises (IMF (a), May 1996, pp. 83f). These have to be subsidised rather than to be profitable. The main economic problems related to such state activities on markets for goods and services are manifold. (1) Domestic relative prices are distorted. This hampers economic dynamics and structural change. (2) Owing to losses of state-run enterprises, expenditures are higher than economically necessary. (3) Due to (1) and (2), tax revenues are lower than economically possible.

Second, the countries in question have difficulties in attaining access to capital markets. Domestic as well as foreign investors are not easily willing to grant governments of these countries a credit. Hence, borrowing is either impossible or very costly: the risk premiums are very high.[16]

Third, in many countries the welfare state has gone beyond economic necessities and fiscal limits. The fiscal burden associated with this development also contributes to the budget deficit. Although it is impossible that it *ceteris paribus* will lead to hyperinflation, a permanent pressure on the government to obtain fresh funds exists. Moreover, the distortions caused by an exaggerated welfare state contribute to future budgetary problems.[17]

The fourth reason for high and persistent budget deficits is a tax system which does not work particularly well. The administration is not able to enforce tax collection properly. Tax avoidance is high. Thus, during the 1990s in some countries accumulated tax arrears amount to a high share of GDP (IMF (a) May 1996, p. 88). In 1998, Russia had severe fiscal problems due to tax avoidance and tax arrears (IMF 1999a, p. 139). As a consequence, tax (and tariff) revenues are by far insufficient to cover all expenditures.

Therefore, it becomes politically necessary to finance public expenditures via monetary expansion. This is usually done by requesting a credit from the central bank which will be used to fill the gap between expenditures and revenues. The revenues generated through monetary expansion are usually called seigniorage, denoted S. We specify S as in equations (2.6) and (2.7) (Cagan 1956, p. 35).[18] The government faces a maximisation problem:

---

16 Cukierman (1995, pp. 150–154) notices that inflation tax is a preferred source of revenue especially in countries suffering heavily from the results of a war. In these cases, there is broad consensus within the public that current consumption is to be preferred over future consumption. If, as in the German case of 1922/23, the burden of reparation amounts to a manifold of GDP, there might be even consensus that inflation tax is to be preferred over bond financing, even if possible and affordable.

17 See Röpke (1966, pp. 270-286).

18 This specification is chosen to make it compatible with the approach selected for the econometric investigation. For a discussion of how to define and measure seigniorage correctly see Klein and Neumann (1990), Honohan (1996) and Baltensberger and Jordan (1997).

$$S \equiv \frac{\dot{M}}{M}\frac{M}{P} = mL(\pi^e) \rightarrow \max_{\pi} \qquad (2.6),$$

$$L(\pi^e) = \exp(-\alpha\pi^e) \qquad (2.7).$$

Since M is the amount of nominal money supply, $\dot{M} = dM/dt$ stands for the change of the amount of money over time. Thus, $L(\pi^e)$ is the demand for real cash balances which depends on the expected rate of inflation π^e. Equation (2.7) shows the assumed functional dependence. Thus, if the expected inflation increases, the demand for money will shrink at rate α.[19] As a consequence, S will decrease, too. Assuming that the growth rate of money equals the inflation rate ($m = \pi$) and maximising S with respect to m yields the standard formulation of the optimal level of monetary growth and inflation:

$$m = \frac{1}{\alpha} \qquad (2.8).$$

Empirical evidence shows that high inflation can – at least partly – be traced back to excessive fiscal deficits. In a simple ordinary least squares (OLS) regression of inflation and budget deficits for a sample of 51 either newly industrialised countries, developing or transition countries, we cannot reject the hypothesis that high inflation is indirectly caused by fiscal problems in that they force the government to excessively increase the money base. We employ the following regression:

$$\pi_t = \beta_0 + \beta_1 bd_{j,s} + \beta_2 bd_{j,s-1} + \varepsilon_j \qquad (2.9),$$

where bd_j denotes the budget deficit of country j in time s and s-1 respectively. The results are reported in *Table 2.1.*

The results have to be handled extremely carefully for several reasons: for one, they contain only federal budget deficits. State and municipal balances are not incorporated. In addition, the values of the exogenous variables are very volatile so that heteroscedasticity cannot be ruled out. Furthermore, the rather low coefficient of determination R^2adj indicates that many other

19 The standard specification is criticised by Bernholz and Jaksch (1989) as well as Bernholz and Gersbach (1992). They argue that it does not lead to a theory of inflation consistent with reality. However, in both papers, no superior alternative is offered. As we are not primarily interested in explaining inflation we use the standard approach throughout the study.

independent variables not included in the estimation also determine the inflation rate. Nevertheless, the results show the expected sign and are significant at the 1 per cent level. To sum up: the regression shows the relationship of budget deficits and inflation, but does not allow for the conclusion that unbalanced public budgets are the only reason for high inflation. Moreover, budget deficits are not even a necessary condition for inflation, as they can be financed on capital markets. If fiscal and monetary policy are properly separated, budget deficits will not contribute to inflation at all. The reasoning is backed by a recent study of Sikken and de Haan (1998) who come to the conclusion that the level of public budget deficits in developing countries is not correlated with commitment (here defined as central bank independence).

Governments depending on seigniorage regularly miss the seigniorage maximising inflation rate by far. Inflation is very high, although seigniorage is not. So the question arises why governments inflate suboptimally. An explanation offered by Cagan (1956) and Cukierman (1995) is that inflationary expectations lag behind the rate of inflation so that in the short run it pays for the government to inflate. Thus a vicious circle can evolve. Depending on the extent of the monetary expansion, inflation will accelerate. Only when the public adjusts its expectations it pays for the government to stop inflation and to set $m = 1/\alpha$. Otherwise this condition does not hold, $m > 1/\alpha$ instead. Again, the problem here is that adaptive expectations have to be assumed, i.e. the public always takes the actual inflation rate as the expected inflation rate in the following period.

Table 2.1: Budget Deficits and Inflation: Empirical Evidence

Endogenous	Exogenous	β_0	β_2 (β_1)	R^2adj	*t*-statistics
π (1995)[1]	bd (1994)	11.72	-264.15	0.091	-2.456
π (1995)[2]	bd (1994)	13.88	-489.35	0.171	-2.562
π (1993)[3]	bd (1993)	474.72	-54.15	0.220	-2.789

Notes: [1]: 51 countries; [2]: 28 countries $\pi \geq 10$ per cent p.a.; [3]: 25 transition countries. See also Appendix 1.

Source: IMF (c)

c) Expectations formation, inflation and credibility

As has been analysed above, expectations play an important role for both the employment motive and especially the revenue motive. Only if the public forms adaptive expectations is it possible to mislead it over a longer period, otherwise, monetary expansion has no stimulating real effects. As long as the public anticipates every monetary expansion correctly, only the prices for commodities and factors will change, that is the economy will be affected neither positively nor negatively. However, it is rather improbable that the public will be able to forecast the effects of expansive monetary policy correctly. It is exceptionally difficult to incorporate every future surprise inflation into e.g. long-term lending contracts.

The foregoing considerations show that the effects of monetary policy strongly depend on the way expectations are formed (Sheffrin 1983, pp. 1–26). Following the theory of rational expectations the public consists of forward-looking actors who know how the economy operates. Expectations about economic variables are formed using exactly the economic model that determines these variables. Applied to monetary economics, the public is assumed to know the objective function of the policymaker and the transmission mechanism. This indicates that actors do not make systematic errors; only stochastic errors can occur. It does not necessarily mean that all individuals have the same expectations (Muth 1961).

The information structure of the actors is of crucial importance as to whether monetary policy has real effects or not. Actors form their expectations about the rate of inflation in $s+1$ on account of the information available in s. Only if they had perfect information, would they anticipate every surprise inflation. Monetary policy would have no real effects, neither positive nor negative. In this case, only inflation would occur (e.g. Cukierman 1992, pp. 29–31) or the government would try to avoid inflation as it knows that no other objectives can be achieved. However, if the policymaker has private information it is possible to deceive the public for a short time. In the long run, the public will adapt and adjust the contracts to the new situation. The real effects will dissolve again.

The assumption of rational expectations has the important implication that it can cause credibility problems for the monetary policy. The exact definition of credibility is complicated. Thus, we agree with Blackburn and Christensen (1989, p. 2): 'Perhaps the most general interpretation is the extent to which beliefs about the current state and future course of economic policy are consistent with the program originally announced by policy makers.' The concept of credibility is related to the notion that governments are only partially interested in overall economic welfare as defined by the Pareto criterion. Instead, it pays off politically for the policymaker to deviate from this criterion and to favour special groups within the economy. Given that the public is – at least broadly – informed about the difference between general welfare and governmental objectives, it may tend not to believe in official statements about policy goals. Policy announcements, for instance an announcement of an inflation target, are inspected by the public for their consistency, i.e. their compatibility with the policy model. In particular, a period of severe inflation will induce the public to scrutinise an announced monetary policy very carefully.

A lack of credibility is closely related to an inconsistent monetary policy regime. If monetary policy announcements are inconsistent, the public will not be convinced. Three types of inconsistencies can be distinguished, with different underlying causes and different consequences. Two of them can be overcome rather easily. The first type is the theoretical or technological inconsistency (Agénor and Taylor 1992, p. 547). It arises when the inflation target will be missed at any rate for theoretical reasons: e.g. monetary expansion is too high to be compatible with the target, or the fiscal deficit remains high without access to international capital markets, or even the model of monetary policy is misspecified to meet the target. Then there is the administrative or political inconsistency (Blackburn and Christensen 1989, pp. 2f). The government in charge is unable to handle the announced monetary policy administratively or to implement the required legislative measures. It is possible to master these problems if the political determination is strong enough. A lack of domestic expertise can be mastered by employing foreign consultants or international organisations.

The third type of inconsistency is the relevant one. Even if a monetary policy announcement is technically and politically consistent, it may not be credible due to time inconsistency. The core of a dynamic inconsistency problem is the following: the government announces a certain monetary policy in period s for the following period ($s+1$) which from its point of view is optimal. After the announcement, the public reacts by choosing wage contracts etc. If the public believes in the policy announcement, these contracts will be consistent with the planned monetary policy. It can be expected that both the objective of the monetary policy and other policy targets with respect to employment etc. will *ceteris paribus* be met. However, if the public does not have confidence in the monetary policy announcement, it is inconsistent. In this case, the reactions such as wage contracts cause the initially announced policy to become suboptimal from the government's point of view in period $s+1$. Therefore, it has an incentive to deviate from the initially announced policy (Kydland and Prescott 1977; Calvo 1978). Monetary policy becomes endogenous in the political process. If the government indeed chooses an inflation rate different from the declared one, the public will not trust the governmental policy announcement any longer. Reaching the goal of stability will grow increasingly difficult.

The macroeconomic literature has developed a certain method to analyse time inconsistency in monetary policy. The starting point of these analyses is an objective function of the incumbent policymaker as generalised in equation (2.5). Normally, monetary policy is modelled as a game to analyse the strategic interaction between policymaker and public. The results differ depending on the information structure of the public (complete versus. incomplete information) as well as the nature of the game (repeated versus one-shot game) and other particularities.[20] As a basic result of the literature, however, it can be shown theoretically that in the absence of commitment time inconsistency is a problem that regularly causes monetary policy to neglect the target of stability. Empirical evidence – though not very rich – also supports this view (e.g. Mastroberardino 1994).

d) Credibility and the economic order

There is a broad consensus among economists from all schools of thought that credibility is an important precondition for the success of economic policy. Due to the fact that money is a store of value, credibility is particularly relevant for monetary policy. Consequently, there has been a variety of contributions on the nature of credibility and about ways to make policy announcements more credible, that is how announcements can be enforced.[21]

To start with, a promising approach to analyse credibility problems is the ORDO approach which is based on the Freiburg School of Law and Economics. Here, credibility is a problem of economic order (Eucken 1955; Issing 1997). The structure of monetary policy is a component of the economic order of a country. This has two implications. On the one hand, money influences the real sector of an economy: because of the interdependence of components of the economic order, monetary stability is crucial to let relative prices indicate scarcity. Eucken (1955, pp. 255–264), thus, argues in favour of primacy of monetary policy over other fields. On the other hand, the success of monetary policy depends on other areas of economic policy. For instance, if fiscal policy is unable to either balance the state budget or to borrow on the capital market, a sustainable stability-oriented monetary policy seems impossible. To put it the other way round: credibility is the higher the less dependent the government is on money growth to achieve other policy goals. If it is possible to attain full employment and to balance the budget or finance all expenditures respectively, without taking recourse to monetary policy, the public has more

---

20 Comprehensive surveys of the macroeconomic literature on credibility of monetary policy can be found in Persson (1988), Driffill (1988), Alesina and Tabellini (1988) and Blackburn and Christensen (1989).

21 The latter will be discussed extensively in the next section.

confidence in any policy announcement. The probability of a credible monetary policy rises with the economic quality of the economic order.

The new institutional economics interprets credibility problems as principal–agent–problems, the policymaker being the agent and the public being the principal. The public engages policymakers to act in its interest. The policymaker is accountable to the public. The principal–agent problem is characterised by the facts that (a) the principal is unable to observe the agent's behaviour completely and (b) monitoring is costly (Richter and Furubotn 1996, pp. 163–171). Thereby, it is acknowledged that information is never without costs. In addition, the problem has a time dimension. Due to the fact that both the formation of expectations and the conduct of monetary policy do not take place simultaneously, we can observe an intertemporal exchange. In period s, the public gives trust to the policymakers. In period $s+1$, the policymakers can justify this confidence by abiding by their own announcement. If they do not, there is a problem of opportunistic behaviour (Richter 1996, p. 122).

Implicitly, the macroeconomic literature also acknowledges the interdependence of the components of economic order by taking into account the costs of inflation in the policymaker's calculus (e.g. in equation 2.5).[22] Nevertheless, an explicit awareness of this correlation can only rarely be seen, at least in formal models. Other publications give credit to what is called fundamentals, but which can also be interpreted as an economic order or more generally an institutional setting.[23] In this case, the analysis as well as policy recommendations are not based on the respective models. It seems plausible that the problem of credibility is more sophisticated in terms of policy consistency and optimal commitment when taking into account components of the economic order or institutions than explicitly stated in the macroeconomic literature.

To conclude: to be sustainably successful, monetary policy requires credibility which not only depends on the quality of the monetary regime implemented through the reform, but also on institutional constraints. This can be derived from different methodological strands of economics. Although they are based on different assumptions, neo-classical macroeconomics as well as new institutional economics and the ORDO approach come to this

---

22 Richter (1999, pp. 109–111) argues that this strand of macroeconomics has been infiltrated by the new institutional economics.

23 See e.g. the following quote: 'Our overall summary of these results is that institutional arrangements do not by themselves seem to be of much help in achieving low inflation. Economic fundamentals, such as openness, political instability, and tax policy, seem to play a much larger role. (Campillo and Miron 1997, p. 356). Note that the monetary regime here is called an institutional arrangement and the institutional setting is labelled as economic fundamentals. Only the diction differs from the one we use (see also below).

conclusion. Credibility, however, is not easy to achieve. This holds especially after a period of severe inflation. One major task for economic policy, therefore, is to provide for an enforcement mechanism for the new monetary regime. The alternative approach would be to rely on reputational forces. Regular elections would discipline the policymakers. As Alesina and Tabellini (1988, pp. 546f) point out it is not possible to enforce announcement through voting behaviour. Therefore, we are looking for a mechanism that enforces prudent monetary policy. Commitment to a certain monetary regime has been generally regarded as the best solution. It will be the subject of the next section.

III. INCREASING CREDIBILITY THROUGH COMMITMENT

a) Various aspects of commitment

In the following, the hypothesis is that a change in the monetary policy regime is credible if deviating from the announced policy imposes costs on the government. These costs can be increased through the design of monetary policy. In the macroeconomic literature, several aspects of such a design can be distinguished (Chortareas and Miller 2000). The most comprehensive approach is the 'legislative approach' favouring an independent central bank. There is no acknowledgement of an explicit inflation target or personal requirements of the central bankers, it is argued that high central bank independence quasi-automatically leads to a good monetary performance. Other approaches are more direct, e.g. the 'conservative central banker's approach', suggesting the appointment of an inflation-averse central banker who imposes his preferences on society. Alternatively, the central bank can be forced to adopt inflation or other targets in the so-called 'targeting approach'. It is not clear whether the central bank chooses the target or whether it is set by the government. The last approach to be mentioned is the 'contracting approach'. It deals with optimal incentive schemes which are introduced to reach a first-best monetary policy.

As will be shown in the following, these four approaches concern different aspects of commitment. They will be discussed in this section. Although they are all meant to solve the credibility problem, it will turn out that neither of them can be regarded as being a comprehensive concept of commitment suited for this purpose. Rather, each is a single element of commitment. In order to develop this argument, several issues will be addressed: first, the assignment problem is tackled. Then, costs of commitment have to be specified. After that, the scope commitment is discussed. The possible scope ranges from an inflation target to a monetary policy regime. Subsequently, the question of who commits to stability is addressed. Finally, some aspects of democratic control have to be discussed.

b) The assignment problem: Tinbergen's law as a basis for monetary policy

Monetary policy and other policies are closely related. On average countries performing badly in one area seldom function well in others. This is very interesting with respect to monetary reforms. It shows that monetary performance cannot be judged separately from other policy areas. Monetary policy is a component of economic order. In economic policymaking, a number of objectives have to be met. Price stability, full employment and growth are the most important ones. Politically, it is very tempting to try to meet several objectives with one policy variable. Policymakers then may hope to get a so-called double dividend.

One of the most attractive policy instruments in the history of economic policymaking has been monetary policy. It has been used regularly to meet other policy objectives besides price level stability. On the contrary, price stability has often been neglected. Instead, monetary policy has been misused as a means to enhance employment and output, to balance the public budget and to improve the current account. Theoretical analysis as well as empirical evidence show that it is practically impossible to meet these objectives with the means monetary policy (see above). The objective of price stability is also missed.[24]

Thus, following Tinbergen (1952), we argue that every policy instrument should be assigned to one policy target. To avoid assignment problems, there should be one agency for each policy objective that should decide independently from other agencies on its policy instruments. This has two advantages with respect to the objective of combating severe inflation. The most important argument in favour of the Tinbergen rule is that it is a strong signal that the government is serious about separating the economic policy areas; the temptation to aim at a double dividend (e.g. an increase in employment and stable prices) is resisted. Besides, the analytical problem of policymaking is neither under determined nor over determined.

These considerations say nothing about the adequate monetary policy. Therefore, it is plausible to assume that the application of Tinbergen's consideration to have as many policy instruments as policy targets is a

---

[24] This was often demonstrated in the literature. Only recently, two practitioners, José Viñals and Javier Valles (1999) have put emphasis on this argument.

necessary, but not a sufficient condition for a satisfactory macroeconomic performance. Tinbergen himself did not write about economic order and rule-bound policy. He treated policymaking as a technical problem which can be solved by setting a target or by maximising a variable. Monetary policy, however, is more than a technical exercise.[25] Despite the theoretically convincing and empirically confirmed costs of inflation, many countries have suffered from severe inflation and still do. This demonstrates that a sufficient condition for a good monetary performance is an adequate monetary regime the government commits to.

g) Commitment and the political costs of inflation

Monetary policy is not pursued by the benevolent dictator. In contrast, it is assumed that policymakers are rational and maximising actors who respond to incentives. This assumption has important implications for the credibility of policy announcement. Monetary policy often suffers from the inconsistency problems which create a need for political constraints. One possible political constraint is the election cycle. The public has the opportunity to vote against the reigning government. However, elections are not useful as a constraint. Rather, especially before general elections there is a tendency to boost the economy via surprise inflation.

The macroeconomic literature has shown in theory that monetary policy without commitment has an inherent inflationary bias (for a survey see Persson and Tabellini 1990, p. 31). A lack of commitment decreases the cost of inflation for the government or the parliament. If the public becomes aware of the inflationary bias it will not trust policy announcements. Credibility of monetary policy then can be regained by commitment. From the point of view of the policymaker, commitment is a means of raising the costs of inflation. This can be seen by specifying the objective function Z (equation 2.4). If the government only considered seigniorage, Z would have the following form (equation 2.6 and 2.7):

$$Z = S = m\exp(-\alpha\pi^{e}) \qquad (2.10).$$

The politically optimal rate of inflation, i.e. the rate of inflation generating maximal seigniorage, would be $1/\alpha$, (2.8). Due to credibility problems, however, governments generally miss the optimal level of inflation. Instead, inflation is higher than $1/\alpha$, and seigniorage below its maximum level. Given an objective function as in equation (2.10), the

---

[25] See Blinder (1997) as well as the volume by von Furstenberg and Ulan (1998) about central bankers.

monetary authorities have a strong incentive to deviate from an announced and seigniorage maximising inflation rate (that is money growth rate).

The time inconsistency problem associated with (2.10) can be overcome by changing the policymakers' incentive structure. In general, this can be done by introducing a factor that induces costs of inflation on policymakers. As long as they have discretionary power, there are no external forces inducing costs on them. Therefore, the only way to make inflation costly for a policymaker is a commitment to a certain monetary policy which reduces discretionary leeway. Equation (2.10) changes: a positive inflation rate is associated with a loss of utility for the policymaker, whereas an increase of seigniorage will raise Z. The objective function then is as follows:

$$Z = \delta S - \phi(\pi, \pi^e) \to \max_{\pi} \qquad (2.11).$$

In (2.11), δ denotes the weight given to seigniorage by the policymaker, whereas ϕ stands for the costs of inflation and expected inflation, respectively. The higher δ, the higher the inflationary bias of the policymaker. The higher ϕ, the lower the inclination towards inflation. Thus, commitment can reduce uncertainty of the public and create transparency. Concerning the first, the public can form expectations more precisely. As for the latter, it is able to observe whether the government abides by the rule or not. This ability raises the cost of inflation.

The reason why expected inflation (π^e) has to be taken into account by policymakers is that the government has to break inflationary expectations. As mentioned above, the starting point of our analysis is a period of severe inflation, sometimes hyperinflation. A monetary reform is pursued by the government to commit to stability. Hence, the government is in an unusual situation: either it is the old government with a reputation of being 'wet' and in this case, it will be hard to convince the public of the honesty of the new policy announcement or the government has just been elected and has no track record at all (Backus and Driffill 1985).

For an alternative perspective on the issue of credibility, Backus and Driffill (1985) suggest interpreting macroeconomic policy as a repeated game between the government and the public in which both sides can establish a reputation of being strong. The result would be a dynamically consistent equilibrium with low inflation. However, there are at least two arguments against this interpretation. The first is a methodological argument why a game theoretical approach may be inappropriate. There are two players, individual policymakers and a collective mass, called the public. Whereas the policymaker is able to develop a strategy and choose an action and react respectively, the public does not have a body to agree on strategies and actions. Thus, it seems inappropriate to model the public as a coherent player (Brunner and Meltzer 1993, p. 12). The two players are not equally endowed with strategies and information. Moreover, it is not clear whether it is at all justified to assume a joint strategy of the public. If this is not the case, there seems to be a fallacy of composition: what seems to be valid for individual strategic behaviour is not necessarily true for collective behaviour (Samuelson and Nordhaus 1985, p. 8).

In addition, it remains unsolved how the resulting commitment of the government can be enforced since it is not explained how the payoffs emerge (Backus and Driffill 1985, pp. 213f). This is particularly relevant given that the status quo ante is characterised by chronic inflation or hyperinflation. No emphasis is put on the type or form of the monetary regime the government employs to meet the inflation target. This is problematic since in an international setting it can be rather difficult to meet a certain target each period. Therefore, no matter whether the government is old or new and regardless of the chosen monetary regime, it is important for the credibility of the announced monetary policy rule that the potential costs of breaking are rather high. Only then will the public believe in the announcement.

The costs of reneging are not easy to specify. In democratic societies they may incorporate diminishing chances for the government to be re-elected. However, given that the theory of the political business cycle is relevant, from a political economy point of view it may even be advantageous for the government to accept a moderate inflation to stimulate economic activity in the short run. Inflation will appear in the medium run and won't hit the public before the election. That is why it is necessary to specify commitment, e.g. by a monetary policy rule which can be observed. Any attempt of the government to break this rule will then be recognised by the public. Hence, such an attempt can be costly for the government.

d) Commitment and the economic order

In the macroeconomic literature, commitment, in general, is not defined as a monetary regime. It is argued that the government can commit credibly to a certain inflation rate, e.g. $\pi^*=0$, which is called a policy rule (e.g. Barro and Gordon 1983, p. 106). For the purpose of showing in a positive analysis that credible commitment to rules leads to lower inflation and less output volatility, this restriction is appropriate. However, to explain how to generate credibility through commitment, such a rule has shortcomings: it is left to the policymakers how to meet the inflation target. There is no observable monetary regime to abide by. Hence, policymakers have discretionary power. It remains an open question why they should not make use of this room to move, as long as the transparency of policymaking is low. Furthermore, and closely related, the problem of enforcement is not solved. How can the public ensure that the government will stick to the inflation target? Without enforcement, commitment cannot become credible (North 1993, p. 12; McCallum 1995, p. 210; Bofinger 1991, p. 24). Therefore, a rule has to be more than an announcement of an inflation target.

Moreover, it is sometimes argued that, instead of creating a rule, the government can try to build up a reputation as being 'dry' (Vickers 1986). In this case, it is not necessary to create a rule. The government is subject to reputational forces inducing it to create a sustainably low inflation rate. The government loses reputation in case the inflation rate increases which may even lead to a lost election. Therefore, the government has the incentive to consider price stability. Eventually, this process yields a so-called reputational equilibrium with a sustainable inflation rate normally being higher than zero (Barro and Gordon 1983, pp. 110–114). However, this approach is unable to generate credibility during a severe inflation. The reputation of the government is already spoiled; it is regarded as being 'wet'. Without an explicit regime switch and without clarity about the nature of reputational forces, it is difficult to imagine a gain in credibility. In other words, how can the public enforce stability in such a situation without a rule? Furthermore, as known from game theory, multiple reputational equilibria can occur (Richter 1996, p. 125). It may be possible that inflation will only be reduced slightly, if at all; there is no guarantee that inflation is sustainably low.

Taking into account the political economy background of inflation, we use an alternative concept of commitment. Commitment is interpreted as a deliberately chosen monetary regime, not as a certain inflation rate, money growth rate and the like (Brennan and Buchanan 1981, p. 65). From a normative point of view, this regime has to meet at least two conditions in order to be sustainable. First, it should reflect the preferences of the members of the society. We assume that on a constitutional level all individuals would prefer a monetary regime that ensures stability.[26] Second, the monetary regime must be independent of time and the monetary policymaker in charge. This is especially important since the quality of monetary policy, i.e. the inflation rate, must not depend on the motives behind the behaviour of the policymaker: whether or not inflation is low should not depend on the personal attitude of the individuals governing the central bank. As Albert G. Hart puts it: 'No form of organization, of course, can obtain wise policy from men who have no wisdom in them. But poor organization can obtain unwise policy from men who have wisdom in them' (Hart 1948, p. 515). Therefore,

---

26 This does not exclude that in a special economic situation a majority might prefer strong money growth to stimulate demand. The rule is a means to keep a long-term perspective.

suggestions to choose a central banker who has a reputation of being 'dry' (Rogoff 1985) do not solve the problem; without a rule there is no certainty that the central banker will withstand pressures exerted on him/her by the government to e.g. finance an excessive deficit in the public budget. Moreover, even if this central banker pursued a stability-oriented policy, there would be the danger that her/his successor is 'wet'.

Consequently, a monetary commitment or rule has to be a part of the overall economic order. It has to be chosen carefully so that it interacts well with other parts of the economic order, e.g. the labour market, fiscal policy or international (monetary) treaties the country has signed. This requirement is the subject of this study. Commitment also has to provide for an enforcement mechanism which makes inflation costly. Both requirements are especially important for those countries pursuing a monetary reform after a hyperinflation. The public will be very sceptical and the danger of dynamic inconsistency prevails.

e) Who commits to stability?

The preceding section has made clear that – from a normative point of view – commitment is particularly necessary when the government actually depends on monetary policy to meet other than monetary policy objectives. Persson and Tabellini (1990, p. 5) distinguish two cases: first, the policymaker's interests differ from the public's interests. This cannot hold for a long time, since the public can elect another government that represents the general interest in a better way. Second, the government lacks policy instruments in other policy areas. For instance, it only has limited access to international capital markets, or it cannot influence the wage bargaining process.

In the second case, it can be attractive for the government to increase inflation as it cannot solve the assignment problem (Chapter2, subsection IV.a). Commitment inflicting costs on the government is appropriate to diminish the political attraction of inflation. Therefore, it is always the government that commits itself to a certain monetary policy rule. This seems to be trivial at first glance. However, it has important implications on the concrete making of monetary policy. Often, economists propose special contracts or restrictions for central bankers meant to guide their behaviour. These economists argue that even central bank independence would not be a strong enough incentive to create a stable currency. Suggestions are made to restrict the discretionary power of central bankers, for instance by giving partial independence (Lohmann 1992), by giving a monetary rule the state of a law (Scheide 1993) or by making contracts with central bankers (Walsh

1995) limiting their personal income (up to dismissal) in case they miss a certain politically given inflation target.[27]

As Wood (1997) has shown, these contracts for central bankers will only make sense if the government itself is committed to stability. It is not enough to guarantee central bank independence and to restrict the discretionary power of central bankers. An inflation-prone government would not punish the central banker if she/he broke the rule or contract. Hence, the problem is not solved by a contract, but only relocated (McCallum 1995, p. 210, 1997). This also is not an argument against commitment, but in favour of an enforcement mechanism. The low relevance of contracts for monetary policymakers with the government can be shown in history as well as with contemporary examples (Wood 1997; Jordan 1995/6).[28]

Another convincing argument against restricting the independence of monetary policymakers by special arrangements is given by McCallum (1995, 1997). He argues that there is no reason to assume that monetary policymakers will necessarily act in favour of discretionary monetary policy which would lead to surprise inflation. Given that their perspective is a long-term one, it would pay for them to act rule bound and to stabilise expectations. Under rational expectations, the public will adjust its expectations if in each period the actual inflation rate equals the pre-announced one. This argument is particularly convincing if the society's preference is mirrored in the pre-announced inflation rate. In a nutshell: as long as the government commits and sticks to a certain policy rule, it is not necessary to force a precommitment technology upon the monetary agency, whether it is in the form of a central bank or another institution.

This leads to the question of who is the principal and who is the agent in monetary policy. Those who argue in favour of a contract, interpret the government as the principal. The monetary authority is the agent (Walsh 1995). However, as long as the government has the incentive to abuse monetary policy to meet objectives other than price level stability, the government itself has to be interpreted as the agent. Society is the principal, for it has an interest in stability as opposed to the government which has more than one objective (equation 2.13). Thus, commitment throughout this

---

27 Such a contract has been introduced in New Zealand in 1992. See Kirchgässner (1996).

28 The optimal contract literature itself adds to this critique. Using the contracting approach under different assumptions, Chortareas and Miller (2000) as well as da Empoli (2000) theoretically show that it may be impossible to define an optimal contract. The former use the concept of common agency to show that if a contract between the government and the central bank is possible, a second (implicit) contract between an interest group and the central bank is also possible, dominating the first contract. Da Empoli shows that a central banker who either has several tasks, e.g. monetary policy and financial market supervision, or is seeking for a post in private business after his/her contract ends, is always tempted to renege on the contract.

study always means commitment to stability by the government via constructing a monetary regime. The fact that central bankers are restricted by law or by a contract can be part of this regime. Without governmental commitment, however, a monetary regime will certainly not become credible.

One could go even further and always define commitment as a constitutional decision which has to be made unequivocal. This definition, however, restricts the scope of possible commitments. Too many different interests oppose to consensus. This is especially relevant, since normally the monetary reform does not coincide with a constitutional reform. Instead, there is not enough time for a public discourse leading to a consensus. Only in transition economies, it could have been possible to give a constitutional status to the monetary regime. Under normal circumstances and for pragmatic reasons, the government as a legal agent of the principal 'public' has to decide on a monetary regime. To sum up: a monetary rule should have constitutional quality, but written with a small 'c' rather than a capital 'C' (Hetzel 1997, pp. 50f). Monetary policy is part of the economic order, but details are not laid down in the constitution.

f) Commitment and democracy: constitutional economics considerations

Decisions on constitutional level as well as decisions laid down in laws can be considered as being democratically legitimated. Nevertheless, many claim that commitment by governments to a monetary rules independent from time and policymakers in charge, is undemocratic in the sense that monetary policy is conducted without control by democratically elected institutions like parliament. It is argued that something as important as money cannot be left in the hands of 'uncontrollable technocrats' in a monetary institution like a central bank or a currency board. For instance, Fischer (1995, p. 202) argues that central bank independence ensures that the preferences of the central banker rather than those of the public determine monetary policy.[29] The question arises whether a monetary commitment implies a lack of democratic legitimation or not. This question is answered by taking a close look at the arguments against commitment.

First, it is argued that a rule-bound monetary policy performed by an independent monetary authority that is not accountable to a parliament cannot meet its macroeconomic responsibilities. It is very likely to miss other objectives than price level stability. These objectives are said to be employment and growth. As a consequence, there should be a macroeconomic dialogue between parliament and the monetary authority which should be fully accountable to the former. Moreover, transparency

---

[29] However, in another paper, Fischer (1994, p. 37) argues that the degree of commitment (central bank independence) reflects the preferences of the society.

should be high, e.g. through the publication of protocols of the decisionmaking process and monthly reports. This would raise democratic control and legitimation (Randzio-Plath 1998; Fischer 1995, p. 202). There are at least two arguments against this reasoning: first, there remains doubt about whether the participation of parliament itself will raise democratic legitimation; the opposite is possible (see below). Second, the reasoning is based on the wrong assumption that monetary policy *not* aiming at price level stability can improve employment and the growth perspective.

Another claim is that if the monetary authority is free to choose its policy objective, the democratic legimitation is low (Prast 1996). This is certainly correct. Goal independence is to be rejected. Independence of a monetary authority can only mean the independence to meet a (politically) given objective with independently chosen instruments. It should not be mixed up with complete freedom in choosing the objective and instruments. Thus, independence can in contrast be described as freedom of arbitrary interventions by the government. The public, represented by the government, must define monetary objectives (ideally price stability) and will delegate the task to an independent institution whose members can be controlled and, if necessary, dismissed.

This leads to the main counter-argument against the claim that commitment to a rule is undemocratic: the crucial questions are (1) whether the process leading to the commitment is democratically legitimated and (2) whether the commitment is reversible in case a new consensus on monetary policy arises. As long as either commitment is made on a constitutional level or those who commit themselves are elected in a democratic process, there is no reason to believe that commitment contradicts with democratic principles (Blinder 1996). Put differently: it is important that the monetary policy regime is agreed on and can be changed democratically. The example of the Bundesbank may clarify this point. Until 1999, the law giving the Bundesbank independence and defining its objective (monetary stability) could be changed with the majority of votes in the German parliament, the Bundestag. The Bundestag and the government, however, had no right to control or even give orders to the Bundesbank. Obviously, there was no need for a further democratisation of German monetary policy prior to 1999. Its policymakers were not acting without control.[30]

In addition, there are two other elements that make commitment and democracy compatible (Blinder 1996, pp. 10–13).[31] The first is that the

30 With the introduction of the Euro, the Bundesbank has become one of 12 partners in the European System of Central Banks (ESCB), including the European Central Bank (ECB).

31 He elaborates on central bank independence and democracy. Nevertheless, his reasoning can be extended to the more general concept of commitment.

monetary policymaker (i.e. the board of a central bank or the chairman of a currency board) is appointed by elected politicians and not by unelected persons, such as other members of the board. The second element is transparency, i.e. the monetary authority explains its objectives, instruments and the reasons behind its actions to the public. It is certainly in the self-interest of the monetary authority to create a certain degree of transparency.[32] If it fails to do so, the authority is at risk of becoming the scapegoat for politicians in case these perform unsatisfactorily in their own policy fields (*The Economist* 1998b, p. 22). Blinder (1996, p. 11) suggests another element: monetary policymakers have to be honest. It goes without saying that civil servants generally have to behave honestly. The monetary regime, however, should be organised in a way that it does not depend on the personal properties of the policymakers. As mentioned above, it has to function independently from the persons involved.

To sum up, it cannot be denied that commitment of the government in a constitutional democracy is normally compatible with democratic principle. To pick up and reverse Fischer's (1995, p. 202) argument, only commitment can make sure that society's preferences are adequately considered. The argument is fortified when we imagine for a moment that monetary policy is not rule-bound. Instead, suppose the monetary authority is dependent from orders of and is controlled by the parliament. Given that parliaments in most modern democracies regularly approve suggestions by the governments, it is not even necessary that governments formally controls monetary policy.

Under such circumstances, monetary policy may become anti-democratic in that it impairs the property rights of some members of society. Let us assume that parliament gives order to lower interest rates in order to enhance economic activity. Some groups, such as debtors and the states will gain at the expense of other groups. Under rational expectations, there will be no long-term increase in employment and growth. Monetary policy without rules can also have the consequence of a chain of interventions (Hetzel 1997, pp. 51–54). For example, unrestricted money growth will cause the prices of politically sensible goods and services like food and house renting to rise. This can lead to the call for price controls which will not only cause a misallocation of scarce resources but also favour certain interests at the expense of others. On a constitutional level, there would be agreement in society to avoid such situations. However, in day-to-day politics it may be impossible to avoid it.

---

32 This does not include the obligation of publishing minutes of the executive board meetings. This would make its members personally vulnerable to public accusations with the potential consequence of decreased transparency through secret meetings etc.

IV. COMMITMENT AND MACROECONOMIC OUTCOME: EMPIRICAL OVERVIEW

At this stage of the analysis, it is worth while to assess the theoretical considerations on credibility and commitment. It is empirically investigated how and to what extent commitment in fact can improve macroeconomic performance. Among the indicators of macroeconomic performance, inflation is of crucial importance. But also the correlation between monetary commitment and growth as well as the cost of disinflation is of interest. There is a rich body of literature assessing in depth the impact of commitment on macroeconomic outcome both theoretically and empirically. In this section, we take a closer look on the empirical literature although it does not perfectly fit to our purpose: commitment in all these studies is narrowly defined as central bank independence (CBI). Moreover, empirical work does not necessarily consider a regime switch, that is a monetary reform. It takes both the degree of CBI and the macroeconomic outcome as given. The role of institutions is not explicitly considered. Finally, most of these studies focus on industrial countries with low average inflation whereas we – necessarily – concentrate on developing or transition countries. Nevertheless, there are lessons to be drawn for our analysis (see below).[33]

There is one study that does not assess whether CBI has a systematic impact on macroeconomic performance, but which is worth mentioning. Schuler (1996) scrutinises the success of monetary policy in 155 countries. He distinguishes three groups of countries: industrialised countries with central banks, developing countries with central banks and developing countries with other monetary arrangements. For the period from 1950 to 1993, he compares these groups concerning the following indicators (ibid., pp. 110–118): growth rates, inflation rates, number of years with high inflation, convertibility restrictions. His results are straightforward: developing countries with central banks have the worst performance of these groups in any respect. He concludes that developing countries do not have comparative advantages in central banking and should rather import their monetary policy, e.g. via a currency board system or by dollarisation (ibid., p. 53). His results are not backed by econometric calculations and do not consider institutional differences between countries. Therefore, to be reliable and meaningful, the analysis is by far too imprecise to back such a proposal. A serious analysis has to assess in detail the level of commitment in each

[33] This section is not meant to be a comprehensive survey. For a survey see Eijffinger and de Haan (1996, Chapter 4 and appendix B).

country before suggesting policy options. This is done in other studies discussed in what follows.

a) How to measure central bank independence (CBI)

The measures of central bank independence are separated into two groups: legal and non-legal measures. Legal measures are based on laws and contracts, whereas non-legal measures normally are based on questionnaires. They have one thing in common, namely that a higher score indicates a higher degree of independence. All indices range between two values, that is they are not infinite. Cukierman (1992) norms his index between zero and one as a weighted and unweighted average of 16 factors grouped into four clusters. Thus, he receives very differentiated scores.

Others have chosen an additive approach: if the central bank has certain properties, these add to the index. The approach of Bade and Parkin (1988) is to ask whether each out of three criteria is valid or not. If it is, the score is one, otherwise zero. The simple unweighted average is calculated and the countries in the sample are ranked. Alesina (1988) proceeds similarly by adding a fourth criterion. Grilli, Masciandaro and Tabellini (1991) construct an unweighted index where they apply two kinds of criteria, political and economic, on the whole 13 criteria. If the criterion is fulfilled, the score is one, otherwise zero. Consequently, the highest score of independence can be 13. In contrast to all indices named so far, Eijffinger and Schaling (1993) use a weighted average of three criteria, out of which one has three solutions. They obtain a range of five policy types with scores between one and five. As compared to Cukierman's index, the scores of these four indices are less differentiated.

As regards the components of the index of central bank independence, all studies quoted here employ the same or very similar factors. These include limitations to lending to the government, appointing and dismissal procedures for the board members, accountability of the central bank, the possibility of the government overriding the central bank's decisions and the objectives of monetary policy.[34] Despite the similarity of different approaches, the results quite often contradict one another. This can be interpreted as a weakness of such indices in general and can have several causes. First, different researchers might interpret the relevant laws or contracts very distinctively (Eijffinger and de Haan 1996, pp. 24f). Second, authors put different emphasis on the same factors, that is the weights given to components of the index differ in the studies (see below). Third, legal measures only tell a part of the story. As long as the government can break the monetary regime without facing high costs, i.e. as long there is no enforcement mechanism,

[34] For an overview see Eijffinger and de Haan (1996, pp. 22–28 and appendix A).

high central bank independence does not guarantee high stability. This leads Eijffinger and de Haan (1996, p. 28) to the conclusion that the indices are better suitable for developed rather than developing or transition countries. Finally, using questionnaires also has its shortcomings: often, it is impossible to obtain an answer from the central bankers in charge. If they answer, there might be a bias in the answer towards being too optimistic about central bank independence because this obviously is advantageous for the central bankers (ibid., pp. 26f).

b) The impact of CBI on inflation

Both the rate and the variability of inflation have been tested regarding their dependence on CBI, the focus of the analyses lying on the rate of inflation. Among the first studies to test the impact of CBI on the inflation rate there is a paper by Parkin and Bade (1977) who employed reaction functions of central banks. They came to the conclusion that (legally) independent central banks are concerned with price stability whereas dependent central banks (as the Bank of England in those days) respond to other macroeconomic variables. Subsequent studies[35] tested the correlation between CBI and inflation econometrically, using different measures for legal central bank independence. For *industrialised countries*, the evidence is (almost) unambiguous: there is a negative impact of the degree of CBI on the inflation rate.

The evidence is less convincing for *developing countries*. The legal measures of CBI do not correlate with the inflationary performance. Hence, Cukierman (1992), Cukierman, Webb and Neyapti (1992) and Cukierman and Webb (1995) employ alternative measures, for instance the turnover of central bank governors and the political pressures exerted on the central bank. The lower these are, the higher is the CBI. Thus the correlation between measured CBI and the inflation rate also is negative. Loungani and Sheets (1997) construct an index of legal CBI for 12 transition countries. In a second step, they compare it to the Bundesbank, finally obtaining a new index. For 1993 they find a significant negative impact of this index on the inflation rate. However, the restriction of the analysis to one year is rather unusual. Therefore, the findings should be handled with care. All other cross-country studies operate with longer periods than one year.

As a consequence of the unsatisfactory results concerning CBI and inflation, some authors have added in other explanatory variables to their estimations of the determinants of inflation. Jenkins (1996) analyses OECD

35 See e.g. Cukierman (1992, pp. 415–431), Grilli, Masciandaro and Tabellini (1991), Cukierman, Webb and Neyapti (1992), Alesina (1988) and Eijffinger and van Keulen (1995). More studies are listed in Eijffinger and de Haan (1996, table B2).

countries. He adds three variables to the measure of legal CBI: the turnover of central bank governors, the regulatory burden of the central bank and a dummy for membership to the EMS. His findings suggest that all variables are jointly significant determinants of international differences of inflation rates. Havrilesky and Granato (1993) test if other variables like strength of corporatism, size of the public sector and the degree of dependence on imported oil explain the differences of inflationary performance in 18 industrialised countries. They come to the conclusion that only CBI affects inflation rates. Anyadike-Danes (1995) elaborates the analysis of Cukierman, Webb and Neyapti (1992) adding a variable for the exchange rate system of the developing countries analysed by the latter. The results show that CBI is less important, if countries fix their exchange rate. Loungani and Sheets (1997) also add some more 'institutional' variables: fiscal balance in 1992, a reform index and average tenure of the central bank governor. The result of their estimation is encouraging, but not very reliable, due to the limited degrees of freedom (ibid., p. 390).

c) Growth rates, sacrifice ratios and commitment

The relationship between economic growth and CBI has also been tested extensively (Eijffinger and de Haan 1996, Table B3). The results suggest neither a positive nor a negative relation between these two variables. The study of Cukierman et al. (1993) is an exception: they report a positive influence of CBI defined as turnover rates of central bank governors in developing countries on economic growth. This outcome has been questioned by Akhand (1998) who tests the robustness of the results. Moreover, the theoretical foundation of this relationship can be doubted.

However, more important for our purpose is the question whether output loss due to the reduction of inflation, calculated as sacrifice ratio, is dependent on the degree of commitment. Several papers have dealt with the cost of disinflation; there is no evidence that these costs are negatively correlated with CBI (Eijffinger and de Haan 1996, pp. 37f). Gärtner (1997) estimates a positive correlation between the sacrifice ratio and central bank independence. Unfortunately, these studies have focused on industrialised countries. Thus, the explanation of Gärtner's result can simply be that inflation was already extremely low. To reduce the inflation rate further was only possible with increasing cost.

The correlation of sacrifice ratios and commitment in case of developing countries and after a reform is not reported. There are developing and transition countries that have brought down inflation rates from three- or two-digit levels with nearly no costs. It would be interesting to learn how the degree of commitment affects the cost of disinflation.

d) Do independent central banks behave tough?

Another, related, question is whether central banks respond differently to macroeconomic performance or political pressure, depending on their degree of CBI. Solveen (1998) tested three hypotheses: first, the higher the degree of CBI, the smaller the response to a sign of decreasing demand; the second thesis is that the more independent the central bank, the worse the chances of the government to abuse monetary policy to cause a political business cycle. Finally, he analyses whether the fact holds that the higher the level of CBI, the more restrictive the central bank reacts upon a growing public budget deficit.

Solveen employs reaction functions of the central banks in the G7 countries. He only finds moderate evidence for the second hypothesis, that is the government can produce a political business cycle more easily, if the central bank is less independent. The other hypotheses have to be rejected. This is consistent with the hypothesis that commitment is only meaningful if it is commitment by the government. Solveen himself admits that these results do not suggest abstention from central bank independence. However, he proposes not to rely solely on CBI, but to also place institutional constraints on both the government and the central bank.

e) Summary and qualifications

To summarise, the results of empirical work are ambiguous. The correlation of central bank independence and macroeconomic indicators is rather weak. In industrial countries, there is an expected negative correlation between inflation, growth rates and other variables. However, in developing countries which are of utmost interest for this study inflation is not correlated with legal CBI.

The empirical studies generally are subject to critique. It has to be mentioned that none of the authors use a theoretically sound econometric model when running the regression. An OLS estimation is applied with inflation or growth as dependent variables and CBI in various forms as independent ones. The hypothesis that high CBI is stability-enhancing is not nested in a thorough theoretical analysis. In other words, the question of why it is that independent central banks are more likely to produce stable money is not raised, let alone answered. Such questions are addressed in the critical contributions by Akhtar (1995) and Cargill (1995). They both raise doubts about the methodological quality, and, therefore normative richness of the studies. Posen (1998) asks whether CBI is a device to enhance credibility at all. He argues that there is no causal relationship between CBI and inflation.[36] Indeed, the evidence does not allow for the conclusion that a high degree of commitment causes stability.

Notwithstanding this critique, there are several lessons to be drawn from the econometric literature on CBI and inflation. First, a theoretical model of monetary reforms has to be constructed. This is not the objective of the existing literature, but is necessary for our purpose. Second, to incorporate institutions into the analysis may enrich the results. Similarly, Eijffinger and de Haan (1996, p. 30) reckon that both CBI and low inflation are caused by the same variables like culture and tradition of stability, that is institutional factors. This is exactly the direction of this study (Chapter 3).

Third, a broader concept of commitment than CBI is needed to cover all components of the monetary regime, e.g. the exchange rate arrangement. One important argument can be covered by a comprehensive concept: it is necessary that the government commits to a monetary regime which in many cases implies an independent central bank. CBI without the government being seriously committed to stability is no guarantee for credibility. Therefore, the empirical studies described here do not significantly reject the (alternative) hypothesis that commitment does not matter to recover credibility.[37] A more comprehensive concept of commitment may help to conquer this shortcoming and lead to a better understanding of the stabilisation process. This concept will be introduced in the next section.

V. THE INDEX OF COMMITMENT

a) Legal, not actual commitment

To measure commitment one has to make a detour. Commitment after high inflation generally is made via a monetary reform that introduces a new

---

[36] Forder (1998) goes even further by questioning the need for credible policy regimes at all. This view implicitly denies the relevance of political economy considerations and the need for rule-bound policy.

[37] A recent study by Banaian, Burdekin and Willett (1998) suggests that the reason for the unsatisfactory empirical performance is that e.g. the Cukierman index is not narrow enough. Instead, they claim that it is necessary to figure out those central bank properties that insulate a central bank from political pressure. As long as CBI forms the core of the analysis rather than political commitment to stability this seems to make sense and does not contradict our argumentation.

monetary regime. Monetary reforms can have a variety of forms. Even if the type of monetary regime in two countries is similar, the level of commitment made by the government can be very different. The degree of stability may be different as well. This can be exemplified by the index of central bank independence (Cukierman 1992, p. 381): although during the 1980s Peru and the Netherlands granted their central banks the same degree of legal independence, their monetary policies differed enormously. Consequently, inflation rates also varied considerably. Therefore, it is impossible to directly compare and rank monetary regimes. Instead one has to separate all those elements that contribute to commitment and construct an index of commitment. This index is a theoretical concept not to be mixed up with different kinds of monetary reforms.

Let us remain with the example of inflation differences in Peru and the Netherlands: besides the differences in monetary policy as such there are other elements adding to contrasting experiences in stability, such as convertibility and external obligations. These are not covered in an index of legal CBI and differed in the countries in question. Thus, CBI does not give a full explanation of different monetary performance in these countries. We aim at an index which contains all legal elements of a monetary regime with influence on stability.

Moreover, it should be noted that monetary commitment as discussed previously is not an objective by itself. Instead, it only makes sense when it refers to price stability. This does not mean that a certain inflation target has to be met each period, but that the government commits to a certain monetary regime thereby aiming at stabilisation. Remember that the focus of this analysis lies on regime switches after a period of severe inflation. Commitment to a certain monetary regime is a device to gain credibility.

Of course, legal commitment is not equal to actual commitment. The case that the government does not abide by its commitment seems to be the rule rather than the exception. Even if the government is determined to stabilise the economy and to stop inflation, it may seem politically useful it to deviate from the chosen commitment. The deviation of the actual monetary policy from the announced policy regime is explained in this study. The higher the credibility of the monetary regime is, the lower the deviation will probably be. Therefore, it is important to note that the index of commitment is not at any rate identical with the credibility of the monetary policy. It is not meant to measure actual commitment. Instead, the index focuses on legal determinants of commitment; it measures what governments promise instead of to what extent governments keep their promises.

b) Construction, criteria and components

Legal commitment can be measured like central bank independence. As the latter, commitment has more than one dimension. It depends on factors such as objectives of monetary policy, the constitutional level which the monetary regime is laid down on, discretionary power of the government, whether or not commitment is backed externally and so on (see below). In the following, we briefly introduce the construction of an index of commitment which is based on such factors.

Although the empirical picture of the relation between CBI and macroeconomic outcome is mixed, it makes sense to construct the index of commitment similar to the index of CBI (Cukierman 1992, chapter 19). Giving independence to the central bank is a special form of commitment. The indices of CBI, therefore, contain a number of factors which are also relevant for the index of commitment. The latter is a generalisation of the first. In what follows, the index is briefly established. Technically, the best way to construct an index is by defining its boundaries as zero and one. The reason to proceed in this way is that the institutional factors, which will be explained in Chapter 3 of this study and which theoretically restrict the success of monetary commitment, can also be normed between zero and one. Hence, we can assess the robustness of the theory empirically. If the index broaches zero, the level of commitment is very low. The highest theoretically possible commitment is expressed by the value one. Hence, $0 < C < 1$, where C denotes the index of commitment. In other words: the higher the C, the lower the discretionary power of the government in monetary policy. There, the index is the (weighted or unweighted) average of all the factors determining legal monetary commitment. These criteria are operationalised by using components with discrete outcomes having numerical codings between zero and one.[38] The codings and the weights are given in Appendix 2 in *Table A.2* and *Table A.3* respectively. In what follows, the criteria and their meanings in respect of the level of commitment are discussed.

1. *Objectives of monetary policy.* As shown in Chapter 2, subsection III, monetary policy cannot raise employment and revenues if rational expectations are prevalent. Instead, only inflation is fuelled by employment or fiscal orientation of monetary policy. Nevertheless, time and again, central banks face demands by the public or by politicians to use monetary policy instruments to boost the economy and to solve fiscal problems. A clear definition of the objective of monetary policy in the legal foundation of the monetary regime, namely price stability, makes it easier to refuse these demands. Thus, commitment varies with the kind

38 The names of the components refer to *Table A.2*.

and number of legally given objectives (component *obj*). It is highest when the monetary authorities are obliged by law to only be concerned about price level stability. The obligation to support the economic policy of the government or to take into account employment as well as stability makes commitment much lower. Commitment is the lowest if no objective is defined.

2. *Where is the monetary regime established?* The commitment to stability has to be put into a legal framework. This legal framework can be fixed on different constitutional levels. At the upper end of the scale, monetary policy can be fixed in the constitution which can only be changed by a qualified majority in parliament or by a referendum. At the lower end of the scale, the monetary regime can be implemented by a governmental decree which of course can be changed much easier than the constitution. In the latter case the government is a great deal less committed to stability than in the first. The more difficult a change of the regime for the government, the higher the commitment (component *const*).
3. *Discretionary power left to the government.* Independence of the monetary authority does not mean it defines its objective. This is done in the legal foundation of the monetary regime. Rather, independence, i.e. the freedom from interventions by the government, is the choice of instruments as well as the timing and magnitude of their use to meet the given objective(s). The more the government intervenes as regards instruments, the less it commits to stability. Another way to intervene in monetary policy is to influence the exchange rate of the domestic currency towards other currencies. Let us assume that the exchange rate between the currencies of two countries, A and B, has been in a long-term floating equilibrium. Due to monetary expansion in country A relative to country B, A's currency depreciates nominally and really. This diminishes the price competitiveness of the international sector in country B. Both governments now decide to agree on fixing the exchange rate on the level prior to the monetary shock in A with symmetric obligations to intervene on the market for foreign exchange. However, A does not reduce the speed of its monetary expansion. The efforts to fix the exchange rate will contradict monetary policy in country B with the likely result that money growth accelerates there as well. To sum up, governmental competencies concerning the exchange rate policy also indicate low commitment to stability (component *gov*).
4. *External pledge of the government.* It is possible to take external obligations which raise the level of commitment (component *extern*) as compared to a situation without these obligations. First, the government can fix the exchange rate ex ante towards an international currency like

the US dollar, the Euro or the Swiss franc. This fixing is completely different from interventions on the market for foreign exchange like those described in (3). It illustrates that the government is willing to keep the exchange rate stable, that is to import stability. Second, the government can accept support for its reform by the International Monetary Fund (IMF) or by the World Bank. This (financial or administrative) support is normally given conditionally. Certain elements of the commitment (like those discussed here e.g. convertibility) are not only promised domestically, but also internationally, that is they are part of a contract between the government and the IMF. Both fixing the exchange rate and conditionality raise the level of commitment.

5. *Conditions of appointment and dismissal of monetary policymakers.* The rules for the appointment of policymakers[39] have been discussed controversially for a long time, in particular with respect to their independence from politics. In general, two aspects are of interest (Cukierman 1992, p. 373). First, the question is who is able to become chief executive officer (CEO), especially whether only a reputed expert or any other person as well can be appointed. The higher the demanded expertise of the CEO, the higher the level of commitment (component *ceo*). Second, how is a potential dismissal organised (component *diss*)? For instance, dismissal can be possible after a change of government or even certain ministers (Cukierman and Webb 1995). It is also possible that only severe violation of her/his duty leads to the dismissal of the CEO. The latter is correlated with a high level of commitment. In *Table A.2*, the outcome: 'No rules for dismissal' indicates that there may be rules but they are so intransparent and inexact that they cannot be made enforceable. Conditions of reappointment and the length of term of the CEO are not incorporated. It is not theoretically clear in which direction and to what extent they affect the degree of legal commitment.
6. *Limitations on lending to the government.* Monetisation of budget deficits by monetary expansion has always been and still is the main reason for hyperinflation wherever it happened. Public budget deficits *per se* are not a threat to stability, as long as they are financed on the (international) capital market. However, financing public deficits have to be avoided by printing money at any rate. This is a necessary condition for the success of any monetary reform and should be made clear by the government from the very beginning. Thus, an important factor that determines the level of commitments is a provision on lending fresh money to the government (component *lim*). Hence, highest commitment is given when the monetary authority is prohibited to buy government bonds both on the

[39] In the following, we concentrate on the chief executive officer of the monetary institution.

primary and secondary market. Even central bank holding of government bonds purchased on the secondary market has fiscal effects as long as the seigniorage is added to public revenues. The state pays itself an interest. In other words: 'interest paid to the Fed is essentially a wash:' (Hetzel 1997, p. 56). Moreover, if the monetary authority is not allowed to buy government bonds on the primary market but may purchase them on the secondary market, it is rather easy to circumvent this regulation. Thus, the easier it is for the government to borrow money from the monetary institution, the lower is the level of commitment.

7. *Convertibility restrictions.* Full convertibility can be interpreted as a signal that the government is really committed to stability for it indicates that the monetary regime is open to competition. This enables individuals to spend their money where they prefer. A lack of convertibility indicates the opposite. The public does not know whether the commitment to stability is earnest (Colombatto and Macey 1996). The dynamic inconsistency problem may again evolve due to inflationary expectations. Besides monetary problems resulting from convertibility restrictions the allocation of resources may be seriously hampered. Most countries that have experienced hyperinflation also suffer from structural problems like a bulk of inefficient state enterprises. In case of foreign exchange control, it may be difficult for young and innovative enterprises to obtain foreign exchange for only old enterprises are awarded. Then, structural change would be repressed; especially in countries of transition, this has been a problem (Bomhoff 1992, pp. 454f). Moreover, foreign and domestic capital investments depend positively on convertibility, that is the opportunity to reallocate the capital whenever wanted. If convertibility is denied, foreigners will avoid investing in the country and domestic investors probably will invest abroad (Röpke 1979, pp. 337 financing public deficits 340). This can lead to further restrictions of convertibility and consequently to capital flight if possible.[40] Therefore, the level of commitment is positively correlated with the degree of convertibility (component *conv*). We distinguish full convertibility of all transactions, restricted convertibility for either capital or current account transactions or no convertibility at all (Schuler 1996, pp. 29–32). A second component (*mult*) shows whether or not the market for foreign exchange is unified.
8. *Competitive elements in the monetary regime.* A few countries allow for monetary competition in that not only their own currency circulates, but also one or more foreign currencies. In Argentina, for instance, the US

40 This view is not shared by all observers. Greene and Isard (1991) argue that convertibility also has risks. Their implicit assumption seems to be that economic policymaking without strict rules does not bear any risks. In other words: their trust in governments is high.

dollar is a legal means of payment besides the peso. The public has the choice between the peso and the US dollar for their transactions. This arrangement is not an application of the free banking approach. The state remains the monopolist or oligopolist issuer of money; private firms are not allowed to issue their own currency and compete with the state. It only means that the public has the freedom to make contracts in any of the two (or more) currencies. Such an arrangement exerts competitive pressure on the domestic monetary authorities to issue a sound currency. If they fail to do so, demand for money will focus on the foreign exchange. This makes the realisation of seigniorage difficult. Therefore, the permission of monetary competition raises the level of commitment to stability (component *comp*).

9. *Financial market regulation.* At first glance, financial market regulation is not necessarily connected to commitment to stability. However, if the monetary authority is involved in regulatory issues, this probably will have an impact on its monetary policy. Insofar, regulatory responsibilities can be a signal of whether or not commitment to stability is high. However, this signal is ambivalent. As regards the political independence of monetary policy, there are both arguments against and in favour of commissioning the monetary institution with the supervision of the domestic financial market (Eijffinger and de Haan 1996, pp. 46–49).[41]

   There are three arguments against such an arrangement. First, the monetary authority can face a conflict of interests in case some banks or other financial institutions have liquidity problems. Adding liquidity to the system may rescue these banks on the one hand. On the other hand, money growth associated with the new liquidity may raise both inflationary expectations and inflation (in the longer run). Second, in case of a failure of a financial institution the monetary authority may receive bad publicity. Its reputation may be harmed which again diminishes the credibility of the monetary regime. A third argument is related to the fact that not just the monetary authority, but also the government is concerned with a potential bailout of a failed bank. Mixed responsibilities would harm the monetary authority. The first argument in favour of an active role of the monetary authority is that co-ordination of monetary policy and prudential regulation will enhance efficiency (ibid., p. 78) The other arguments are restricted to independent central banks: central banks act as lender of last resort. Therefore, it makes sense that they control the financial system to recognise as well as to prevent financial crisis as early as possible. Moreover and similarly, the central bank smoothes the payment system. A good knowledge of the system helps with this task.

41 See also De Beaufort Wijnholds and Hoodguin (1994, pp. 76–79)

However, a monetary reform is not restricted to the foundation of an independent central bank that at any rate acts as lender of last resort.

Therefore, we do not give much credit to the arguments in favour of commissioning the supervision of the financial system. The counter-arguments are stronger, especially after a severe inflation when the main task of commitment is to recover credibility. Hence, separating monetary policy and financial supervision indicates high commitment, whereas both tasks being carried out by the same institution show a lower level of commitment. The lowest commitment, however is made when there is no financial market regulation (component *reg*).

10. *Accountability of the monetary authority.* As with the supervision of the financial system, the correlation of commitment to stability and the accountability of the monetary authority to the government or parliament is not clear. On the one hand, the monetary authority has to create transparency; an informed public is more likely to form realistic expectations than an uninformed one.[42] On the other hand, accountability must not lead to the right of the government or parliament to participate in monetary policy. Although criterion (3) already elaborates on this danger, the boundaries between accountability and government intervention cannot be drawn unequivocally. The level of commitment is the higher, the less influence government and parliament can exert. The highest level is given when the public has to be informed by at least quarterly reports of the monetary authority (or a detailed website on the Internet). It is the least when no information is required. A medium level of commitment is achieved when instead of a public report hearings at the parliament have to take place (component *acc*).

The index of legal commitment contains ten elements. These elements are chosen because they cover all pertinent aspects of a monetary regime. Technically, the higher each component of the index, the higher the degree of legal commitment. It takes into account that commitment only makes sense if it is the government who commits to stability. This chapter has shown that they play an important role for a monetary regime to work. Monetary commitment can be credible only and, therefore, successful if it is accepted and deliberately chosen as part of the economic order of the country. However, to broaden the concept of commitment was only a first step towards a theory of monetary reform. In the following chapter, the role of institutions defined as formal and informal rules isanalysed. A detailed

---

42 For a recent discussion of this topic see Deutsche Bundesbank (2000). See also the controversy between Willem H. Buiter (1999) and Otmar Issing (1999).

analysis of the institutional constraints of commitment will enhance knowledge about how to make a monetary reform credible and successful.

3. Institutional Constraints to Monetary Policy

I. INSTITUTIONS AS CONSTRAINTS

The term 'institution' is difficult to circumscribe. It has a variety of meanings. The most common meaning of an institution in the macroeconomic literature is that of an organisation, a body having a name and consisting of persons. We do not focus on this meaning. We concentrate on institutions as sets of formal and/or informal rules including their enforcement mechanism (Richter and Furubotn 1996, p. 6). Institutions can be interpreted as economic goods and act as incentives or constraints (Leipold 1998, p. 27). Whereas formal institutions definitely require an enforcement mechanism, informal institutions normally don't. Nevertheless, there is no distinctive boundary between the two (Raiser 1997, pp. 2f.). Institutions can evolve either spontaneously or they are the result of deliberate efforts to construct them.[1] Along these lines, one can draw the borderline between institutions and components of economic order. We define institutions as the comprehensive concept. All sets of rules – formal and informal, spontaneous or created – are included. The economic order will be seen as a subset of institutions, namely those that are formal and created by political will.

Economic policymakers have to take into account the role of institutions in at least two respects. First, they have to design institutions that are allowed to pursue an adequate economic policy. These deliberately created institutions form the economic order of a country. The monetary regime is part of the overall economic order. From this perspective, a monetary reform has the objective to build a designed institution. This kind of policymaking is of a general, rather abstract nature, best described with the term *'Ordnungspolitik'* or as making the 'rules of the game' (Vanberg 1998, pp.

1 In this study, we are only slightly interested in the way they evolve. Instead we focus on how much and in what way they affect the monetary regime. Moe (1990, p. 215) argues that knowledge about the effects of institutions gives an idea of how they evolve, presuming that individual self-interest leads to the creation of institutions.

173f). After the decision has been made on which kind of economic order to establish, this order has to be sustained as a matter of commitment. We have dealt with this issue in Chapter 2. The results of this analysis imply that the design of a monetary institution does not automatically guarantee low inflation. Instead, the monetary performance differs across countries even given the same degree of commitment.

This leads to the second role of institutions which also is important. Institutions are constraints for the design of components of the economic order. These constraints can be the result of a purposeful process of policymaking, as discussed above, or they emanate spontaneously without an official mandate. Such institutional constraints are to be considered when the monetary reform after chronic or hyperinflation is made. Only by doing so, can the government improve the chances of a monetary reform to stabilise expectations and bring down inflation sustainably (Ábel, Bonin and Siklos 1994).

The second feature of institutions[2] will form the main part of this chapter: in that we take institutions as given, we can model them as constraints for the policymakers who design the monetary regime. These institutions are exogenously given for the government when it reforms the monetary regime. This even holds for institutions that have to be created simultaneously with the monetary regime, for instance fiscal discipline. Apart from the methodological advantage of taking other institutions as given, it is theoretically striking that the design of one part of the economic order has to take into account other institutions, that is other parts of the economic order.[3] The fact that rules rather than organisations are the main focus of this study does not imply that organisations do not play a role in creating or enforcing institutions. Monetary commitment can be described as a part of the economic order. As such, commitment is an institution (set of rules) purposely created by the government. It does not work, however, without an organisation run by individuals. This organisation certainly has an influence on the rules, either on their creation or on their enforcement or both.

---

[2] It is worth mentioning that a third feature of institutions also refers to their role as constraints. Monetary policymakers have to act within the rules or within the economic order to behave credibly.

[3] Although commitment may also influence institutions or even enable the government to change other institutions, for instance labour market regulation, we neglect this side of the story at this stage. It is considered in the discussion of policy options (Chapter 8).

II. INSTITUTIONS AFFECTING THE SUCCESS OF MONETARY REFORMS

In this section, we look for those institutions that affect the success of a monetary reform. Several ways to analyse the influence of institutions on credibility and success of monetary reforms are possible. First, one can exclusively assess the contribution of the institutional setting to the fortune of monetary reforms. This would mean questions like: is high political stability in general beneficial for the success of a monetary reform? How does the openness of a country as such affect the success of the reform? Another way to incorporate institutions into the analysis of monetary reform is slightly different to the one mentioned above. The relation between the type of monetary reform (expressed in terms of the degree of commitment) and institutional factors to be identified soon is searched for. This leads to the following question: given a certain degree of openness, political stability etc., which is the optimal degree of commitment to make the monetary reform credible and to reach stability? Such questions also form the background of the following considerations and are discussed in the empirical part as well.

Some factors affecting the success of monetary reforms are rather similar. For instance, following Cukierman (1992, pp. 450f) the outstanding internal public debt and the ability of the government to raise funds to balance its budget are two determinants of central bank independence. However, it is fair to assume that these factors are highly correlated. In a theoretical as well as an empirical analysis, their weight would be overemphasised if they were both used. Therefore, the number of institutions has to be limited to avoid the possibility that two or more institutional factors deal with similar phenomena. In addition, this is very important to prevent multicollinearity when estimating the effects of the constraints on the success of reforms in the sixth chapter. Technically, the factors are calculated like the index of commitment: they are restricted between 0 and 1.[4] Moreover, they consist of formal and informal as well as spontaneously evolved and politically created institutions. We identify five institutional factors:

- political stability
- fiscal stability
- labour market regime
- openness of the country
- public attitude to inflation.

---

4 For different specifications of these factors see Appendix 2, section 2.

The first factor (political stability) is a summary of the formal and informal rules that affect the way in which the political system in general responds to incentives and constraints. The second, third and fourth institutional factors regard other relevant fields of economic policy. Nevertheless, they indirectly influence most governments in their decision on whether or not to allow for inflation (Chapter 2, subsection II.b). The fifth factor (public attitude to inflation) shows how much the public responds to an inflationary bias of policymakers. In case the country chooses to peg its currency towards another currency or a basket of other currencies, the choice of this reserve medium has to be made very carefully. Fixing the exchange rate sometimes makes the economy vulnerable to external shocks. Therefore, as a sixth optional institutional factor we introduce some properties of the reserve country which will make a commitment successful.

It seems necessary to take into account the comprehensive institutional setting. It would not be satisfactory to concentrate on single aspects, i.e. single institutions. Alternatively, the broad concept of economic freedom can be used to model the complete institutional setting in one variable. For it is a concept which contains variables incorporated in some of the other institutional factors we analyse. Thus, economic freedom seems to be a mix of all institutions relevant for the success of monetary reform (Klump and Reichel 1994, pp. 449f; Gwartney and Lawson 1997).

a) Political stability

The first institution relevant for monetary stabilisation is political stability. It is difficult to define and even more difficult to measure. For a definition various questions are important.

1. Does political stability only focus on the political class or does it also take into account the general public and its attitude towards politics?
2. Does political stability include virtues like the general acceptance of law or even morale (Leschke 1996)?
3. Does political *in*stability mean a change in the political regime (*coup d'état*) or partisan change in government (Eijffinger and de Haan 1996, pp. 44f)?

These three questions can be answered together. A narrow concept of political stability would interpret frequent partisan changes in the government as a sign of political instability. This concept would not deal with the public's attitude towards politics and with the general acceptance of basic rules. Even a democratic system can such as the United Kingdom – would be called politically unstable. It would be an open question whether political stability defined that way would be compatible with a high or a rather low degree of monetary commitment. On the one hand, politicians may wish to restrict the political power of their possible successors. As a consequence, a high degree of de jure commitment would be chosen. Hence, political instability thus defined would be positively correlated with monetary commitment. On the other hand, with a high probability of being removed from office, politicians may be inclined to make use of the short-term benefits of inflation. Consequently, they will not commit to a rule-bound monetary policy. Political instability then would coincide with low legal commitment.[5]

Furthermore, this concept of political stability is not problem-oriented. Partisan changes are usual in democracies. Thus, an adequate concept of political stability can be defined as the long-term survival of a political system. Such a definition gives credit to the question of whether or not the system is democratic. It also considers the degree to which the rule of law and informal moral standards are accepted in society. Thus, a political system cannot be regarded as being stable, if the stability is a result of a repressive and undemocratic government. Normally, such a system does not represent the will of the people. Similarly, a civil war is an indicator of low political stability. Only if the political system has been subject to an open discourse among the citizens leading to a set of rules or a (political) order, political stability is regarded as being high. Indicators of political instability are the number of unsuccessful and successful *coups d'états* and the existence of political reprisal.

A high political stability enhances the chances of a monetary reform being successful. As for the compatibility of political stability as defined here and the monetary commitment, a monetary reform is most successful if political stability and the degree of commitment match. For a monetary commitment to be credible and to stabilise, it is helpful if the political system has been stable for some time. This raises the probability of the new monetary regime being sustainable. Put differently, if political stability is low, there may be the danger of a high monetary commitment not being credible.

b) Fiscal stability

Fiscal stability is – at least compared with political stability – easy to define. It is the ability of the state to run a sustainable fiscal policy. In general, higher public budget deficits imply lower fiscal stability. In a federal system, all levels are included. High fiscal stability *ceteris paribus* can help with stabilisation efforts because the fiscal authorities can finance their expenditure more easily. Pressure on monetary authorities to accommodate

---

5 It seems plausible that the second option would have a higher probability.

do not arise.[6] Moreover, the relationship of fiscal stability and monetary policy is unambiguous. High fiscal stability is compatible with a high degree of monetary commitment. It also seems to be plausible that low fiscal stability leads to low probability of a successful monetary reform.

This institutional factor seems to be measured easily. The public budget is a good approximation. It can be put in relation to the GDP. Two constraints have to be considered. For one, the government can run budget deficits, namely if it is able to finance its budget deficits on international capital markets and to pay a market interest rate. At least a few years of fiscal deficits do not necessarily impede the credibility of a monetary reform. However, deficits cannot be run for a very long time. In addition, in a situation of severe inflation and prior to a monetary reform, fiscal stability cannot be assessed by looking at the historical performance. This is due to the fact that economically bad fiscal policy has made the state dependent on monetary policy. Public budget deficits may even have been monetised which has led to inflation. Analysing only the past would be misleading.

For these reasons, fiscal stability has to be judged by considering a longer period of fiscal policy. The indicator to be calculated is an average of the actual fiscal policy as well as prospective future one (Sargent 1982, pp. 45f). A good approximation is made by analysing the fiscal deficit per GDP over some years before and after the monetary reform.

c) Labour market regime

As in the case of public budgets, monetary policy has often been abused to meet employment objectives.[7] As in the first case, it has also proven to be an inadequate tool to meet these objectives. Despite this evidence, there are still demands for lose monetary policy to boost employment – not only in countries having a need for monetary reforms, but also in OECD countries.[8] With a labour market flexible enough to adjust to supply or demand shocks, the need for accommodation is low; monetary policy can concentrate on price stability, especially after a monetary reform.

Concerning the relation of the degree of commitment and labour market flexibility, Schaling (1995, pp. 185–223) argues that the optimal degree of central bank independence is dependent on the labour market regime. By

---

6 They do not need monetary policy to meet their financial needs. However, low fiscal stability is not the same as relying on seigniorage, i.e. on the money press. See also Chapter 6.

7 It may be justified for the monetary authority to temporarily consider the labour market, especially in a cyclical downturn or when an external price shock like in 1973/74 occurs. These cases are not considered in this subsection.

8 During the introduction of the Euro in late 1998/early 1999 such demands by governments could be observed (*The Economist* 1998a).

using Rogoff's (1985) model and assuming that the dryness of central bankers is finite, he examines the relationship between the aggressiveness of labour unions and the optimal degree of central bank independence. His results are straightforward: the more aggressive the labour unions are, the more independent the central bank should be. The intuition behind this result is that an independent and dry central bank that under no circumstances accommodates wage increases above productivity growth provides credible monetary policy. Moreover, it disciplines the labour market participants. Schaling implicitly assumes the independent central banker is successful in doing so.

In Schaling's analysis, the central bank does not take into account the outcome on the labour market. Unions and employers are responsible for the outcome, and the responsibilities are divided and known to all players. So, there is a first–best world in the tradition of Tinbergen (1952). It is fair to assume that the situation in a country implementing a monetary reform is not that clear. It may be rather difficult for the monetary authorities to exert influence on other groups. It has been shown for industrial countries that more independent central banks do not have a credibility bonus in the labour market (Debelle and Fischer 1995). Therefore, for our purpose, the causality is reversed: commitment does not restrict the labour unions' behaviour. If anything, the success of commitment is contingent on the labour market regime.

We conclude that a monetary reform is increasingly successful if the labour market regime is more flexible. Flexibility in this context is equivalent to contestability: insiders on the labour market have to fear competition from the outside.[9] This restricts their aggressiveness as regards wage demands. As a consequence, political pressure on the monetary authority to accommodate higher wages in order to prevent growing unemployment will be moderate. Thus, a high labour market flexibility is compatible with a high degree of commitment.

The government has to take into account that this relationship also holds in case of a low labour market flexibility. Commitment then should be less ambitious to make the reform a success. The public would not expect the monetary authorities to stick to a strong commitment. In this case, high wage increases would cause a dilemma for the monetary authority. Some discretionary power could be beneficial in that it stabilises the expectations. The public knows that a certain wage increase would be followed by roughly the same inflation rate. The time inconsistency problem would be moderate. In the long run, such an arrangement could even induce the labour unions to

---

9 This definition of flexibility shows that the institutional factors are interdependent. Therefore, it makes sense to analyse them commonly (p. 60 and subsection 3.II.g).

admit that there is no money illusion. Hence, lower labour market flexibility would make lower monetary commitment more credible.

d) Openness of the country

Another institutional factor determining the success of monetary policy is the openness of the country. Openness in this context does not mean openness by contract, e.g. through membership in the World Trade Organisation or IMF rules like convertibility requirements. Rather, we focus on the factual integration of the country into the world economy. A high integration into the international division of labour can also be interpreted as a sign that the internal price mechanism, which we do not consider separately, works. If there is intense competition in internationally tradable goods, one can assume that domestic and international price relations are similar. This may be different for non-tradable goods, like public services, house rents, food etc. It can be taken for granted that in many countries in the developing world these prices always have been highly regulated. Thus, over a sample of reform countries, only a few institutional differences in this respect can be notified. Therefore, it makes sense not to add a separate institutional factor for the functioning of domestic relative prices. Such a factor seems to be highly correlated with openness. In addition, price regulation is taken into account when public opposition to inflation is determined (see below).

The more open a country is towards foreign trade and capital flows, the more competitive pressure is laid on the government. Therefore, the inflationary bias will probably be smaller in an open economy than in a closed one. As regards empirical evidence, Romer (1993) as well as Campillo and Miron (1997), show that openness and inflation are negatively correlated. Concerning the degree of commitment, it has to be high in order to be credible if openness is high as well. For instance, a currency board system (CBS) can only work if markets for goods, services and capital are open. This includes convertibility as a necessary, but not sufficient condition. A sufficient condition for the success of a CBS is that the country is integrated into international markets. On the other hand, restricted openness sometimes correlates better to low commitment. Therefore, to make monetary policy successful, the degree of commitment should approximately match the degree of openness.

e) Public attitude to inflation

Finally, the credibility of a monetary reform is influenced by the preferences of the society as regards inflation in general. A society on average can be either very inflation averse or very inflation biased or something in between. Naturally, the individual attitudes within a society vary, depending on whether a person can gain from inflation or not: a net debtor will probably favour a higher inflation rate. Thus, a personal attitude can change intertemporally, depending on the financial status of an individual. Nevertheless, one can differentiate between countries. There was an intense debate about the so-called culture of stability during the preparation of the European Monetary Union. Culture of stability can best be defined as the average attitude towards inflation in a country. High culture of stability means that the public opposition against inflation is high, and vice versa. Needless to say that strong public opposition to inflation can be a cause for inflation to be low. This has been shown in an empirical analysis by Hayo (1998).

The causes for different degrees of culture of stability are manifold. One important cause for a country's aversion against inflation may be past experience. If a country has suffered from one or several hyperinflations in the past, it will probably express much opposition against an inflationary policy. Germany is such a case. Politicians who in the past questioned the independence of the Bundesbank were subject to severe criticisms by the public and there have been many examples in the history of the Bundesbank. In other countries that have not made such devastating experiences the attitude towards moderate inflation is much more relaxed.

However, the culture of stability certainly is subject to change.[10] The experience of several years or decades of stability may on the one hand raise the consciousness of the public for the benefits of stability, i.e. culture of stability grows. On the other hand, getting used to low inflation can create unawareness for the virtues of stability and the importance of a commitment to a monetary regime that guarantees stability. Both developments evolve over time. It is also possible that a change in the culture of stability is caused by a deeper integration between countries. The inhabitants of one country take the opportunity to learn from the behaviour in other countries (Grüner 1998, p. 39).

This indicates that it seems difficult to define the public attitude to inflation unambiguously. However, it has to be taken into account that the study deals with severe inflation experiences. Thus the measurement of the public attitude to inflation in these cases is easier than it would be in OECD countries with a long history of relative stability. Hence, it is measured as public opposition to inflation based on three criteria: first, if prices are repressed people do not have an adequate feeling for the costs of inflation. Public opposition to inflation is low. Second, the same holds with indexation. If wages, taxes etc. are indexed the public consciousness for inflation is

---

10 Neumann (1998, pp. 343f) argues that a central bank statute can help with keeping culture of stability high. In his view, there is an interdependence.

generally lower than without indexation. Finally, past inflation experience increases public opposition to inflation.[11]

The higher public opposition to inflation is, the more successful a monetary reform can be. Finally, it has to be answered how culture of stability affects the optimal degree of commitment. We argue that if it is high, commitment has to be high to be credible and to allow for stabilisation, otherwise, the public won't believe in a new monetary regime and the time inconsistency problem cannot be solved.

f) Properties of the reserve country

Often, monetary reforms are combined with fixing the exchange rate towards a hard currency. A nominal anchor implies a high degree of commitment. However, an exchange rate peg does not guarantee stability. The East-Asian monetary crises in 1997/98 again have raised doubts about the virtues of a peg. The critique has to be qualified. The success of fixed exchange rates depends on the choice of the reserve currency. It has to be sound, which was not the problem during the crises of the 1990s, neither in Mexico nor in Asia or Russia. In addition, it is important that the choice of the reserve currency protects the reform country from external shocks. Two kinds of disadvantageous external real shocks can be distinguished: a rise in productivity in the reserve country and a capital flow into it (Freytag 1998a). In the following, the reserve (anchor) country will be called country AC and the committing country will be called country CC.

Positive productivity shock in the reserve country: a positive productivity shock (e.g. due to innovations) in the tradable sector of country AC affects country CC in several ways. First, it raises both the relative price competitiveness and non price competitiveness of firms in the tradables sector in AC. Consequently, their sales will increase. Given that country AC is part of a system of flexible exchange rates (or dirty floating), its currency *ceteris paribus* will nominally appreciate. The international sector in country CC will be affected both by the rise in competitiveness of the firms in AC and the nominal appreciation of AC's currency. If the structure of production in both countries is similar, the firms in country CC will directly lose market shares since at the pegged exchange rate, their competitive position has been weakened by the relative productivity loss. But even if no firm in CC competes with any firm in AC, i.e. substitution elasticities are zero, the tradable sector in country CC will lose – via the nominal appreciation of currency AC which will be immediately followed by a nominal appreciation of currency CC. No matter through which channel, *ceteris paribus* exports will decrease and imports will increase. If the fix is a currency board system,

11 See also Vaubel (2000, section 2).

the money base in country CC, then, *ceteris paribus* will also decrease. If this situation continues for a while, a deflationary pressure is placed on country CC. Only if price and wage flexibility in CC is perfect will there be no recession or even depression. An income loss is inevitable in this scenario.

A surge in capital inflow into the reserve country: another external real shock for country CC follows from a sudden and huge net capital flow into the reserve country AC. This inflow can be driven by factors either inside or outside AC. In any case, it will cause AC's currency to nominally appreciate. Again, this has negative consequences for the competitiveness of firms in CC towards a third country since CC's currency will also nominally appreciate. Again, in case of a currency board the money base *ceteris paribus* will decrease. In contrast to the first scenario, this time no structural disadvantage for firms in CC occurs. The opposite may happen. Since the surge of capital inflows causes a real appreciation in AC, the competitive position of firms in the international sector of AC relative to other countries including CC is weakened (Dluhosch, Freytag and Krüger 1996, pp. 55–59). Firms in CC may experience growing demand for their goods. It is, however, not likely that this effect outpaces the negative effect caused by the nominal appreciation.

The appropriate reserve currency has to meet three conditions: first, other countries in a similar situation are also pegged to this currency; second, the reserve country is a major trade partner of the committing country; third, the production structures of the reserve country and the reform country are rather dissimilar. The fact that those third countries where most competitors of the reform country's firms come from, also peg their currencies to the reserve currency, protects the domestic firms in the international sector from a nominal appreciation. This is because their relative competitive position does not change in comparison to the firms of the other countries. A high share of foreign trade with the reserve country can also protect the committing country from the effects of a nominal appreciation of the reserve currency if the trade pattern does not change significantly after the appreciation.. A different production structure as compared to the reserve country shelters the committing country from a productivity shock in the former since the firms in both countries do not compete with each other.

g) Economic freedom and commitment

In the following, we discuss an alternative approach to the calculation of five (six) institutional factors, taking into account their probable interdependence. One also can construct an overall measure of economic freedom as the institution constraining the success of a monetary reform. The higher the economic freedom is in a country, the higher is the probability of a successful monetary reform. The argument for this proposition is straightforward: more freedom for the citizens means less discretionary room to manoeuvre for the government. The citizens have several exit options, the strongest being the possibility to move away. However, e.g. the threat of capital exports may be enough to discipline the government. Thus, a high degree of economic freedom enables the policymaker to run a monetary policy dedicated to stability. Obviously, high economic freedom is compatible with a high degree of commitment.

The measurement of economic freedom is similar to the measurement of commitment. The index of economic freedom is the average of a number of criteria like trade policy regime, tax policy, monetary policy etc. In the literature several different concepts exist. Two of them which are calculated very sophistically and carefully have been considered for use in this study. The first to be mentioned is the study by Johnson, Holmes and Kirkpatrick (1999) who use ten criteria to measure economic freedom of 160 countries. These concern the regulation of the following areas: trade policy, taxation, government intervention in the economy, monetary policy, capital flows and foreign investment, banking, wage and price controls, property rights, (general) regulation, and black market activities (ibid., pp. 51–68). The index is restricted between 1 and 5; the norm could be easily transformed into a range between 0 and 1 needed for a potential comparison to the index of commitment. The book compares the period 1996 through 1998.

The second concept is the index of economic freedom as constructed by Gwartney and Lawson (1997) and by Gwartney, Lawson and Samida (2000). The former base their index on 17 criteria summarised in the four following groups (ibid., p.4): money and inflation, government operations and regulations, takings and discriminatory taxation, and restraint on international exchange.[12] The index is restricted between 0 and 10 making it even easier to compare the indexes of freedom and commitment. The authors calculate the economic freedom of 115 countries over a period of 20 years between 1975 and 1995. The potential sample monetary reforms for the econometric analysis is much larger than in the study of Johnson, Holmes and Kirkpatrick (1999). This is one reason why the Gwartney–Lawson index is used in the empirical part of this study. The second reason is that their database can better be assessed by other researchers.[13]

As regards the newer version by Gwartney, Lawson and Samida (2000, p. 7), it consists of 23 components in the following seven groups: size of government. structure of the economy, monetary policy, freedom to use alternative currencies, property rights, international trade and international

---

[12] For further details see Appendix 2, section II.

[13] For a detailed description and critique see Henderson (1999).

exchange in capital. This study includes 123 countries for the years 1970 to 1997. In other respects, there is no difference to the Gwartney–Lawson index.

Naturally, to be useful for the goal of our analysis, the criteria for monetary policy have to be eliminated from both indexes since theoretically it does not make sense to constrain monetary commitment with elements of this same commitment. Moreover, it is necessary to avoid statistical interference. If the original index was used, the dependent variable would be on both sides of the estimation equation. Thus, the index of economic freedom as calculated by Gwartney and Lawson and Gwartney, Lawson and Samida respectively, will be used in an adapted version.

h) Other 'institutional' aspects

The impression may be given that important institutional factors have been neglected so far. In particular, the regulation of the banking and financial sectors may well contribute to the success of monetary reforms. This is true to a limited extent as the empirical analysis will reveal. In the first few years, a reform can be successful without an appropriate financial regulation. However, the lack of a prudential regulation can be harmful in crises after the reform, even when these crises are imposed externally on the country (Freytag 1998a, pp. 394f). Apart from this argument, financial regulation is part of the monetary commitment (Chapter 2, section V and Appendix 2, section I). Instead of analysing it as a constraint to successful commitment, it is seen as part of the legal commitment.

The same reasoning holds for external help which of course can either constrain or support a reform seriously. Most monetary reforms in the past have been supported generously by foreign countries or international organisations. Such a support has only seldomly been granted without conditions. These conditions are part of the legal commitment which is documented in the index of commitment. Therefore, external pledges and support cannot be part of the institutional setting. Remember that for analytical reasons institutions are interpreted as being exogenously given to the monetary reformer, whereas the choice of commitment is not.

III. COMMITMENT AND INSTITUTIONS: SUMMARY AND OUTLOOK

Commitment is a device to prevent governments from raising inflation in order to meet other than monetary objectives, such as higher employment, higher revenue and a surplus in the current account. Without commitment, credibility of monetary policy remains low. It has been theoretically argued in this study (Chapter 2) that monetary commitment is part of the economic order and that commitment as a concept is more comprehensive than the concept of central bank independence (CBI). Empirical evidence supports this view since most regressions only show a weak impact of CBI on inflation (Chapter 2, section V). Both theoretical considerations and empirical evidence have led in two directions of research in this study.

First, we have broadened the concept of commitment and have constructed a measure for (de jure) commitment which for good methodical reason is based on one of the indices of CBI, the Cukierman index. The index of commitment is considerably more comprehensive than any index of CBI. It can be incorporated into a theoretical model on the success of monetary reform and be used to empirically test whether high commitment is correlated with low inflation. Furthermore, the empirical findings about the relation between CBI and macroeconomic performance suggest that it is obviously not sufficient to commit to a rule–bound monetary policy. High commitment does not necessarily lead to low inflation. Especially in developing countries no legal measure of CBI has had a significant impact on macroeconomic performance. This weak empirical evidence cannot be traced back solely to the fact that CBI is not a good and comprehensive indicator for commitment. Rather, the problem seems to be that the monetary regime must be incorporated into the overall economic order (Eucken 1955). The economic order, however, is only a fraction of all constraints to be considered during monetary reforms. In addition, it is difficult to model. Thus, in this chapter, we have discussed (de-facto) institutional factors affecting the success of a monetary reform. There are a variety of institutions influencing the outcome of monetary policy. Many of these depend on each other. Therefore, we have distinguished five domestic factors and one property of a potential reserve country. Alternatively, an index of economic freedom can serve as a constraint that represents the institutional setting in a country.

The theoretical considerations made so far in this study suggest that a monetary reform which takes into account the institutional setting in the country can properly interact with the economic order. The chances of a monetary reform being a success theoretically rise. These considerations have to be put together to form a positive theory of monetary reform combining both the reasoning about commitment and institutions. This will be done in the next chapter.

4. The Positive Theory of Monetary Reform

I. INTRODUCTION

The public debate on monetary regimes very often is rather unrefined. During the Asian financial crises, for instance, the policy of nominal anchors for developing and newly industrialised countries was generally questioned by some observers. The reason for this sudden dislike was simply that many countries got into trouble although they had pegged their currencies to other (hard) currencies. Other observers suggested currency boards for nearly all countries that got into financial turmoil. They argued that the actual pegging was not credible and should be replaced by a more credible commitment. Both views are myopic. They pretend that simple solutions can be found for such a complex phenomenon as a monetary crisis. The myopia can be taken as a sign that there still is not enough attention given to institutions. The relevant question is whether a monetary regime is compatible with other components of the economic order, or more generally, with institutions defined as formal and informal rules in the respective country.

A government planning a monetary reform, therefore, should be very careful when committing to a monetary regime after a period of severe inflation. The level of commitment has to be chosen very cautiously. One main hypothesis of this chapter is that to exclusively choose a high level of commitment does not guarantee high credibility and automatic stabilisation. Instead, there is a link between the institutional setting and the optimal monetary commitment. Compatibility of the new monetary regime with the institutional setting can make a monetary reform credible and a success.

This relationship is analysed in this chapter. First, we give a brief overview about possible monetary regimes implemented by a reform. Three forms can be roughly distinguished: a central bank system with and without an external peg, a currency board system and the denationalisation of monetary policy, be it via dollarisation, via free banking or via the involvement of international organisations. Second, the considerations about commitment are briefly applied to prototypes of monetary regimes.

Consequently, Chapters 2 and 3 are put together and highlighted in a model of monetary commitment and institutions in the course of a regime switch.

II. PROTOTYPES OF MONETARY REGIMES AFTER INFLATION

a) Monetary reform and commitment

Defining monetary reforms is not an easy task, as neither a clear explanation nor a classification exists in the literature. Bähr (1994, pp. 9–16) provides for a comprehensive overview about definition and types. Based on her description, but with a different focus, we identify two probative elements of a monetary reform:

1. introduction of a new currency and;
2. establishment of a new monetary regime.

The first element is not as important as the second. It is, however, very difficult to define precisely what can be understood under 'establishment of a new monetary regime'. As Sargent (1982, p. 48) puts it: 'While the distinction between isolated actions and strategy regimes is clear in principle, it is admittedly a delicate task to interpret whether particular historical episodes reflect isolated actions within the same old rules of the game or whether they reflect a new set of rules or government strategies'. We include all efforts to change the monetary regime that go slightly beyond a mere removal of some decimal places on the notes or just changing the name of the currency. It is not necessary for the country to introduce a new central bank law or statute. We also do not exclude all those attempts of the government to worsen the money in order to earn more seigniorage or devalue public debt.[1] To neglect these reforms would certainly produce a bias in our sample towards successful monetary reforms. Nevertheless, we do not follow the rather pessimistic view of Mas (1995). His summary of the post-war history of monetary reforms is: 'all for naught' (ibid., pp. 508–510). In his opinion, monetary reforms are mainly made for confiscation. This view is by far too

1 Bähr (1994, p. 13) calls this a manipulating reform which is a bit misleading. In the general understanding the expression 'reform' is associated with an attempt to improve on the situation (Bernholz 1995, p. 262).

pessimistic and misses the point of a political economy analysis which is about politically rational behaviour rather than about political strong-arm methods. Without a contradiction to political economy reasoning, it can be argued that the government pursuing a monetary reform is determined to end the inflation process. Under this assumption, a failure is not due to malice of the government but on the contrary to a lack of policy instruments or missing credibility. The consequences are equivalent in both views.

As regards types of monetary reform, all reforms are excluded that create a new monetary regime after the foundation of a (post-communist or post-colonial) nation state, after the separation of two or more formerly united countries or after monetary integration (Mas 1995, p. 487). In these cases, it is difficult to separate whether the reform is triggered by monetary problems or by political circumstances. Thus, we focus on monetary reforms after periods of severe inflation even if we miss a number of potentially interesting cases.

In general, three prototypes of monetary regimes can be constructed unilaterally in a monetary reform. First, the most common monetary regime has a central bank that pursues monetary policy. The degree of commitment associated with a central bank theoretically varies strongly: the central bank can be more or less independent; the currency can be pegged to a foreign one or not and so forth. A second monetary regime is a currency board system. Monetary policy is tied to the monetary policy of a reserve country. The currency board system has regained importance in the last decade. A third, and rather rare, monetary regime can be at best described as a denationalisation of money (von Hayek 1990). Several options are possible: dollarisation, free banking or monetary policy pursued by an external agency like the IMF.[2] All of these types of monetary regimes are related to different degrees of commitment. The index of commitment, as developed in Chapter 2, is constructed by calculating the (weighted and unweighted) average of ten criteria so that it is impossible to rank the prototypes without knowledge of the details of the monetary regime.

b) Central bank system

By the end of the 20th century, most countries in the world had established central banks, approximately 160 countries by 1998. A central bank is an agency pursuing monetary policy on the behalf of the government. It should be independent of daily political business. Two kinds of independence can be distinguished: goal independence and instrument independence (Debelle and

---

2 Meltzer (1983, p. 95) distinguishes only three types of monetary reform, namely a gold or commodity standard, a rule *á la Friedman* (1951) and free banking. This is too narrow for our purpose.

Fischer 1995, p. 197). A central bank with goal independence chooses the policy target itself, for instance price level stability or a constant nominal exchange rate towards another currency. From a constitutional economic perspective, such an arrangement is highly undesirable. The final objective of monetary policy should not be left in the discretion to central bankers. Rather, it has to reflect the preferences of the society. Therefore, the objective of monetary policy has to be legally codified (see above).

However, a central bank should have instrument independence. A central bank being independent in this sense has the freedom to meet the given objective with the instruments it regards as the most suitable. There is no rule limiting the discretionary power in this respect. The timing and intensity of the use of these instruments is left to the central bank. This arrangement is completely compatible with the concept of commitment since it is the government who commits to a monetary regime (Chapter 2, section III). Thus, the central bank is enabled to react to shocks if necessary. It also has the freedom to reject political demands for easy money, interest rate lowering or foreign exchange interventions.

An important feature of the central bank systems is the exchange rate arrangement of the country. As regards the degree of commitment, the exchange rate arrangement is of importance. If the exchange rate is in the responsibility of another agency such as the treasury, CBI can be restricted. It cannot be ruled out that the central bank has to aim at a certain inflation rate and at a certain nominal exchange rate simultaneously. In such a case, the system is underdetermined: one instrument is assigned to two objectives. There may (not necessarily) be a trade-off between these two objectives. Whether or not this trade-off exists clearly hinges on the construction of the exchange rate arrangement. If the exchange rate is set due to the fundamentals – which of course is not easy – the risk is relatively small.[3]

The easiest but also rarest case is a system of *flexible exchange rates*. The exchange rate as the relative price of two currencies on the foreign exchange rate market is exclusively determined by supply and demand. The central bank has no obligation to intervene in this market. Given that the purchase power parity (PPP) doctrine holds (Dornbusch 1992; Meier 1997), in the long run exchange rate changes reflect differences in the inflation rates of two countries. However, even under flexible exchange rates most central banks intervene to avoid great fluctuations. Inasmuch as the interventions can be sterilised, the inflation target can be met.

---

3 The following paragraphs are not meant to add to the general discussion of whether flexible or fixed exchange rates are superior from a welfare economic standpoint. For a basic and still relevant theoretical discussion see Sohmen (1969) and the contributions in Dreyer, Haberler and Willett (1978).

A central bank system can also be run under a formal or informal *fixed exchange rate arrangement*. Such an arrangement can in general have five different forms. These differences have consequences for the degree of commitment – not necessarily for the degree of CBI as defined in the literature – and the danger of a trade-off between nominal exchange rate stability and price level stability.

1. Governments can sign a treaty fixing the exchange rate of all participating currencies to one currency ('hegemony currency'). We assume that the exchange rates are fixed in a political process rather than after an economic analysis of which is an equilibrium exchange rate. The bilateral exchange rates of the other currencies are redundant. The 'hegemony country' only tries to meet an internal objective of monetary policy. The responsibilities to keep the exchange rate stable lie completely in the hands of the other countries. Thus, if the monetary policy of the 'hegemony country' is not compatible with the internal objective of one of the other countries, this country will import either inflation or stability, depending on the stability orientation of the 'hegemony country'. Under such an arrangement, an individual long-term monetary policy for smaller countries is impossible (Johnson 1972). Whether the independence of their central bank is enhanced or restricted depends on whether or not the arrangement can be used by the central bank to resist political pressure for easy money. In the Bretton Woods system, many countries imported inflation rather than stability from the USA. As a lesson from this experience, such an agreement should allow for exchange rate adjustments if inflation rates differ across countries.
2. A variation of this is a fixed exchange rate arrangement that distributes the burdens of keeping the exchange rate stable symmetrically among the member countries. There is no 'hegemony currency'. Under such an arrangement, monetary co-operation that allows to minimise frictions seems to be possible. Depending on how different the cultures of stability in the member countries are and how close the exchange rates set in the political process are to equilibrium exchange rates, CBI in the member countries is on average higher than in the asymmetric case with a 'hegemony currency'. The European Monetary System (EMS) was intended to be an example for this type of agreement.
3. Another variation of a fixed exchange rate arrangement is designed in a way that the burden of exchange rate stabilisation completely lies with the countries whose currencies tend to depreciate, in other words, whose long-run money growth exceeds that of other member countries. The independence of central banks is not restricted, at least as long as they aim

at price level stability.[4] For this regime to work it is not necessary to sign a formal international treaty. The reform country only has to announce that it fixes its exchange rate to another currency and thereby uses this currency as a nominal anchor.

4. Similarly, a reform country aiming at a disinflation process fixes its exchange rate to another currency, but depreciates its currency regularly and by a pre-announced rate (crawling peg). A basic rate towards the reserve currency is set, with an exchange rate band of about ±10 per cent. It will not be intervened if the exchange rate does not tend to fall short of this band on the market for foreign exchange. Every month or quarter, the currency will be depreciated by a fixed percentage. This will be done by raising the base rate (in domestic currency per reserve currency). It is aimed at reducing the costs of disinflation by a crawling peg. Poland has been applying this regime since 1995; Argentina made use of it in the 1970s.
5. Besides these types of formal agreement there is an informal exchange rate fixing. One country decides to choose another currency as a nominal anchor. This could be either due to political will or the central bank chooses to fix the exchange rate towards another currency. The Austrian central bank unofficially followed the Bundesbank in monetary policy from late 1981 (Hochreiter and Winckler 1994, p. 34) until December 31, 1998, when monetary policy in Euroland was handed over to the ECB.[5] As long as the nominal anchor is chosen to import stability, there is no reason to believe that CBI is restricted by the fixing. A nominal anchor can be to run both with definitely fixed exchange rates or as a crawling peg, with a constant pre-announced depreciation of the domestic currency. The latter seems sensible if the costs of disinflation are very high. The necessary adjustment can be distributed over several periods. Obviously, there is a trade-off between this and credibility.

The degree of commitment to stability obviously depends on the form of the exchange rate arrangement. This has not been acknowledged by the literature on CBI (Chapter 2, section IV), but in the index of commitment (Chapter 2, section V). However, the problems mentioned here have in the past only applied to industrialised countries that had to import an inflation rate of about 5 to 8 per cent. Therefore, this problem does not directly affect a country planning a monetary reform after a chronic or hyperinflation. In case they decide to found a central bank and to fix their exchange rate, they will

---

4 If a central bank permanently wants to keep inflation high it could argue that its independence is restricted. Remember that our normative basis is price level stability: the question then is why does the country join a fixed exchange rate system?

5 Because of its original application through the Austrian central bank, this type is sometimes referred to as 'Austrian solution'.

certainly choose a nominal anchor with or without a crawling peg, formally or informally, in order to import stability. At the same time, it is rather unlikely that other countries will agree on a Bretton Woods or EMS-style monetary arrangement with the reform country. Therefore, we restrict the analysis to unilateral regime switches.

c) Currency board system

A currency board system is an extreme form of an informal fixed exchange rate arrangement.[6] When introducing a currency board, the government fixes the exchange rate towards a reserve currency and guarantees full convertibility of its own currency. Monetary policy is pursued by a monetary institution called a currency board rather than by a central bank. Contrary to the latter, the board only has a couple of tasks. Whereas a central bank has a variety of monetary instruments with which it can influence either quantities or prices on the market for money and credit, a currency board has none. It issues notes and coins exclusively against foreign currency. The board merely reacts to the supply or demand of market participants. The monetary base is fully backed by foreign exchange.

Besides issuing money on demand the currency board has another task. The reserve currency does not have to be held entirely in cash. The board can invest part of the reserves in order to earn interest payments. These can be either added to the reserves in order to protect the board from possible future losses[7] or it can be handed to the government as additional revenues. It is self-evident that the board has to invest the foreign reserves in secure assets which can be changed into cash very quickly in case many people want to cash in domestic notes and get foreign currency in cash.

Consequently, the board has no control of the money supply in the country. High-powered money is created endogenously in the market for foreign exchange depending on balance-of-payments transactions. A trade surplus *ceteris paribus* raises the stock of high-powered money, a trade deficit diminishes it. Net capital inflows *ceteris paribus* increase the money base, net capital outflows decrease it. These transactions depend on factors like international competitiveness of the tradables sector and the extent to which the country is able to attract foreign capital. Broader money is created in the banking sector which normally functions like the banking sector in a monetary system with a central bank. It can be shown in a multiplier analysis that the money supply in a currency board system can be compared to that of

6 For a comprehensive description see Hanke and Schuler (1994).

7 The West-African Currency Board (1913–1971) for instance created a backing of 110 per cent of the money base by adding seigniorage to the reserves (Schuler 1992, p. 59). Thereby, it tried to protect itself from losses from its portfolio. See also Freytag (1999).

a central bank system. Moreover, the board cannot act as a lender of last resort. In case a commercial bank goes bankrupt, the currency board cannot bail out this bank. This, too, is different for a central bank. The absence of a lender of last resort makes it even more necessary to introduce prudential banking regulation than in a central bank system (Baliño, Enoch et al. 1997, pp. 20–23). The money supply can be made more regular and predictable if foreign banks are allowed if not encouraged to operate branches in the CBS country.

Different forms of currency board systems exist in reality.[8] What has been described above is often called an orthodox system. Usually, it is not adopted in practice. This can be illustrated by three examples. In Argentina, for instance, the money base only needs to be backed with a minimum of 70 per cent of foreign assets. The rest may be backed by USdollar denominated Argentine government bonds (BONEX). Estonia has accumulated foreign reserves that approximately double the money base (Eesti Pank various issues). Those reserves exceeding the money base can be used to act as a lender of last resort. Hong Kong's currency board has been equipped with a number of monetary instruments that make it increasingly appear like a central bank (Greenwood 1988a, 1988b, 1995).

Another important question regarding a currency board system is its duration. A currency board normally is not meant to be a permanent institution. Rather it is introduced to create credibility and stability. Some of the countries that recently have established currency board systems, lacked the professional expertise and the financial institutions needed to run a central bank system. During some years with a currency board system, expertise can be gained and financial institutions can evolve or be set up (Baliño, Enoch et al. 1997, pp. 24f). If, and only if, monetary policy has reached credibility, it may be advantageous for a country to proceed a step and to introduce an independent central bank.[9] A politically independent central bank has more flexibility than a strictly rule-based currency board. Flexibility and discretionary power may be especially important when the country that proceeds in the debt cycle becomes a net capital exporter (Röpke 1930). In this case it will become difficult to acquire the money base necessary for a growing economy. It then would be dangerous to rely on the balance of payments concerning the money supply unless there is full price flexibility.

A very important aspect of a CBS is the choice of the correct reserve currency. A currency board can import stability by fixing the exchange rate

---

8 For a recent overview see Baliño, Enoch et al. (1997). See also Bennett (1993 and 1994), Schuler (1992), Freytag (1998a and 1998b), Hanke (1996) and Cavallo (1993).

9 To abandon a currency board before the monetary system has been strengthened may have the same effect as to default.

with respect to the reserve currency. If a sound currency (like the US dollar, the D-Mark or the Swiss Franc) has been chosen, a necessary condition for stability is fulfilled. Hence, the soundness of the reserve currency is a necessary condition for the success of a currency board system.[10] Contemporary currency boards (with the exception of Brunei Darussalam) have pegged their currencies either to the US dollar or to the D-Mark. The success of a currency board, however, is not only to be expressed in terms of the inflation rate and its change, respectively. By choosing the right (wrong) reserve currency, the country can protect (fail to protect) itself from external real shocks (Chapter 3, section II).

There is one severe criticism, namely that the introduction of a currency board is equal to a loss of sovereignty. The government or its agent can only react. No scope for action is left. Although this is a serious objection, the argument has a weakness which should not be overlooked: it implicitly assumes that discretionary power of governments always means sovereignty (Willgerodt 1990). It is highly questionable if the government by its own will runs budget deficits which then contribute to inflation (Chapter 3, section II). Rather, it should eagerly try to bring down inflation quickly. Thus, it can be taken for granted that vested interests are very strong and make it impossible for the government to pursue a policy which is compatible with higher price stability. In a nutshell, unless the economic and political system limits the power of interest groups, the sovereignty of the government is also limited. Or, as Jan Tumlir (1985, p. 71) has put it: 'governments are becoming the servant of rent-seeking groups'.[11]

d) Denationalisation of money 1: dollarisation and free banking

The issuing of money is not necessarily a public task to be fulfilled by the government or its agency. It is also possible that foreign money circulates in the country (dollarisation), that money is issued by private suppliers (free banking) or that an international organisation (IO) pursues monetary policy. In practice, there are only few contemporary examples for dollarisation; free banking was practised in the 19th century, particularly in the British Empire; and so far monetary policy has not been pursued by an IO.

---

10 This does not necessarily mean that the inflation rate in the currency board country is as low as it is in the reserve country. If productivity in the currency board country grows faster than in the reserve country, its currency normally appreciates in real terms as compared to the reserve currency since the prices for non-tradables rise faster than in the reserve country. Therefore, inflation in the currency board country is higher.

11 A country that introduces a CBS can hide this fact from the public by naming the monetary authority central bank which Estonia and Argentina did. The latter was so successful that even experts were misled and did not call the board a board (e.g. Mastroberardino 1994).

Dollarisation means that the country does not issue an own currency. Instead a foreign currency, normally the US dollar, circulates and is used for all purposes, i.e. cash holdings, banking accounts, credits and so forth. In the context of this chapter, dollarisation is a deliberately chosen monetary regime, as opposed to cases where due to instability the US dollar has driven out the official currency. In particular, during hyperinflations currency substitution can be observed. It usually takes place prior to a monetary reform. Often, it is the immediate stimulus for a reform.

The country where only a foreign currency circulates cannot pursue its own monetary policy. Monetary sovereignty is completely abandoned. In this respect, dollarisation is similar to a currency board system. However, the country has no source of interest payments which can be used for the public budget. As long as such payments exceed the cost associated with a currency board, dollarisation has opportunity cost. Moreover, sometimes it is seen as a disadvantage that a country does not have its own currency. Again the problem of sovereignty applies. In contrast to a loss of sovereignty associated with a currency board or a nominal anchor, this argument is more significant since many people may regard the exclusive circulation of foreign exchange, especially the US dollar, as somewhat humiliating. Nevertheless, in some countries, the US dollar is an official currency, for instance in Panama and (besides the Peso) in Argentina and since September 2000 in Ecuador (see Chapter 8, section V). In Panama, the people did not accept the domestic currency, the balboa (Schuler 1992, pp. 82f).

As long as the circulating currency has a reputation of being stable, the degree of commitment of this monetary regime *ceteris paribus* is obviously very high. The government has no chance to intervene on the foreign exchange markets and the domestic money markets since monetary policy is pursued abroad.

Whereas dollarisation relies on money that is issued by a state monopoly, albeit a foreign one, the proponents of *free banking* argue that privately and competitively issued money is superior.[12] Their argument rests on two pillars: first, as empirical regularity governments are always tempted and in history often successfully have tried to abuse their monopoly power to depreciate the money and to expropriate their people. The proponents of free banking seem to distrust governments in general. Second, as an assumption, banks in a competitive banking system are profit maximisers and, therefore, provide stable money (Dowd 1994, pp. 409–411). The proponents argue further that this makes banking regulation superfluous. Concerning financial crises, they

12 See for the general argument for instance Smith (1936), von Hayek (1990) and Dowd (1994) and for an application Selgin (1988).

also argue that in free banking systems these crises were always caused by excessive banking regulation (Smith 1936, pp. 42–56).

In practice, any bank or individual, domestic or foreign, is allowed to issue money. The relative price of different moneys – the expression currencies is misleading – is determined by their relative scarcities. There is no official monetary policy and there is no central bank or similar monetary authority. The government has no influence on monetary variables like prices, interest rates etc. The degree of governmental commitment to stability can be regarded as being high at first glance. There are competitive elements and the government cannot intervene. However, some qualifications remain: how easily can the government change the system if it needs money? How is the regulation of the banking system organised? If these questions are settled, free banking is a strong commitment by the government.

e) Denationalisation of money 2: IMF as monetary agency

Finally, we discuss the *role of international organisations* in a monetary reform. The most important IO to think of in this context is the International Monetary Fund . The rationale for its founding in the late 1940s was on the one hand to prevent balance-of-payments problems and to help with the supply of international capital for developing countries given that the private international capital market does not work properly. Whereas the IMF has its main task in case a country faces balance-of-payments problems, its fellow organisation, the World Bank, is supposed to give development aid. In what follows we concentrate on a possibility of making use of the IMF's comparative advantage, i.e. assistance of those countries suffering from high inflation rates and losses in foreign reserves. The proposal made here has a different focus as compared to the actual debate and the suggestions made there to improve on the IMF's role as international 'lender of last resort (e.g. SVR 1998; Siebert 1999).[13]

The IMF today advises governments, trains officials, surveys economic policy and provides financial assistance in case a reform is needed. Naturally, the work of the IMF is not restricted to monetary reforms. One of the main tasks in the 1990s has been the surveillance of its member countries. In recent years, the IMF has successfully tried to raise transparency: since 1998, a tri-annual periodical, the *IMF Economic Review*, has been published to report on bilateral consultations with member countries under Article IV (IMFe, January–April 1998, p. V). Much information can also be extracted from the IMF's website (http://www.imf.org). Concerning the second pillar of the Fund's policy, financial help is only given contingent on reforms of

[13] Nevertheless, the suggestions of especially these two contributions make sense and should be followed at any rate. This, however, is a different issue.

economic policy in the country (Fischer 1997).[14] The emphasis on conditionality has been increased in recent years, especially after the Asian crisis and problems in Russia and Latin America in its aftermath. It has been suggested that the IMF should increase its emphasis on conditionality even further (Krueger 1998, pp. 2010–2012). This is consistent with the view that conditionality raises the degree of commitment; the government commits externally and makes its actions more transparent.

Conditionality has an interesting and important property. It relieves the internal political pressure from the government involved. The government has a better chance to pursue the monetary reform since it can claim that all unpopular aspects of the reform – especially sacrifice ratios – are due to the conditions the IMF has 'forced' on it. If the reform is successful in the medium run, i.e. inflation decreases and economic growth increases, the government can take credit for the success. Many governments have taken advantage of this 'dirty-work' strategy (Vaubel 1991a) in the last decades.

Notwithstanding, the dirty-work strategy has risks. The first risk is that private investors undermine the conditions the IMF imposes on the country. For instance, they are too generous with new credits for the government being sure that the IMF will bail out the country and the investors another time. Moral hazard has been a regular – but not permanent – problem of IMF programmes. During the public debate about the virtues of IOs in the late 1990s it was a main argument of the Fund's critics.[15] Another danger is that the government of the country in trouble may try to swindle by not meeting the conditions although they are part of the deal. Many reforms failed because of either the inability or the unwillingness of governments to meet the requirements of the IMF (James 1996, pp. 330–335).[16]

Third, risks may evolve from the IMF itself. One reason is that conditionality always is ex-post conditionality, i.e. the IMF reacts only after a crisis (Siebert 1999, pp. 9f). That is why an even better surveillance is often demanded (e.g. Fischer 1998). This is necessary in two respects: first, better surveillance helps to avoid the crisis from the very beginning. However, it cannot be excluded that it triggers a crisis as international investors take the Fund's report as an incentive to leave the country. There is no easy way out of this dilemma. Second, the help given to countries in crises has to be put under scrutiny as to whether it was effective in overcoming the problems that led to the crisis. The IMF itself regularly assesses the programme it launches.

---

14 For a brief overview about the IMF's potential arrangements see Schadler et al. (1995, p. 3).

15 However, others argue that the IMF – at least during the Asian crisis in 1997/98 – focused too much on moral hazard and thus demanded too much austerity from the Asian countries (Nunnenkamp 1998).

16 For similar experiences see also the case studies of the monetary reforms in Greece 1944 and Paraguay 1943/44 (Chapter 7).

It has been criticised for being too enthusiastic about the effects of the conditionally given support (Killick 1995). Following Killick, this enthusiasm stems from a lack of statistical evidence; the Fund only applies case studies which do not allow for separating possible causes for the measured macroeconomic outcome after the reform package.[17] Killick's (1995) criticism is methodical rather than general in nature. He does not object to the work of the Fund as such.

This leads to a slightly differentiated criticism of the IMF. A more general approach applies public choice considerations to international organisations (Vaubel 1986) and asks questions such as the following: why should IMF staff be interested in reports showing a low impact of IMF programmes? There are two reasons for the IMF for not being too critical with its own work: first, the staff does not necessarily want to attract disapproval for their actions. This would endanger the future role of the whole organisation. Second, the governments of the countries supported simultaneously are recipients of financial aid and supervisors of the Fund. Their interest in critical reviews certainly is low. A proof of this thesis is given in the IMF Economic Reviews (IMFe) where critical remarks about a country's future prospects are made only implicitly, if at all.

Public choice considerations also suggest that the IMF staff may be only partly interested in strong commitment in order to keep some discretionary power (Vaubel 1991b; Frey 1991). Such behaviour has been reported, for instance, by Domingo Cavallo, the Argentine Minister of Finance, who planned and pursued the Convertibility Law in 1991. He complained that the IMF was not in favour of a strong commitment such as a currency board which Argentina introduced (Cavallo and Cottani 1997).[18] The interest in less than optimal commitment may be fostered by the fact that competencies and responsibilities are not delegated properly if the IMF conditionally gives assistance but is not involved in policymaking.

A better acknowledgement of these incentive problems can enhance both the Fund's interest in rule-bound policy and the domestic monetary policy in countries facing chronic inflation and hyperinflation and in need of monetary reform. Hence, in the remainder of this subsection we discuss – as a theoretical possibility – that the IMF by contract runs the monetary policy of the country implementing the monetary reform. Such an arrangement may totally change the incentive scheme for the IMF staff. It not only suggests a

---

17 See the debate between Killick (1995) and Schadler (1995) about the assessment of the application of the 'enhanced structural adjustment facilities' (ESAF) to 19 low-income countries (Schadler, Rozwadowski et al. 1993). See also Schadler (1995) and Schadler et al. (1995).

18 See also Chapter 7. In other instances, e.g. in Bulgaria 1997, the IMF argued in favour of stronger commitment than the respective government (Gulde 1999).

policy mix and forces it upon the country in question, but is also involved in day-to-day business. It can gain the status of an independent central bank.[19] Under this arrangement, the IMF's affinity towards rule bound monetary policy and strong governmental commitment probably will be strengthened. Thus, more use could be made of the expertise and experience of IMF staff members. In a formal agreement the IMF is given the task to pursue monetary policy in the respective country. The complete monetary regime, including targets and instruments of monetary policy as well as the exchange rate arrangement, is also subject to the agreement. Thereby, the commitment remains a domestic issue; the government of the reform country decides to commit itself to a rule-bound policy and delegates monetary policy to an international agency instead of a national one.

The most important characteristic is that the government has no means to intervene in monetary policy and that the monetary authority is run by a foreign institution, but not a foreign government. As regards day-to-day business, the IMF as the monetary authority is not directly responsible to the government. Nevertheless, the monetary authority is responsible for the monetary objectives being met. Besides, the country can denounce the treaty when needed. At first glance, the most striking disadvantage of this regime is the loss of sovereignty which even exceeds the loss associated with a currency board system. Again, the argument applies that the government can gain internal sovereignty by giving it up externally. Moreover, the government can announce that it commissions the IMF with this task on its own will. Or – depending on the domestic political climate – it can be announced that the IMF insists on this arrangement. Otherwise, it would not assist the reform process with financial aid. As regards the degree of commitment, it seems to be rather high. The domestic government completely dismisses all means of discretionary power.

Like the currency board system, this solution is a transitory regime. The agreement can be designed in a way that domestic monetary specialists are involved in monetary policymaking from the very beginning. They can also increase their involvement in an ex-ante fixed schedule. This includes that they increasingly take part in decisionmaking. Thus, they benefit from training on the job. After some years, they completely take over monetary policy and the IMF restricts itself to surveillance.

---

19 In a recent paper, Schneider and Wagner (1999) emphasise this role of the IMF. They also make a detailed proposal including the policy instruments needed by the IMF to master such a task.

III. MONETARY REGIMES AND THE DEGREE OF COMMITMENT

It is a priori unclear which of these prototypes should be introduced by a monetary reform. At this stage of the study we will assign a degree (or a range of degrees) of commitment to each prototype. However, before we start, we will briefly explain why free banking is not an appropriate monetary regime implemented via a reform.

a) Free banking does not help

One prototype of a monetary regime after a period of high and volatile inflation relies on competitive forces to ensure credibility and eventually stability. We argue that free banking is no appropriate regime to guarantee a success of the monetary reform. There are several serious criticisms of free banking which are particularly valid after hyperinflation or during a transition from socialism to a market economy. The first criticism refers to one argument of the proponents of free banking after hyperinflation. Since the relative prices are completely distorted and no bureaucracy is able to predict the correct price relations there is uncertainty about the price relations. A competitive monetary regime is said to create stable money almost by itself with a price structure reflecting the relative scarcities. The claim then is that certainty is higher under free banking than under any other monetary system (Wentzel 1995, pp. 70–71). However, it can also be argued that a competitive monetary regime creates high uncertainty in the public since it had to bear losses of wealth during the inflationary process. These losses were not distributed equally among the public; instead there were winners and losers. In a competitive private currency system the danger of individual bankruptcies is evident. Again, some people will lose at least parts of their assets if bankruptcies occur. Uncertainty will rise and the credibility of the reform will suffer.

A competitive monetary system demands for new banks to enter the market and old, unsuccessful banks to go bankrupt and exit. On markets for goods and services this would be no problem; in the contrary it is a normal element of structural change. In the worst case, a customer of a bankrupt firm loses his right of compensation and cannot buy replacements. This is a foreseeable risk. However, the danger of bankruptcies in a system of free banking can have a severe disadvantage. In particular after a regime switch, those people holding money of a bank that fails lose their wealth or at least parts of it. Whereas on other markets a bankruptcy is a normal thing, in the banking sector it might lead to a bank run and a chain reaction. The whole system may crash (Wentzel 1995, pp. 69f). The people would experience the second monetary crisis after the inflation period.

Moreover, it cannot be completely excluded that competitive issuers of fiat money have an incentive to create a hyperinflation. If the present value of a stable money supply in the future is lower than the one-shot gain of a hyperinflation, hyperinflation today is attractive for single issuers (White 1999, pp. 227f). It is difficult to construct enforceable contracts which prevent the issuers from this behaviour (ibid. pp. 238f). Hyperinflation of one issuer's money will also certainly increase the danger of a crash, especially after a monetary reform.

These arguments are more or less restricted to free banking as a monetary regime after an inflationary phase. If the monetary system was intact before the introduction of free banking, the case against a competitive currency system then may be weak. However, given that people are faced with huge informational problems and losses of wealth, free banking as an intellectually demanding monetary regime seems to be rather incredible. Another argument against free banking is that it produces high transaction costs since consumers have to inform themselves comprehensively about the banks and have to calculate a variety of prices. In a functioning market economy, however, it will lose importance because e.g. rating agencies will help to overcome informational problems.

To sum up, as an appropriate regime introduced by a monetary reform free banking does not make sense because regardless of the institutional setting its credibility probably will remain low. This is due to the unquestionable risks of the system. In such a situation, the chances of the system cannot develop properly. Therefore, we do not take free banking into consideration in the following analysis.

b) Monetary regimes and the index of commitment

Finally, the index of commitment has to be applied to the monetary regimes discussed in this chapter. For a country planning a monetary reform, seven alternative prototypes of a monetary regime are conceivable. These regimes are central bank system with: (1) flexible exchange rate; (2) crawling peg; (3) unannounced exchange rate fixing ('Austrian solution'); and (4) fixed exchange rates; (5) a currency board system; (6) dollarisation; and (7) delegation of monetary policy to the IMF. Each of these regimes can be restricted to a certain range of commitment, albeit a rather huge one. Without knowledge of the details concerning the ten criteria (12 components) of the index, it is impossible to restrict the degree of commitment further.

Nevertheless, it is possible to rank the regimes in principle by calculating a theoretically possible degree of commitment C_{uw} with the help of *Table A 2*.

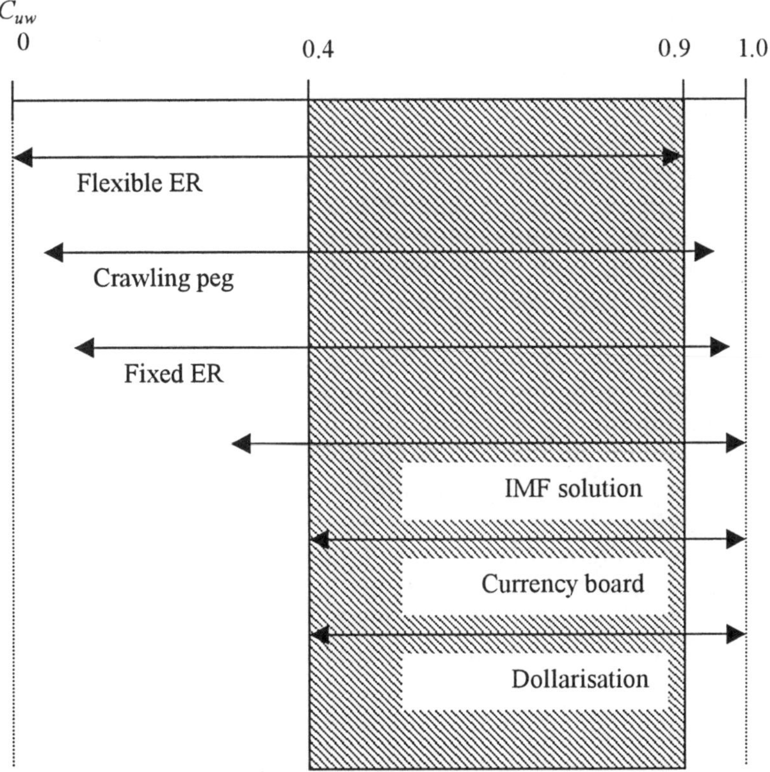

Figure 4.1 Monetary Prototypes and the Degree of Legal Commitment (C_{uw})

Figure 4.1 shows the range of different prototypes as some examples illustrate. For instance, although a purely theoretical case, a central bank with flexible exchange rates can be introduced by a government that does not commit to anything at all. All components of the index obtain the value 0 (C_{uw} = 0).[20] At the other end of the range, C_{uw} with a flexible exchange rate arrangement can at most have the value 0.9. In this case, all components of the index except for *extern* (its value is 0) have the value 1. The monetary regime applied by Austria for more than 20 years (independent central bank with unofficial exchange rate fix) has the same potential range of formal commitment as flexible exchange rate and is not mentioned separately. With the same logic, a crawling peg can be combined with a formal degree of

20 For the calculation of C_{uw} see Appendix 2, section I. *Table A.2* explains the components and *Table A.3* shows the weights given to each of them.

commitment between 0.05 and 0.95. For a central bank system with fixed exchange rates the possible range is $0.075 \leq C \geq 0.975$.

The possible range of legal commitment in case of delegation to the IMF is smaller. The degree of commitment reaches at least the value of 0.3 as the components *gov*, *ceo* and *diss* have the value 1. Since it seems plausible that the IMF tries to conduct a monetary policy that avoids the problems which caused the inflation, other components (*lim*, *mult* and *conv*) will probably also obtain the value 1. A currency board system has an even greater minimum degree of commitment ($C_{uw} \geq 0.4$) as *gov*, *extern*, *lim*, *conv* and *mult* are at any rate equal to 1. Dollarisation has not only exactly the same minimum degree of legal commitment as a CBS, but with the same components having the value 1. These prototypes can even be introduced with a maximum degree of commitment ($C_{uw} = 1$).

Figure 4.1 also reveals the problem associated with a formalised procedure to measure legal commitment. There is a broad range between 0.4 and 0.9 where each of the monetary regimes discussed above can be located (grey area in *Figure 4.1*). This certainly has consequences for the empirical part of the study. The explanatory power and policy relevance of a purely econometric assessment may be limited. This is a first indication that the empirical work has to include detailed case studies in addition to econometric analysis.

IV. DETERMINANTS OF A SUCCESSFUL REFORM: A FORMAL ANALYSIS

a) Introduction into the analysis

In this section, we develop our theoretical framework further to derive a model for calculating the relation between the degree of commitment, the institutional setting in the country and the resulting level of inflation. The model presented here is founded on a model by Barro (1983) on the optimal inflation rate from the point of view of a policymaker with and without commitment.[21] A novelty in macroeconomic models is that it reflects the influence of the institutional setting. This is done by incorporating institutional factors into an objective function. The formal analysis should elaborate more precisely the main result of Chapters 2 and 3 which is that the success of a monetary reform depends on monetary commitment and institutional factors. Moreover, it should allow for an empirical assessment of the theoretical findings of Chapters 2 through 4.

The analysis begins at a point in time of severe inflation which may even be hyperinflation. Therefore, the main goal of commitment is to break inflationary expectations. It can be taken for granted that the public strongly wishes a lower than the actual inflation rate. We also assume that policymakers have at least implicitly accepted that stabilisation is needed. Under this assumption, commitment in our analysis is commitment of governments rather than commitment of monetary policymakers like central bankers.[22] The degree of commitment in the following describes a monetary regime rather than monetary instruments or a special rate of inflation the government commits to. The choice of monetary policy is the choice of a set of rules (Chapter 2, section III). That does not exclude the fact that policymakers in charge act according to personal utility considerations.

Given that consensus about the need for disinflation has been reached within the society,[23] we deviate from the method often applied in such models: inflation there is modelled as the outcome of a strategic game between the policymaker and the public. This reflects the interaction of

---

[21] See also Cukierman (1992, chapter 4).

[22] Cukierman (1992, p. 53) also concludes that this is adequate. His argument is different: the policymaker is the government as it is in its interest to receive seigniorage. Considerations about economic order do not play a role in this reasoning.

[23] Végh (1995) shows that consensus can be reached more easily after hyperinflation than after chronic inflation because of the social chaos in case of the former. Credibility of an announced stabilisation programme is higher.

policymakers and the public. Because of the assumed consensus about the necessity of a reform, we do not have to model strategic interaction in a game theoretic approach. Instead, we model the policymaker's utility maximisation under constraints.[24]

We construct an objective function for the government which it seeks to maximise. It has to take into account direct costs of inflation and costs of expected inflation. The latter will be modelled in three ways: (1) as being equal to the degree of commitment; (2) as the sum of commitment and the institutional factors; (3) as the degree of commitment adjusted for the institutional setting. We model the optimal inflation rate as a function of commitment and institutional factors IF_1 to IF_n, i.e. $\pi^* = f(C, IF_1..IF_n)$ in a first step.[25] Thus, we try to explain why monetary reforms succeed or fail.

By proceeding this way, we make the results comparable to the standard literature and we furthermore avoid the problem of causality. It is not adequate to argue that a certain institutional setting causes a certain degree of commitment to be optimal in that it reduces inflation. It can be justified to use exactly the opposite causality: a certain degree of commitment causes a certain institutional factor to be in line with low inflation. By making π^* an endogenous variable that depends on both exogenous variables, it is considered that the components of economic order (C, IF_i) are interdependent. Nevertheless, in the formal analysis, we treat institutions as given. This assumption has to be relaxed for the discussion of economic policy conclusions.

b) The analytical framework

We assume that the main reason for high inflation has been the need for revenues (Bernholz 1995, pp. 263f). Other sources of revenues such as income tax or value added tax have proven to be insufficient to cover the government's expenditure. Therefore, it seemed attractive for governments to inflate. They try to issue enough money to maximise the amount of seigniorage S. Following Cagan (1956, p. 35), it is defined as in equation (4.1):[26]

$$S \equiv \frac{\dot{M}}{M}\frac{M}{P} = mL(\pi^e) \qquad (4.1).$$

---

24 For a purely methodical critique of a game theoretic analysis of monetary policy see subsection 2.III.c.

25 The term 'optimal inflation rate' means a politically optimal rate.

26 Equations 4.1, 4.2 and 4.5 are equivalent to equations 2.6, 2.7 and 2.8, respectively.

$$L(\pi^e) = \exp(-\alpha\pi^e) \qquad (4.2).$$

M is the amount of nominal money supply, $\dot{M} = dM / dt$ therefore stands for the change of the amount of money over time. Thus, m denotes the growth rate of money. Since P denotes the price level, $L(\pi^e)$ is the demand for real cash balances which is assumed to depend on the expected rate of inflation π^e. Equation (4.2) specifies the assumed functional dependence. Thus, if the expected inflation increases the demand for money will decrease at rate α.

We assume rational expectations.[27] The public makes use of all information available in period s (I_s) to form expectations about the rate of inflation in period $s+1$.

$$\pi^e = E(\pi_{s+1} | I_s) \qquad (4.3),$$

where E denotes the expectation operator .

We also assume that $s=t$ is the moment of the monetary reform. The public has been informed about the planned monetary reform and bases its expectations on these plans. The period $t+1$ is not defined as an exactly given time span or a moment. [28] It is defined as an amount of time after the monetary reform which is long enough to prove whether the reform was successful or not. Under this assumption, the growth rate of money equals the actual inflation rate, presuming that the quantity theory of money holds and that the economy does not grow:

$$m = \pi \qquad (4.4).$$

Let us first look at the case where the government only tries to maximise its seigniorage as the tax revenues are insufficient to cover all expenditures. Assuming the expected inflation rate equals actual inflation at period t and maximising (4.1) with respect to the inflation rate π gives the optimal level of monetary growth and inflation:

$$m = \frac{1}{\alpha} \qquad (4.5).$$

27 It can be taken for granted that the public has learned about the negative consequences of hyperinflation and, therefore, is aware of the mechanism that leads to inflation. Consequently, the assumption of fully rational expectations is justified.

28 In the econometric analysis, the notation is changed: t remains the moment (year) of the reform, but $t+1$ is the following year, $t+2$ the year after that and so on.

However, the government also faces costs of inflation, ϕ, dependent both on actual and expected inflation. If, due to dynamic inconsistency, $m > 1/\alpha$,[29] the political costs of inflation even rise. Then the policymaker's problem is given by:

$$Z = \delta S - \phi(\pi, \pi^e) \rightarrow \max_{\pi}{}^{30} \qquad (4.6),$$

$$\text{where: } \frac{d\phi}{d\pi} > 0 \text{ and } \frac{d\phi}{d\pi^e} > 0.$$

The weight the government places on seigniorage in (4.6) is denoted by δ with $\delta \geq 0$. This factor can also be interpreted differently from the usual macroeconomic framework. Whereas it normally indicates the importance the government gives to seigniorage relative to inflation (e.g. Cukierman 1992, p. 53), here it also shows the intensity to which the need for stabilisation and the causes of inflation is politically perceived. The smaller the value of δ, the higher the acceptance of the need for price level stability.[31] Since we take a long-term perspective we can set $m = \pi$ (equation 4.4). We define $\phi = \exp(\pi^2 + k(\pi^e))$ where $k(\pi^e)$ describes the costs of expected inflation. Increasing expected inflation raise the political costs associated with inflationary expectations. The government takes the expected inflation rate as given. The fact that actual inflation is introduced into the cost function in a quadratic form takes into account the costs of deflation as well (Chapter 2, section II). Thus the objective function becomes:

$$Z = \delta\pi \exp(-\alpha\pi^e) - \exp(\pi^2 + k(\pi^e)) \qquad (4.7).$$

c) The governmental utility maximised without and with commitment

Now (4.7) can be maximised with respect to π. It then becomes: $Z = \delta\pi \exp(-\alpha\pi^e) - \exp(\pi^2 + k(\pi^e)) \rightarrow \max_{\pi}$. The first order condition of this maximisation problem is given by the following equation:

---

29 It has been shown theoretically and empirically that in the absence of commitment the rate of inflation regularly is above the optimal level. Seigniorage is not at its maximum. See for instance Calvo (1978), Barro (1983) and the survey in Cukierman (1992, pp. 51–55).

30 Alternatively, a loss function could be minimised.

31 A third way to interpret δ is that the lower it is, the more the government accepts the fact that monetary stabilisation contributes to fiscal stabilisation as it allows tax revenues to rise.

$$\frac{dZ}{d\pi} = \delta \exp(-\alpha\pi^e) - 2\pi \exp(\pi^2 + k(\pi^e)) \stackrel{!}{=} 0 \qquad (4.8).$$

Maximisation of Z leads to:

$$\delta \frac{M}{P} = 2\pi \exp(\pi^2 + k(\pi^e)) \qquad (4.9).$$

Equation (4.9) shows that the optimal inflation rate in this setting can only be derived implicitly. Using the total differential of (4.9) and interpreting the politically optimal rate of inflation as: $\pi = g(\delta, \frac{M}{P}, k(\cdot))$ leads to the following partial derivates:

$$\frac{d\pi}{d\delta} > 0;$$

$$\frac{d\pi}{d\frac{M}{P}} \geq 0 \text{ and}$$

$$\frac{d\pi}{dk(\cdot)} < 0 \text{, if } \pi > 0 \qquad (4.10).$$

Equation (4.9) also illustrates that the optimal inflation is non-negative, since δ, M and P are non-negative. Indeed, the model does not explain negative inflation rates which is irrelevant since we consider a period after high and volatile positive inflation rates. It, therefore, can be excluded that the disinflation process leads to deflation within a reasonable time span. Following (4.9) and (4.10), the optimal inflation rate π^* (from the point of view of the government) depends positively on δ and the demand for money, and negatively on the costs of inflationary expectations. This is intuitively plausible.

Table 4.1 Optimal Inflation Rate under Extreme Assumptions

if	$\delta = 0$	$\delta \to \infty$	$k(\pi^e) \to \infty$	$k(\pi^e) = 0$
...then π^*...	... $\to 0$	...$\to\infty$	... $\to 0$	...is strictly positive

Before proceeding by introducing institutional constraints and commitment, we can distinguish four special cases: first, the weight given to seigniorage is zero ($\delta = 0$), and second, the government does not commit to price level stability ($k(\pi^e) = 0$); the third and the fourth case are the other two extremes ($\delta \to \infty$) and ($k(\pi^e) \to \infty$). *Table 4.1* shows how the optimal inflation rate depends on different outcomes of δ and k. The optimal rate of inflation is higher without costs of expected inflation ($k(\pi^e) = 0$) than with them. High costs of expected inflation reduce inflation close to zero (it cannot be zero for this range is not defined). A low inflation rate is also reached when the government attributes no importance to seigniorage ($\delta = 0$). Accordingly, inflation is very high when the government gives a prominent weight to seigniorage even after the reform, i.e. when it is less concerned about disinflation.

Finally, (4.9) can be rearranged into (4.11) which can be seen as a basic equation for an econometric analysis (Chapter 6):

$$\ln 2\pi + \pi^2 = \ln \delta + \ln(M / P) - k(\pi^e) \qquad (4.11).$$

d) Different specifications of commitment and institutional restrictions

We now analyse the case that the government commits to a monetary regime. Governments can commit and will do it after a period of chronic inflation or hyperinflation. To be credible, commitment has to generate high costs for the policymaker in case of reneging (Barro and Gordon 1983). These costs are associated with expectations: by changing inflationary expectations, the costs of disinflation can be diminished. The costs of commitment can be specified in different ways. We distinguish three options which all seem rather similar at first glance, but turn out to be substantially different when one takes a closer look.

Variant 1: comprehensive commitment

First, we model the costs of commitment in a more traditional way. We assume that the costs of commitment are equal to its degree. Equation (4.9) can be expressed as follows.

$$\delta \frac{M}{P} = 2\pi \exp(\pi^2 + C)\text{, leading to (4.13)} \qquad (4.12),$$

$$\ln 2\pi + \pi^2 = \ln \delta + \ln(M/P) - C \qquad (4.13).$$

The higher the degree of commitment C, the lower the politically optimal inflation rate. This is a well-known theoretical outcome of the standard macroeconomic literature and by no means surprising. The problem of this specification is that it is well suited to explain the success of monetary reform relying on a high degree of commitment, but it has difficulties in explaining the failure of such a reform, provided a high degree of commitment has been chosen. In this – in reality rather common – case both inflation and commitment are high. To solve this problem, in the second and third variant, the costs of commitment are a function of commitment itself and of institutional factors:

$$k(\pi^e) = f(C, IF_1..IF_n) \qquad (4.14).$$

Variant 2: commitment and institutions added

We have distinguished six institutional factors: political stability, fiscal stability, flexibility of the labour market regime, openness of the country, opposition against inflation and a variable reflecting properties of a possible reserve currency. In general, the measurement of institutional factors has to be equivalent to the calculation of the index of commitment. Thus, it is possible to assess the influence of the institutions on the success of the monetary reform. Therefore, we restrict the institutional factors between zero and one, that is $0 < IF_i < 1$, where IF_i stands for the institutional factor $i \in \{1,...,n\}$. These institutions restrict the discretionary power of monetary policymakers.

The second specification of the costs of commitment is simply to add C and the institutional factors IF_i (4.15) and (4.16).

$$\delta \frac{M}{P} = 2\pi \exp(\pi^2 + C + IF_1 + ... + IF_n) \qquad (4.15),$$

leading to (4.16)

$$\ln 2\pi + \pi^2 = \ln \delta + \ln(M/P) - C - IF_1 - ... - IF_n \quad (4.16).$$

In this specification, the relationship between commitment and institutions is rather lose. Their influence on politically optimal inflation has the same direction. The higher the degree of commitment and the higher political stability, fiscal stability, labour market flexibility etc. are, the lower the inflation rate will be. However, the interaction of commitment and institutions does not explain the inflation rate after a monetary reform. As in variant 1, the simple formula holds: more commitment equals less inflation. Moreover, in this setting, a low degree of commitment does not necessarily lead to high inflation. Other variables can bring down inflation. Again, the economic message is ambiguous. On the one hand, it is appealing that commitment and institutions have common influence. On the other hand, it is not very striking that a monetary reform can turn into a success without commitment which is easily possible given equation (4.16). This weakness will be eliminated in the third variant.

Variant 3: difference of commitment and institutions

This specification tries to avoid problems having turned up in the first two variants: in this variant, the costs of commitment are a function of the compatibility of the degree of commitment and the institutional setting. Technically, they are reflected by the difference between the degree of commitment and the average of the institutional factors i, all restricted between 0 and 1. The costs are the higher, the smaller the difference between the level of de jure monetary commitment C and the average level of the de facto institutional factors IF_i.. Whereas in case of the index of commitment a value close to zero (one) means low (high) commitment, in case of IF_i a value close to zero (one) indicates low (high) compatibility of the institution i with high commitment. Low (high) compatibility leads to the probability of a success of the monetary reform being low (high). We have chosen a quadratic form to clarify that big differences between the commitment and the optimal individual institutional factor will cause high costs and to make sure that the summand is positive. As a result of (4.17), the costs of commitment decrease when compared to the highest costs not only if the degree of commitment is too low for a successful stabilisation, but also if it is too high. To take them into account properly, we specify the costs of commitment as follows:

$$(k\pi^e) = \frac{1}{(C - \frac{\sum_{i=1}^{n} IF_i}{n})^2} \tag{4.17},$$

which can be expressed as $k(\pi^e) = -f(C - IF_i)$. It is also possible to take the absolute value of the difference without a quadratic form:

$k_2\pi^e = \frac{1}{\left|C - \frac{\sum_{i=1}^{n} IF_i}{n}\right|}$. Large differences are not emphasised and the summand remains positive.

The economic reason for this specification is that the public has rational expectations and is well informed about the interaction of monetary commitment and other institutions. It recognises deviation from an economically sound design of the monetary regime under given constraints and adjusts its expectations adequately. This has consequences for the consistency of a monetary regime. Equation (4.17), therefore, has another interesting property. The expression $(C - \frac{\sum_{i=1}^{n} IF_i}{n})^2$ can be interpreted as a proxy for credibility. Credibility does not only depend on the degree of commitment, but also on the compatibility of commitment and institutional circumstances in the country. The lower the squared differences between the two values is, the higher the credibility of the monetary regime will be and vice versa. Thus, here we have an ex-ante proxy for credibility which is important for policy conclusions. It enables the policymaker to assess the credibility of a monetary reform in advance. By way of contrast, other proxies for credibility used are ex-post measures which can only be applied after the reform has been made.[32]

Finally, let us determine the optimal inflation rate of a policymaker under commitment which is specified according variant 3 (4.18) and (4.19).

$$\delta \frac{M}{P} = 2\pi \exp(\pi^2 + \frac{1}{(C - \frac{\sum_{i=1}^{n} IF_i}{n})^2}) \qquad (4.18),$$

[32] See section 4.V below.

$$\ln 2\pi + \pi^2 = \ln\delta + \ln(M/P) - \frac{1}{(C - \frac{\sum_{i=1}^{n} IF_i}{n})^2} \quad (4.19).$$

The higher the credibility is, i.e. the better the monetary reform acknowledges institutional constraints, the lower the optimal inflation rate will be, following (4.19). The introduction of institutional factors does not change the principal results of the foregoing analysis, reported in *Table 4.1*.

e) Implications of the model

The structure of the model implies that economic policymaking is an endogenous process. This is consistent with political economy considerations: after choosing a degree of commitment policymakers determine whether a high or a low rate of inflation is beneficial to them. In detail, the analysis leads to the following (provisional) conclusions.

To allow the monetary reform to be successful, the government – as the policymaker in our model – in any case should not take recourse on money to finance its expenditure. The less weight the government attributes to seigniorage, the lower the politically optimal post-reform inflation rate is. Given that the need for revenue was the main motive for inflation, this result makes perfect sense. Its normative implication is also clear: without a determination to finance a budget deficit on the (international) capital markets, a government will be unable to turn a monetary reform into a success.

Furthermore, the demand for real money has negative effects on the success of a monetary reform. The more real money the public demands, the more likely the government will give in and produce fresh money, contributing to a higher price level.[33] Moreover, by breaking inflationary expectations the government can improve the chances of the reform to succeed. For this purpose, the government has to commit to a policy rule. Commitment itself is an important device to bring down inflation. In general, the analysis shows that commitment can change the optimal inflation rate from the point of view of a government. Without commitment, inflation is higher than with commitment.

However, the exact direction and strength of effects generated by commitment depend on how the costs of commitment are specified. We have offered three alternatives. First, we set the costs of commitment equal to the

---

33 It has to be remembered that the model assumes a static economy. In a growing economy, increasing demand for money does not necessarily lead to inflation.

degree of commitment ($0 \leq C \leq 1$). The message then is very simple: the higher the commitment, the lower the policymaker's inclination to inflation. Institutions in this specification are irrelevant. They are taken into consideration in the second and third variant. The second specification adds the influence of each institutional factor. An institutional factor compatible with high commitment raises the probability of the success of a monetary reform. The policy lessons to be learned from this specification are ambiguous: it makes perfect sense that a reform is successful if commitment is both high and compatible with the institutional setting, i.e. if the institutional factors have a high value. This result has interesting implications for the policy reform. It shows that not only a reform of the monetary regime but also of other parts of the economic order can contribute to stabilisation. However, variant 2 has one puzzling result: despite a low degree of commitment, the reform can be a (relative) success, provided the institutional factors have a high value. By intuition, it does not seem possible to reach stability without any monetary commitment.

This problem is overcome by the third specification. It explicitly models the interaction of commitment and institutions. The interesting by-product of this specification is an ex-ante proxy for credibility. Low commitment and high values of IF_i produce low credibility. The result of variant 2 is qualified. The main conclusion to be derived from variant 3 is that strong commitment is not necessarily a perfect device to stabilise successfully via a monetary reform. Instead, credibility of commitment can be low if the deviations of C from IF_1 to IF_n are great. For instance, low budget discipline regularly leads to fiscal problems. Governments then are considerably tempted to monetise such a deficit. A strong commitment sometimes does not prevent them from doing so. Thus, the optimal inflation rate for policymakers can be high despite a very strong commitment if the interdependence of the components of the economic order is neglected when making a commitment. In other words, institutions constrain the optimal degree of monetary commitment. If the public knows about this problem, it will not regard a monetary reform as being very credible in this respect. The positive result of the analysis is that only the appropriate interaction of all parts of the economic order will make monetary reforms credible and successful.

The normative conclusion of the model's outcome, naturally, cannot be to choose a low degree of commitment if the institutional setting cannot support a monetary reform. Political chaos for instance does not imply monetary chaos as the proper policy option. Rather, as regards the policy option, the implication is that any monetary reform has to be made in accordance with the institutional setting, or alternatively to the economic order. There is no general first-best solution of monetary problems. Which monetary regime fits a country best can be assessed with the model before the monetary reform takes place. Technically, policymakers should set a certain rate of inflation π^*, as a target. In order to achieve this target, the level of commitment C then can be chosen according to the institutional setting IF_1 to IF_n by simulating the model (Chapter 6, section V and Chapter 8, section IV). This is a new result which has not appeared explicitly in the literature yet.

V. AN EX-ANTE PROXY FOR CREDIBILITY

a) The concept

To assess whether a monetary reform has a positive impact on the expectations of the public and consequently on the inflation rate, it is necessary to measure credibility of the monetary regime after the reform. Otherwise, one cannot easily separate the effects of the reform from other determinants of the inflation rate. The main problem associated with this task is to find an appropriate proxy for credibility as it naturally is unobservable directly. Several studies measure credibility of regime changes (in the cases of e.g. Denmark and the UK) and monetary reforms (in the cases of e.g. Chile and Argentina). The results of these studies are promising in that they show a weak, albeit apparent relationship of credibility and macroeconomic performance. These studies use different methods and proxies for credibility. In the following, we will discuss some properties of these methods and proxies in general.[34] Three methods can be distinguished: (1) the error prediction-method; (2) the Bayesian approach; (3) an *ad hoc* approach.

1. Using the error prediction method two periods are distinguished: the pre-reform period and the reform period. A model of the economy for the pre-reform period is estimated. On the basis of the coefficients for the exogenous variable the values of the endogenous variable, for instance the inflation rate or a domestic interest rate, are predicted for the reform period. The differences between the predicted and observed inflation rates or interest rates are used as a proxy for credibility. The reform can be interpreted as being credible if the observed value is smaller than the predicted one. This procedure has two major shortcomings. First, if the institutional design in the reform period strongly differs from the pre-reform period, the model may be misspecified (Mastroberardino 1994, p.

34 For an overview see Mastroberardino (1994, pp. 72–108) and Blackburn and Christensen (1989, pp. 35–40).

74). Second, the Lucas critique applies: the public may change its behaviour due to the reform. The coefficients of the pre-reform model might then be poor predictors of the reform period (Agenor and Taylor 1992, pp. 553f).

2. The Bayesian approach also employs a pre-reform model. However, the coefficients of exogenous variables are not used as predictors. Rather the public has knowledge of them and employs them to assess the probability with which the monetary reform is likely to succeed. Following Baxter (1985) in her analysis for Argentina and Chile, fiscal deficits and domestic money creation are exogenous and observable by the public. An exchange rate rule is the announced policy. Agents are assigned a probability to believe in the announcement of the government. In the Bayesian learning approach, the compatibility of the pattern of budget deficits and monetary development with the exchange rate rule is computed. A low probability of failure of the monetary reform indicates its high credibility. The assignment of probabilities to believe in the governmental announcement by the analyst is problematic since it makes the result somewhat arbitrary (Mastroberardino 1994, pp. 75–78, 214). Moreover, the criticism of the error prediction method holds as well. In addition, it is highly questionable whether the public has a knowledge of macroeconomic data as profound as assumed in the approach (Agénor and Taylor 1992, p. 551).
3. The third approach is not a deliberately chosen method. The weaknesses of the other methods have led some economists to base their estimation of credibility on variables that are selected *ad hoc*, i.e. without a theoretical underpinning. These are variables such as the interest rate structure, the difference of the interest rate between the reform country and other countries, a surcharge for the exchange rate on the unofficial market, the price of governmental bonds and the dollarisation ratio. The problem of this technique is that the variables might not exclusively be explained by the monetary regime, but also by other determinants not specified in the analysis.

All proxies for credibility mentioned here are ex-post measures. They allow to estimate how credible a monetary reform is in practice after it has been made. This surely is very helpful for an assessment of monetary reforms. Nevertheless, it only tells part of the story. It would be better if credibility in a comprehensive manner could be assessed ex ante, i.e. before the reform is made. Thereby, costly experiments could be avoided.

As an outcome of the model presented here, a new measure for credibility has been worked out. The costs of commitment $k(\pi^e) = f(C, IF_1..IF_6)$ are specified in a way considering the expectations of the public. As we assume rational expectations, the public can assess the probable credibility of the monetary reform by comparing the degree of commitment incorporated in the planned monetary policy with the institutional setting. It then builds its expectations about how credible the regime will be. This is captured in the expression $(C - \sum_{i=1}^{n} IF_i / n)^2$. The smaller it is, the higher the credibility of the policy will be. On the other hand, low credibility is indicated by a high sum of squared deviations of commitment and the institutional setting.

This measure has some advantages over the measures described above. First, a pre-reform model is not necessary, since the measure does not compare two periods. Instead, only the post-reform model is applied. Therefore, using this measure of credibility is not subject to the Lucas critique. In an econometric application, coefficients of the estimators are probably stable since the behaviour of the agents is analysed under the post-reform policy framework. Second, different to various measures used in the literature it is a theoretically sound measure. It has been elaborated in an analytical framework that takes into account the behaviour of policymakers and the public. Third, the proxy can be used to measure the credibility of monetary reforms prior to the reform, i.e. ex ante. As long as the data of the pre-reform period and projections of the post-reform period are available for a country that opts for a monetary reform, different regime options can be evaluated in advance as regards their probable future inflation rate.

b) Credibility of different monetary policy regimes

In this subsection, some hypotheses about a systematic relationship between institutions and a legal monetary regime are developed, using the results of variant 3. The prototypes of monetary regime described here are not equally credible. It cannot, however, be said a priori whether one monetary regime is more credible than others. There are two arguments for this assessment. First, we discussed prototypes which have to be designed in detail. These details may vary strongly so that central banks with equal properties in two countries still appear very different: the degree of commitment of similar monetary regimes may vary. Second, the institutional setting also varies among countries. Thus, even if the design of two central banks is completely identical, one cannot be sure that credibility and subsequently the monetary performance is also identical. Consequently, the outcome of proxy for credibility is dependent on both commitment and the institutional setting.

In *Table 4.2* we show the necessary properties of the institutional setting for the prototypes of monetary regime being credible. *Table 4.2* is read as follows: in column 2 assumed values of C_{uw} are assigned to the real monetary regimes. These values are plausible since they are located in the middle of the possible range (*Figure 1*). Column 3 indicates the necessary magnitude of the institutional setting defined as the average value of each factor required for a legal monetary regime (column 1) to be credible. This information can be obtained from the expression $(C - \sum_{i=1}^{n} IF_i / n)^2$ and equation (4.17) which both hold that the credibility of the reform negatively depends on the magnitude of this expression. The expression $\sum_{i=1}^{n} IF_i / n$ does not give all the information necessary to judge the credibility of a reform, for the average of an institutional setting has to be disaggregated again to make sense economically. This is done in columns 4 through 9. They indicate the magnitude the individual de-facto institutional factors possibly require in order to generate credibility of the chosen monetary regime.

Table 4.2 Interaction of Monetary Regime and Institutional Setting for High Credibility of the Reform

1	2	3	4	5	6	7	8	9
Prototype/IF_i[1]	C_{uw}[2]	Σ*IF*/5	*PS*	*FS*	*LM*	*OP*	*POI*	*RC*
Central bank								
flexible ER	0.40	med	high	med[4]	low/ med	low	med	no[5]
fixed ER[3]:								
Nominal anchor	0.60	high	high	high	high	high	high	high
Crawling peg	0.50	med	high	med	med	high	med	high
Austrian type	0.50	med	high	high	med	med	med	high
CBS	0.75	high	high	high	high	high	high	high
Dollarisation	0.75	high	high	high	high	high	high	high
IMF runs Central bank	0.65	med/ high	med	med/ high	med/ high	med	med	?

[1]Notes: The abbreviations stand for the following: $\Sigma IF/5 = \sum_{i=1}^{n} IF_i / n$; ER = exchange rate; PS = political stability; *FS* = fiscal stability; *LM* = labour market flexibility; *OP* = openness; *POI* = public opposition to inflation; *RC* = reserve currency. For further details of IF_i see Chapter 2, section III; [2]: assumed values of C_{uw}; [3]: exchange rate arrangement of Bretton Woods or EMS style are excluded. For reasons see Chapter 4, section II; [4]: med = medium level; [5]: no = no reserve currency necessary; ? = exchange arrangement not clear.

Two examples illustrate the logic of *Table 4.2*. For instance, imagine the following institutional setting: political stability (*PS*) is high, and fiscal stability (*FS*) and public opposition to inflation (*POI*) are on a medium level. Openness (*OP*) and labour market flexibility (*LM*) are lower. In such a setting, a monetary reform introducing a central bank with flexible exchange rates is likely to be credible since the exchange rate may function as a (albeit weak) substitute for flexible labour regulations. No reserve currency (*RC*) exists.

For a currency board system to be credible, all institutional factors should have a reasonably high magnitude. In particular, the country should be open to foreign trade and the labour market should be flexible. The latter is important in case the monetary base decreases in the course of a current account deficit to avoid increasing unemployment (Chapter 4, section II). As for political stability, the hypothesis derived from the analysis here is that it should be high across all possible monetary regimes to avoid the regime being subject to frequent changes.

Only if the government signs a contract with the IMF it can be assumed that a medium value for political stability may also generate credibility since it may be rather difficult for the government – regardless of whether the old or a new one – to break this contract.

The results yielded in *Table 4.2* can be seen as a confirmation of conventional wisdom. Eichengreen, Masson et al. (1998, pp. 20–23) draw similar conclusions concerning the criteria for the choice of an exchange rate system. They distinguish floating exchange rates (pure and managed), target bands, a crawling peg, a CBS and a currency union. The criteria for the choice of an adequate exchange rate system are the following (either high or low): inflation, level of reserves, capital mobility, labour mobility and nominal flexibility, trade integration, political integration and preponderance of shocks. The general conclusion is that a high outcome of these criteria is correlated with a higher degree of commitment which is compatible with the results obtained in this chapter.

5. The Empirical Analysis: Some Facts and Figures

I. INTRODUCTION

Chapters 5 through 7 provide an empirical assessment of the positive theory of monetary reform developed in the preceding chapters. Before commencing with hard evidence, Chapter 5 is intended to give a brief overview on the history of monetary reform after World War I. It is also dedicated to a brief introduction into the reforms that are analysed in more detail in Chapters 6 and 7 where two methods are be applied. First, we pursue a cross-sectional estimation of the model set up in Chapter 4. This model is transferred into an econometric model where some of the restrictions of the theoretical model are be lifted. The sample consists of 29 monetary reforms after World War II. For these reforms, enough data could be collected. Chapter 6 is dedicated to the econometric analysis.

Second, some of the monetary reforms of the 20th century are discussed in case studies. Case studies make sense since they allow us to describe some of the features shown in the theoretical and econometric analyses in greater detail. They show the importance of institutional aspects in economic policymaking. In addition, there are also some interesting reforms to be analysed for which the data set could not be completed. The reason is simply that either these cases date back to the time before World War II or that the reforms have only been made recently. Nevertheless, there is enough evidence to assess some of our theoretical considerations. This is done in Chapter 7.

II. MONETARY REFORMS AFTER WORLD WAR I AT A GLANCE

The following *Table 5.1* gives an overview on monetary reforms after World War I. It has to be mentioned that not all monetary reforms are included in this list. Sometimes, it seems rather difficult to distinguish whether the institutional change in monetary policy has all the properties of a monetary reform or not. Thus, we restrict the list to undisputable monetary reforms as defined in Chapter 4, section I. Moreover, since the theoretical model focuses on those countries needing to overcome severe inflation,[1] the empirical analysis is also limited to these cases.

Therefore, monetary reforms during the period of transition from a centrally planned to a market economy and after a split-up of two formerly united countries (e.g. the Czech and Slovak Republics) are not incorporated unless they were meant to end a hyperinflation. The latter was the case in Slovenia, Russia, the Ukraine, Lithuania and Estonia. Similarly, African countries which gained independence in the 1950s and 1960s are excluded from the empirical analysis. In many of their cases, there just was the perceived need for an autonomous monetary policy after a long period of monetary co-operation with their mother countries. This point of view was backed by the then predominant Keynesian approach of macroeconomic policy. This approach was favoured in academia, politics and also in international organisations like the IMF.[2]

For the econometric analysis, only the monetary reforms in those economies are considered, where those institutional factors are observable that theoretically contribute to the success or failure of the reform. This sample consists of 29 observations which is enough to get significant results. In *Table 5.1*, these reforms are marked with a star.

The 20th century was a century of monetary disaster and reform. In some countries, monetary reforms were made just about annually. Especially in some Latin American countries one can observe a sequence of monetary reforms (e.g. Argentina and Brazil). As mentioned above, this list is incomplete; not all reforms are documented in this study. For instance, in Argentina, monetary policy was not only subject to reform in 1985 and 1991, but was also changed in 1976 and 1983. Moreover, monetary policy was adjusted four times after the 1985 reform. However, the changes were not as substantial as in the subsequent years. Another striking example for a permanent process of changes in the monetary framework is Paraguay (Triffin 1946). After its independence in 1842, for a century Paraguay experienced two major wars (1895–1870 and 1932–1935) which contributed to a large monetisation of public spendings and very high inflation rates. As a

1 Only very few reforms in this sample were not meant to stop high inflation.

2 See e.g. some contributions to the *IMF Staff Papers* of the late 1950s. Birnbaum (1957) argues that a currency board with a 100 per cent covering of base money is inappropriate. In the opinion of Laso (1958) at least three objectives of monetary policy (price stability, external equilibrium and higher growth) exist. Ahrensdorf (1959/60) does not even see the danger of monetised budget deficits.

consequence, Paraguay made at least a dozen piecemeal changes of monetary policy between 1870 and 1943. However, it was not before 1944 that a central bank statute under foreign (US) assistance was created. This was the first Paraguayan monetary reform that was substantial and that can be assessed with the tools developed in this study.

Latin America has experienced 23 of the reforms listed in *Table 5.1.* In particular after 1982, efforts to reform the monetary regime and to stabilise the economy have been increased enormously and with considerable success. Since the early 1990s, many observers are likely to attest many Latin American countries an almost sustainable stabilisation process (e.g. Corbo 2000).

Table 5.1: Monetary Reforms in the 20th Century: An Overview

Country	Year
Albania	1965
Argentina	1983, 1985*, 1991*
Austria	1922
Bolivia	1963*, 1987*
Brazil	1986*, 1989*, 1990, 1993, 1994*
Bulgaria	1952, 1962, 1997,
Chile	1956, 1960, 1975*
China	1948, 1949,1955, 1969
Czechoslovakia	1953
Estonia	1992*
Germany	1923/24, 1948*, 1990* (East Germany)
Greece	1944, 1946, 1954*
Hong Kong	1983*
Hungary	1924, 1946
Indonesia	1957, 1965
Israel	1980*, 1985*
Kyrgyzstan	1993
Korea	1962*
Laos	1979, 1996
Latvia	1992*
Lithuania	1994*
Morocco	1959
Mexico	1916, 1987*, 1993*
Nicaragua	1988*, 1990/91*
Paraguay	1943/44

Table 5.1 (continued)

Country	Year
Peru	1985*, 1991*
Poland	1920, 1924, 1950, 1995
Romania	1947, 1952
Russia	1994*
Serbia	1994
Slovenia	1991*
Soviet Union	1924, 1947, 1961
Taiwan	1949
Tunisia	1958
Ukraine	1992*
Uruguay	1975*, 1993*
Yugoslavia	1966, 1990
Zaire	1967

Notes: * These reforms are subject to econometric analysis.

Source: Dornbusch and Fischer (1986); Mas (1995); Bernholz (1990); own research.

In Europe, more monetary reforms (33 in total) have been made than in any other continent. Whereas in the 1920s, mainly countries suffering from World War I, such as Germany or Austria, had to reform their monetary regime, the second wave can be observed in the 1990s when the former socialist countries did not manage the transition process very well and had to correct their monetary policies. During the socialist era, instead of price increases, queues indicated scarcity (Wentzel 1995, pp. 15–20). State enterprises gave credit to each other so that money growth was high. Fixed prices and money growth had created the potential for an adjustment inflation. This can be easily demonstrated when looking at the Fisher equation:

$$gv = gY - gM \text{ , with } gP = 0 \qquad (5.1).$$

After prices had been freed, the surplus money was reduced by raising these. Put it another way: the velocity of circulation increased.

$$gv = gP + gY \qquad (5.2).$$

If there is no economic growth, the increase in velocity will lead to an increasing price level. This cannot be regarded as an inflation which made a monetary reform necessary, at least if it had stopped after a while. Rather it was necessary to adjust domestic relative prices to world market price relations for the sake of the overall reform process. However, in some countries, prices did not stabilise after the end of the adjustment inflation. Their governments were not able to keep money growth moderate thereafter. Instead, monetisation of public budget deficits contributed to further inflation.

Other continents did not witness as many monetary reforms. Only 11 monetary reforms reported in *Table 5.1* took place in Asia, and only five in Africa. That does not necessarily indicate that on average the monetary performance there was significantly better than in Latin America or Europe. It only was better in the sense that inflation rates on average were lower and less volatile than elsewhere. Hyperinflations did not occur as regularly as in Latin America or in the countries of transition. However, two-digit inflation rates over many years are also harmful for economic development. Although between 1975 and 1995, for instance, average inflation in the Western hemisphere was about sevenfold as compared to Africa, GDP growth in Africa was only 80 per cent of that in the Western hemisphere.

As regards the distribution of currency reforms over time, until the late 1960s, the number of reforms per decade has remained stable (approximately ten reforms per decade). The need for reform emerged mainly in countries of the Eastern hemisphere. During this period, the fixed exchange rate regime of Bretton Woods may have contributed to the relative sound monetary policy in the Western hemisphere as compared to the 1970s and 1980s. In the 1970s, the role of monetary policy in the policy mix slightly changed. Many policymakers and economists thought it could also be used for other targets than price stability. This assessment caused higher inflation across the world. Some countries, especially in Latin America, which by that time was also hit by political turmoils, experienced ever rising inflation. Finally in the 1980s, governments became increasingly aware of the problems and began to combat inflation. Many attempts, however, failed so that the 1980s and the 1990s witnessed a growing number of monetary reforms (about 21). In the 1990s, in addition, many of the monetary reforms pursued in former socialist countries during the transition process failed.

a) The Sample of 29 Monetary Reforms

The sample for the econometric assessment consists of 29 monetary reforms. The sample size and structure is determined by the availability and quality of the data.[3] As suggested by the theoretical chapters, inflation after a monetary reform depends on commitment, institutions and the determination to stop

3 All data is given in Appendices 3 and 4.

monetisation of budget deficits. A few other determinants are be added in Chapter 6. Some of these determinants are backward-oriented, some are forward-looking. This requirement indicates that reforms directly after World War II cannot be considered since the data for the war period is missing in great parts. Similarly, reforms after 1994 cannot be assessed as it would be rather speculative. For instance, the interesting cases of Paraguay in 1943/44, Poland in 1995 and Bulgaria which introduced a currency board in 1997 are lost. Partly, they have to be analysed as case studies.

The sample includes countries from three continents and a period of nearly 50 years and, therefore, is rather diverse. On the one hand, this makes it difficult to generate a comparison and to find reliable data. On the other hand, it shows that in different areas and through different times, the basic problems of monetary policy are comparable. Most of the countries in the sample have similar basic problems, namely high inflation rates and huge public budget deficits. Hence, it can be expected that important lessons about success and failure of monetary reforms can be learned.

Given this common feature of the reforms, the theoretical model is well tailored to fit the cases in the sample. Only a few reforms do not completely correspond: the German monetary union in July 1990 analysed here as a monetary reform of East Germany is not caused by explicit budget deficits and a high inflation rate. Rather, the budget deficit was implicit, and inflation manifested itself in queues. Inflation was undoubtedly repressed. However, this reform is an excellent example of how institutions and commitment can bring about stability. It also has to be taken into account that the German unification was very expensive. The German government could have had an incentive to monetise the resulting budget deficits. The second case that does not completely match the framework is the reform in Hong Kong in 1983. It was not a fiscal problem that caused Hong Kong to commit to a currency board based on the US dollar. Rather, during the negotiations between the UK and China about Hong Kong's accession to the latter in 1997 inflation rose for many people felt very insecure about the near future and started to panic-buy food and other basic products. To break further inflationary expectations, the Hong Kong authorities established the board at short notice (Greenwood 1983). Thus, Hong Kong would not fit in with another theoretical framework like the Phillips trade-off either. However, like Germany, it is a good example for the relevance of monetary commitment and institutions.

There are some other countries where inflation was rather low before the reform. In particular, Greece 1954 and Korea 1962 are cases in point. It has to be mentioned, however, that in the 1950s and 1960s world-wide average inflation was much lower than in the following decades. Two-digit inflation rates were recognised as being a great deal more worrying than was the case in subsequent decades.

Table 5.2: Pre-reform Inflation, Post-reform Monetary Regime and the Degree of Commitment in the Sample

Countries	Year	CPI in t-1	Monetary Regime	C_{uw}	C_{w1}	C_{w2}	C_{w3}
Argentina	1991	2,313.7	CBS	0.798	0.882	0.873	0.898
Argentina	1985	549.4	CB[1], fiER	0.462	0.479	0.462	0.474
Bolivia	1987	277.0	CB, fiER	0.540	0.545	0.466	0.450
Bolivia	1963	5.9	CB, fiER	0.540	0.545	0.466	0.450
Brazil	1994	1,000.0	CB, fiER	0.495	0.520	0.482	0.507
Brazil	1989	1,431.7	CB, flER	0.238	0.225	0.188	0.175
Brazil	1986	226.1	CB, fiER	0.346	0.354	0.317	0.342
Chile	1975	511.1[2].	CB, fiER	0.474	0.412	0.350	0.350
Estonia	1992	1,069.0[2]	CBS	0.787	0.825	0.837	0.825
Germany	1990	n.a.	CB, flER	0.665	0.624	0.649	0.599
Germany	1948	25.4	CB, fiER	0.707	0.687	0.712	0.699
Greece	1954	9.1	CB, flER	0.424	0.341	0.312	0.299
Hong Kong	1983	10.1[2]	CBS	0.674	0.750	0.804	0.833
Israel	1985	374.9	CB, fiER	0.503	0.495	0.478	0.490
Israel	1980	75.0	CB, flER	0.495	0.441	0.411	0.374
Korea	1962	12.1	CB, fiER	0.441	0.396	0.308	0.283
Latvia	1992	243.6[2]	CB, flER	0.632	0.658	0.628	0.616
Lithuania	1994	409.7[2]	CBS	0.715	0.783	0.829	0.850
Mexico	1993	15.5	CB, fiER	0.628	0.687	0.641	0.624
Mexico	1987	87.3	CB, fiER	0.378	0.345	0.291	0.275
Nicaragua	1990 /91	7,475,8	CB, fiER	0.662	0.704	0.649	0.624
Nicaragua	1988	911,5	CB, fiER	0.441	0.412	0.358	0.333
Peru	1991	7,592.3	CB, flER	0.578	0.637	0.624	0.641
Peru	1985	110,5	CB, fiER	0.445	0.454	0.383	0.375
Russia	1994	874.6	CB, fiER	0.611	0.653	0.632	0.641
Slovenia	1991	n.a.	CB, flER	0.511	0.516	0.507	0.491
Ukraine	1992	n.a.	CB, fiER	0.187	0.266	0.266	0.291
Uruguay	1993	68.4	CB, fiER	0.457	0.479	0.425	0.433
Uruguay	1975	77.3	CB, fiER	0.440	0.445	0.391	0.400

Notes: [1] CB = central bank, fiER = fixed exchange rate, flER = flexible exchange rate; [2]: CPI in t.

Source: See Chapter 6, section VI.

Table 5.2 shows the inflation rate, defined as consumer price inflation (CPI), in the year before the monetary reform (*t*-1), the monetary regime established through the reform and the degree of commitment both unweighted and weighted.[4]

It can be seen that the degree of commitment differs across the sample whereas the variety of monetary regimes is rather small. This is in line with *Figure 4.1.*

Concerning the interdependence of the chosen monetary regime and the degree of commitment, there is one interesting feature worth mentioning. Whereas central banks are connected with a wide range of the degree of commitment, the currency board system is inevitably connected with a relatively high degree of commitment. It can be shown that the degree of legal commitment of the currency boards in history exceeds the theoretical minimum (C_{uw} = 0.4) by far. The governments of those countries which chose a currency board (Argentina 1991, Estonia, Hong Kong and Lithuania), strongly committed themselves to stability (*Table 5.2*, fifth column). However, as shown in the following chapters, this is no guarantee for immediate success.

III. THE CASE STUDIES

In addition to econometric estimations in the following chapter, the empirical part of this study contains 12 case studies of individual monetary reforms in Chapter 7. The reason for carrying out some case studies is to obtain some detailed knowledge of the monetary problems and the planned and executed reform in different countries. Normally, the problems and their proper solution differ among countries. Moreover, by applying case studies the situations can be made comparable and policy conclusions for similar countries with actual problems can be drawn.

These cases are included in *Table 5.1* and discuss monetary reforms in Argentina (1985 and 1991), Brazil (1986), Estonia (1992), Germany (1923/24 and 1948), Greece (1944), Hungary (1924), Israel (1985), Lithuania (1994), Paraguay (1943/44) and Poland (1995). The choice of the reforms is determined by five criteria. First, these reforms are decisive turningpoints in the monetary policy of the countries. They are unmistakable reforms. In addition to the change in commitment, we can identify institutional factors.

---

[4] See Appendix 2, section I, for the detailed codings of the index *C* and the weights.

This makes the case studies good examples for analysing; to test the theoretical considerations of Chapters 2 through 4.

Moreover, both success and failure of the reform should be documented. In this study, it turns out that it is not so easy to distinguish both. Whether one regards monetary policy after a reform as being satisfying or as being disappointing depends on the expectations and on the goals associated with the reform. In particular, different inflation rates are consistent with the perception of the price level being relatively stable (Blinder 1997, pp. 4f). Nevertheless, the cases discussed in Chapter 7 consist of unambiguous successes and clear-cut failures. Interestingly, Argentina is a case in point: whereas the reform in 1985 was a complete failure (which had been forecast by many experts), the convertibility plan in 1991 restored credibility and led to remarkably low inflation in due course. Besides, cases of moderate successes are analysed in Chapter 7.

Third, the case studies cover several continents and regions. Certainly, monetary problems and their cures differ enormously between countries, especially between Latin America and Europe. Further, different periods of time are included. Two reforms took place after World War I (Germany, Hungary), two others during World War II (Greece and Paraguay), one three (long) years after the War (Germany), three reforms were made during a huge world-wide debt crisis in the 1980s (Israel, Argentina, Brazil), and finally four reforms were made in the 1990s, three of them in transition economies (Estonia, Lithuania, Poland). It may be interesting to see how the problems in different historical contexts demand different solutions. Finally, some of the cases are included in the sample for the econometric analysis, others not. The case studies are meant to show the relevance of our theory even without the complete data set.

There are other cases of monetary reform in *Table 5.1* which contain much information and many lessons for policymakers to adhere to. To name a few: Hong Kong and Bulgaria chose currency boards in completely different economic situations. Whereas in Hong Kong, inflation in autumn 1983 was only approximately 10 per cent, Bulgaria in 1997 was in a situation close to a hyperinflation. Nevertheless, due to political insecurities, the credibility of the monetary regime in Hong Kong was declining. So one can find both political and economic causation for monetary reforms.

Latin America is but a laboratory for monetary reformers. Argentina, Bolivia, Brazil, Chile, Nicaragua and Peru have experienced many reforms as monetary policy has been abused throughout the 1970s, 1980s and 1990s, mainly to finance public budget deficits. The people in these countries have seen many currencies and stabilisation plans. The majority of the reforms failed, partly for similar reasons and partly for different reasons. After World

War II, many countries were reforming their monetary regime. Hungary had to manage two hyperinflations within a generation which it handled quite well. All these examples would be interesting to analyse. However, the sample of 12 reforms chosen as case studies represent most economic peculiarities before and after a reform. Little seems to be added by including more cases, however exciting their history may be.

6. Cross Country Studies: Commitment and Institutions Matter

I. THE ECONOMETRIC MODEL

Of the 72 monetary reforms identified in *Table 5.1*, we have chosen a sample consisting of 29 monetary reforms made after World War II. For these 29 reforms, the relevant data has been available. The estimation is cross-sectional as we analyse different countries performing monetary reforms at different times. The method applied here is ordinary least squares (OLS). The econometric analysis is based upon the theoretical model developed in Chapter 4. This chapter is organised as follows: methodical foundations are laid in this section. In the subsequent section, the choice of the variables for the measure of commitment, institutional factors and all other variables are explained, respectively. In section III, we estimate the model in variants 1 through 3. The results of the estimation procedure are discussed and interpreted in section IV. Section V indicates how the results can be used for policy simulation.

a) Introduction

The straightforwardness of the theoretical model is very helpful for an econometric analysis in that we can use the maximised monetary policymaker's objective function as the basic equation for the OLS estimation. The objective function has a standard form (4.7): $Z = \delta\pi \exp(-\alpha\pi^e) - \exp(\pi^2 + k_2(\pi^e))$. The costs of commitment are related to both actual inflation and inflationary expectations. In the theoretical analysis, the expression $k(\pi^e)$ is specified as follows:

$$k(\pi^e) = C \qquad (6.1),$$

$$k(\pi^e) = C + IF_1 + ... + IF_n \qquad (6.2),$$

$$k(\pi^e) = \frac{1}{\left(C - \frac{\sum_{i=1}^{n} IF_i}{n}\right)^2} \quad \text{or}$$

$$k(\pi^e) = \frac{1}{\left|C - \frac{\sum_{i=1}^{n} IF_i}{n}\right|}, \text{ respectively} \qquad (6.3).$$

In the theoretical model we apply a political economy framework for the success of monetary reforms. The main hypothesis is that inflation can be kept on a low level if the monetary reform creates a credible commitment to stability. The first specification does not allow for a judgement of how credible the commitment is. The second one corrects for institutional factors, but the relation between commitment and these factors is very lose. Theoretically most appealing, in the third case $k(\pi^e)$ is modelled as an ex-ante proxy for credibility. Credibility itself depends on how well the chosen commitment harmonises with the institutional setting in the country. The better the degree of commitment and the institutional setting suit each other, the higher the credibility of the reform and the lower the inflation rate will be. To assess how credibility affects the success of a monetary reform, we have to further specify the commitment C and various institutional factors IF_i.[1] In addition to these, there are other determinants of the success of the reform.

b) Other determinants of the success of monetary reform

Seigniorage. in the theoretical model, the success of the reform also hinges on the degree to which the government is in the self-made need of seigniorage (δ) and on the demand for money (M/P). An actual attitude of the government towards seigniorage δ cannot be observed.[2] Instead, a measure of seigniorage itself needs to be applied. There is no clear concept of seigniorage, the difficulty being to link monetary and fiscal aspects. Klein and Neumann (1990) incorporate both aspects and show that the correct magnitude of seigniorage transferred to the government cannot be determined by a simple formula such as the Cagan-type we used in the theoretical model

---

1 The specifications of both the index of commitment and the institutional factors is documented in Appendix 2, section I and II, respectively.

2 This holds regardless of whether the government has committed to a rule that prohibits direct loans to it by the monetary authority or not.

(equation (1): $S = mL(\pi^e)$). The same holds for the two concepts of seigniorage which are generally used, the so-called opportunity cost concept and the monetary seigniorage concept. Instead, a correct measure of seigniorage has to consider legal, institutional and operational details of money creation (Klein and Neumann 1990). Only then, the contribution of seigniorage to the public budget in different countries can be made fully comparable.

The demand for real money is defined as $L(\pi^e) = \exp(-\alpha\pi^e) = M / P$. The problem is that we cannot observe $(-\alpha\pi^e)$. Thus, we have to operate with M / P. However, both M and P are already incorporated in other variables. M is part of any measure of seigniorage, whereas P is a component of the endogenous variable, the inflation rate. Thus, it is very probable that multicollinearity occurs. Therefore, one remedy is to not include the demand for money. The technique of dropping a variable is one possible answer to this problem, but not the best since information is lost if the variable's estimators differ from zero (Kennedy 1992, pp. 180–186).

An alternative is to form a principal component, i.e. a composite variable consisting of the two multicollinear variables (ibid.). In a heuristic way, this is done by constructing the variable *SEIGN*. This is calculated as the annual increase in base money over the sum of public revenues and the increase in base money for the same year (see Appendix 2). Thus, it bundles the information of the demand for money and the dependence on seigniorage. This can be seen when looking at the expected sign of both variables. Both the reliance on seigniorage δ and demand for real money (*M/P*) positively contribute to post-reform inflation (4.11): $\ln 2\pi + \pi^2 = \ldots \ln\delta + \ln(M / P) + \ldots = \ldots \ln\delta + \ln M - \ln P + \ldots$. The variable *SEIGN* includes both δ and M with the theoretically shown direction of causation. Rearranging equation (4.11) and bringing *lnP* to the left-hand side leads to P being included in the dependent variable. It again has the theoretically expected sign. Next, we approximate $\pi \approx \pi + \ln P$ and $Seigniorage \approx \ln M + \ln\delta$, respectively and find that inflation positively depends on *SEIGN*. It is a good approximation and allows to not compose a special variable for the demand for real money. The theoretically expected impact this variable has on the success of the reform is negative, that is the expected influence on inflation is positive.

International capital mobility. one factor that may also be of importance for the policymakers' calculus, is the degree of capital mobility. Capital mobility is determined by the legal (national and international) framework and by technical opportunities. In recent economic history, increasing capital mobility is closely related to the end of the Bretton Woods system. During its existence, capital mobility was rather modest, due to political and technological obstacles.

On the one hand, it is theoretically convincing that higher capital mobility contributes to a lower inflation rate since the capital owners can avoid the country with a high inflation rate more easily. If they do so, investments are lower than possible, eventually leading to unemployment. This provides a strong disincentive for governments to raise the rate of inflation above a certain level. Given the relatively low degree of capital mobility, one could argue that the inflationary bias during the existence of the Bretton Woods system was higher than afterwards.

On the other hand, the Bretton Woods system may have had a disciplining effect on governments.[3] Many countries fixed their exchange rate towards the US dollar. For many of them, this fixing gave a strong disincentive to raise inflation. But even without being part of the system, governments were always reminded of monetary discipline. Consequently, the average inflation rate during the era of Bretton Woods was lower than afterwards. Until 1973, the average CPI in the world was below 10 per cent. From 1974 until 1995 (with the exception of 1978) it was on a two-digit level. Additionally, the increasing average inflation rate can certainly be traced back to supply shocks, particularly the huge price increase of oil in 1973/4 and 1979/80, respectively (IMF (a), October 1996, pp. 100f). Only recently, average inflation moved beyond 10 per cent again. Thus, without the empirical results it remains an open question in which direction capital mobility affects the politically optimal inflation rate.

Capital mobility is difficult to measure. Ideally, one should use an ex-ante measure rather than an ex-post one, such as the capital account. Using the latter one easily could confuse cause and effect. Thus, we employ the variable *PostBW*, a dummy which measures the effect of the Bretton Woods system. Its value equals 1 if the reform was made after 1973 and 0 if it was made before then. The impact on inflation is theoretically ambiguous.

International growth differentials. in reality, the rate of inflation after a monetary reform can also be affected by the difference in productivity growth between the sectors in the reform country (Balassa 1964). Productivity growth is normally higher in the tradables sector than in the non-tradables one. Productivity growth in the tradables sector causes factor prices to rise without output price increases for tradables as long as the law of one price holds internationally. As a consequence, factor prices in the non-tradables industries also rise leading to higher prices for non-tradable goods and

3 Others, e.g. Germany, regarded the average inflation rates as being too high during this period, as their fundamentals were compatible with lower rates.

services. Thus, even without money growth exceeding real growth, there will be a positive rate of inflation. Inflation will be the higher, the higher the productivity growth in the tradables sector is. International differences in inflation can be partly explained by the so-called Balassa–Samuelson effect. To avoid a misspecification of the econometric model, we have to consider this factor.

However, growth rate differentials are not only causes of inflation. They can also be its effects. In some of the countries of the sample, the monetary reform completely failed. In most instances of failure, inflation decreased briefly and rose again sharply. In such a situation, high inflation can contribute to low or even negative economic growth, at least if inflation is very high (Barro 1995)[4]. Both high inflation and low growth are caused by an inappropriate economic policy mix. Thus, the explanation derived from the Balassa–Samuelson effect[5] does not necessarily hold in such a situation. We will test whether it makes sense to add a variable for the Balassa-Samuelson effect (*BAL*) into the econometric model.[6]

In addition to these two economic factors, there may be a third one influencing the politically optimal inflation rate after monetary reforms, especially in emerging countries: an external shock leading to a depreciation of the capital stock. Such a shock can be both economical and non-economical, for instance a price increase for crucial import goods on the one hand or an earthquake on the other hand. Both may cause the government to delay the stabilisation and to print more money than compatible with the targeted inflation rate. A situation like an oil price shock or an earthquake certainly diminishes the relative importance of an incredible monetary policy. It has turned out, however, that explicitly considering this situation with a dummy variable would not make sense because in the first few years after the reform a vast majority of reform countries have been hit by a shock in one way or another. Moreover, we already have introduced *PostBW*. Thus, we do not make use of this factor.

c) Some methodical remarks

The OLS estimation can produce a 'good' econometric result in the sense that the estimators are unbiased and have minimum variances. Estimators with these properties are called BLUE (best linear unbiased estimator). However, the goodness depends crucially on whether the model is well specified. The quality of the specification itself depends on the economic foundation and

---

4 See also Chapter 2, section I.

5 See Balassa (1964) and Samuelson (1964).

6 See also Appendix 2, section III for the specification of *SEIGN*, *PostBW* and *BAL*.

some features of the econometric model.[7] However, not all difficulties one may think of, are relevant for this study. For instance, autocorrelation can be largely excluded since the sample consists of very different cases of reforms having been made in different continents at different times. A systematic economic relationship between the residuals is not very likely.

As opposed to autocorrelation, heteroscedasticity, i.e. the variances of the residuals not being uniform, cannot be ruled out. If the absolute magnitude of the residuals varies with the magnitude of the variables, both dependent and independent, heteroscedasticity is highly probable. The sample of 29 monetary reforms is very heterogeneous as regards the magnitude of the variables. Heteroscedasticity leads to still unbiased but inefficient estimators. Their variances no longer are at a minimum, but are bigger than without heteroscedasticity. White's heteroscedasticity test and if necessary White's correction for heteroscedasticity are applied. The interesting feature about White's correction is that even in the presence of heteroscedasticity the OLS method can produce consistent estimators (White 1980). The computational task can be handled more easily than with a generalised least squares estimation (Kennedy 1992, pp. 118f).

The econometric analysis can be prone to another difficulty, namely multicollinearity. The explanatory variables can be correlated with each other. It is important to acknowledge the fact that the independent variables do not have to be related through economic theory for multicollinearity to occur. It is given when the variables are related nearly linear. It is often suggested not to be concerned with this for the estimators are still unbiased. The negative consequence of multicollinearity is that the informational content of a single estimator is low when this estimator systematically varies with another one. The effects of each of these estimators cannot be distinguished. This situation can be compared with fewer degrees of freedom as opposed to a situation without multicollinearity (Kennedy 1992, pp. 177–179). It cannot be completely precluded that the data we make use of to compose the institutional factors is correlated. Given the rather small sample, this is reason enough to avoid the problem.

There are several ways to cure multicollinearity which all try to add information (ibid., pp. 181–183). Among them there are some that are not very promising for our purpose. The best remedy is to drop a variable if and only of the multicollinearity is perfect. If not, the remaining estimators are biased. Another cure is to obtain more data, i.e. to enlarge the sample size. If this was possible, we certainly would have taken this opportunity. The difficulties to obtain data for this study have turned out to be considerable. Obtaining even more data is impossible. A third unurable cure is to

7 For a general overview see Kennedy (1992, in particular the synopsis on p. 45).

incorporate results from other studies. This study explores unknown territories and cannot refer to other work. Nevertheless, there are two suggestions which in general make sense: the first, not used in this study, but worth mentioning, is to formalise the relationship between the two or more independent variables and to change the OLS into a simultaneous equation estimation. The cure used in this study is to form a new variable as a component of the two or more variables that are highly multicollinear (see above). Other problems concern the stability and linearity of the parameters. It is assumed that the relationship between explanatory variables and the dependent variable is linear. This needs to be tested. We apply several stability tests to check whether the parameters are robust, e.g. the Ramsey-reset test, the cusum of square-test and recursive residuals.

The parameters of all reported estimators (*Tables 9* through *11* below) proved robust. Moreover, subsamples, are estimated separately, e.g. the Latin American countries. We also test whether it is critical to drop countries that do not perfectly fit theoretically such as Germany 1990 and Hong Kong 1983. In both cases, hyperinflation was not the reason for the reform. Unless individually reported, the parameters of all regressions have proven robust in these tests as well. For the choice of the variables, we also calculate the correlation coefficient of the regressors (see below).

II. CHOICE OF VARIABLES

The next step is to operationalise the determinants of expected inflation and inflation itself. Two difficulties need to be solved: first, the nature of the variables, in particular *C* and *IFi*, does not allow to directly observe these. They have to be composed of different elements. Such a composition always bears the danger of arbitrariness and a lack of interpersonal comparability. Both the choice of elements and the outcome can be biased. Second, the sample consists of monetary reforms at different times and in different countries. The quality of data is not homogeneous: in countries such as Germany and Hong Kong, the data seems to be reliable whereas in other countries, especially in Latin America and the former socialist countries, doubts seem to be justified. To make these reforms comparable, one often has to look for a common denominator diminishing the average quality of the data. We have elaborated different specifications of both the independent and the dependent variables which are introduced and explained in full detail in Appendix 2. Before we start with the econometric work and its interpretation, in this section we look for those specifications of each variable that produce the most reliable results, that is which goodness of fit is the highest.

a) Inflation as the dependent variable

The rate of inflation after the monetary reform is the endogenous variable in the model. Policymakers announce a monetary policy, subsequently react to certain signals and choose an inflation rate which is optimal from their personal perspective. In general, the variables are based on the concept of consumer price inflation. This is the best approximation given the goal to break inflationary expectations in the public, and it is an internationally comparable indicator. Moreover, the data is available for the whole sample. The theoretical model does not allow to separate the rate of inflation on the left-hand side. Instead, the expression $\ln 2\pi + \pi^2$ (equation 9) overemphasises high inflation and huge differences within the sample. This makes the estimation increasingly difficult. Given the diversity of the sample, it therefore makes sense to eliminate π^2 and to approximate $\ln 2\pi + \pi^2 \approx \ln CPI$.

Instead of this specification, one can think of applying a completely different approach, namely a binary choice model. The outcome of the reform process is not defined in terms of inflation but as success (value 0) or failure (value 1) of the monetary reform. Different to the OLS regression applied here, a logit or probit estimation would have to be applied in such case. However, this approach has methodical shortcomings: for one, the outcome is not directly observable. Whether the reform is a success or not has to be decided by the researcher on the basis of the observed inflation rates. One way to overcome this problem is to use an index function (Greene 1997, pp. 880f). One has to choose a rate of inflation *CPI** which distinguishes success from failure: $y = 1$ if $CPI > CPI^*$, and $y = 0$ if $CPI \leq CPI^*$. Furthermore, the binary choice approach is based on the assumption that the outcome of y (0 or 1) is due to the choices of the acting individual. Since we can take it for granted that the monetary policymaker would in any event choose success (value 0), we do not use this technique. In addition, the number of observations is too small to generate meaningful results of a logit or probit estimation.[8]

Disinflation with the help of a new monetary regime is a process which needs time. It can hardly be expected that the annual inflation rates drops down close to zero within a year or an even shorter period. Inflationary

8 To control for the results of the estimations of variant 1 through 3 (see below), we have run logit and probit models, yielding results similar to the OLS model, but insignificant. This is probably due to the methodical problems of this approach.

expectations may be very resistant especially when the public has experienced a few unsuccessful reforms before. People are used to rising prices. Moreover, many contracts may be indexed so that there is an inflationary pressure. Even if the monetary reform is credible (*C-IF* close to zero), the stabilisation process will be time-consuming. Thus, we assume a period of five years as being sufficient for the stabilisation process. It can be expected that a success of the reform will be visible within five years. Of course, disinflation can be achieved earlier with the inflation rate being low afterwards. Moreover, a failure can be identified easily within five years. Even if in the first few months or years after the reform a slight stabilisation is observed, this period is long enough to recognise a failure.

Hence, we use two different specifications of the dependent variable.[9] The first is a weighted average of annual inflation rates during a period of five years after the reform (*WCPI*). The highest weight is given to the final year. The second specification is the average inflation rate during this period (*ACPI*). Both are tested in logarithmic form (Appendix 2, section IV).

b) The independent variables

Commitment is specified as the degree of commitment. We first calculate the correlation between the four specifications C_{uw}, C_{w1}, C_{w2} and C_{w3}. It turns out that the weighted forms C_{w1}, C_{w2} and C_{w3} of the index are higher correlated with one another than any of them is correlated with the unweighted form of the index of commitment. The lowest correlation exists between C_{uw} and C_{w3} (0.922). In sum, the different specifications of *C* are highly correlated with each other, but not identical. Therefore, we apply all of them for the estimations.

The individual institutional factors are also specified differently. To figure out which seems to be the best specification of each factor is necessary for the second and the third variant of the model: we look for those specifications that add most to the explanation of inflation after a monetary reform. In a first step their fit for variant 2 is tested. For this purpose, we run a regression with each specification of the institutional factors on different specifications of the dependent variable. It turns out that – with the exception of the index of economic freedom – individually the institutional factors do not contribute much to the explanation of the post-reform inflation. However, in common estimations (not reported in *Table 6.1*) their influence cannot be rejected. In addition, the logarithmic form of either *ACPI* or *WCPI* are explained in a more preferable way by the regressors than the non-logarithmic forms, which theoretically makes perfect sense. *Table 6.1* shows the result of the univariate regression on *lnACPI*.

9 Detailed definitions and explanations are given in Appendix 2.

Table 6.1 Regressions on lnACPI

Independent	Coefficient	t-statistic	R^2adj	Intercept
*PS*1	-2.283	-0.57	-0.023	5.85
*PS*2	-3.749	-2.937***	0.243	6.7***
*FS*1	-6.295	-3.124***	0.057	6.844***
*FS*2	-3.298	-3.194***	0.054	4.347***
*FS*3	-1.232	-0.822	-0.016	3.751***
LM	0.673	0.432	-0.032	3.442***
*LM*73	-4.566	-0.941	-0.011	4.332***
OP	-0.925	-0.834	-0.014	4.335***
*OP*2	-2.21	-2.86***	0.062	4.069***
*OP*3	-0.88	-0.979	-0.006	4.071***
*OP*4	-2.17E-04	-2.917***	0.065	4.074***
*OP*5	-0.89	-1.31	-0.004	4.135***
POI	-4.114	-2.887***	0.22	5.358***
RC	-4.181	-2.451***	0.124	4.924***
EF	-5.709	-3.791***	0.341	6.7***
*EF*2000	-7.549	-7.088***	0.634	8.393***

Notes: *, **,***: significant at 10 per cent level, 5 per cent level, 1 per cent level, respectively.
For an explanation of the variables see Appendix 2, sections I and II.
Source: See Appendix 2, section V.

The variables' specifications in bold face are used in the estimations of variant 2 in Chapter 6, section III. As compared to other specifications of the same variable they provide the best explanation of post-reform inflation. Before proceeding, the correlation matrix of these variables is shown. The less they are correlated with one another, the more the estimations are unbiased. The correlation can be regarded as being rather low. An exception is the correlation between the index of economic freedom, *EF* (*EF*2000), and the rest. Because *EF* (*EF*2000) is a composition of institutional features, although others than we use, it is - and should be - highly correlated with the other institutional factors. Naturally, *EF* (*EF*2000) and the other factors are used in separate estimations.

Table 6.2 shows the correlation between the institutional factors used in variant 2 of the model. The (partially) high correlation of *EF* (*EF*2000) with other factors is encouraging. It is an external test since the degree of economic freedom is based on the data generated by Gwartney and his colleagues (Appendix 2, section II.g). We take this as evidence that the data for the institutional setting seems reliable.[10]

Table 6.2: Institutional Factors for Variant 2: Correlation Matrix

	*PS*2		*FS*1	*OP*4	*POI*	*RC*	*EF*	*EF*2000
*PS*2	1.000	0.063	0.202	0.489	0.070	0.155	0.515	0.485
*LM*73	0.063	1.000	-0.154	-0.219	0.701	-0.085	0.141	0.077
*FS*1	0.202	-0.154	1.000	0.743	0.104	-0.095	0.766	0.612
*OP*4	0.489	-0.219	0.743	1.000	-0.129	-0.315	0.467	0.427
POI	0.070	0.701	0.104	-0.129	1.000	-0.160	0.350	0.172
RC	0.155	-0.085	-0.095	-0.315	-0.160	1.000	0.132	0.226
EF	0.515	0.141	0.766	0.467	0.350	0.132	1.000	0.833
*EF*2000	0.485	0.077	0.612	0.427	0.173	0.226	0.833	1.000

Source: See Appendix 2, section V.

For the calculation of the proxy for credibility (variant 3), the choice of specifications is a little different. The variables that individually contribute to the explanation of inflation do not necessarily have a similarly strong influence when estimated commonly or when even composed into a common indicator. The proxy for credibility has the form $1/(C_{uw} - IF)^2$ or $1/|C_{uw} - IF|$. *IF* is the arithmetic average of the following specifications: *PS*1, *FS*1, *LM*73, *OP*3 and *POI*. They are less correlated than the sample of variables used for variant 2 as *Table 6.3* shows. Moreover, the estimations of this specification of *IF* provide the best results (reported in *Table 6.6*).

Table 6.3: Institutional Factors for Variant 3: Correlation Matrix

	*PS*1	*LM*73	*FS*1	*OP*3	*POI*
*PS*1	1.000	0.146	0.115	0.341	0.174
*LM*73	0.146	1.000	-0.087	0.175	0.619
*FS*1	0.115	-0.087	1.000	0.284	0.101
*OP*3	0.341	0.175	0.284	1.000	0.119
POI	0.174	0.619	0.101	0.119	1.000

Source: See Appendix 2, section V.

[10] Even if the data is less reliable, it can be regarded as proof of how difficult it is to generate good data. Obviously, other researchers have the same problems.

One of the other potentially independent variables is of interest, namely the influence of growth differences on inflation. As mentioned in section I of this chapter, it is not clear in the sample whether growth differences to other countries cause high inflation (Balassa–Samuelson effect) or whether high inflation causes economic growth rates to diminish. Both scenarios can be found in the sample. We test it by running two regressions:[11]

$$\ln ACPI = \beta_0 + \beta_1 BAL + \varepsilon \quad (6.4a),$$

$$BAL = \beta_0 + \beta_1 \ln WCPI + \varepsilon \quad (6.4b).$$

It turns out that both inflation and growth differences to the US depend significantly (the five per cent level) on each other. The coefficient β_1 shows the correct (negative) sign in both cases. There is no clear answer to the question of causality. Because of this result, we do not use *BAL* in the following section.

Finally, the expected direction of influence of the variables used in the following section on post-reform inflation has to be mentioned. The index of commitment, institutional factors and the proxy for credibility are expected to have a negative impact on inflation, whereas the influence of *SEIGN* on inflation is expected to be positive. The dummy for the post Bretton Woods era, *PostBW*, can theoretically have a positive or a negative impact. Both can be explained and understood in an economic context.

III. EXPECTED SIGNS IN ECONOMETRIC ESTIMATIONS CONFIRMED

a) Specification 1: showing the importance of commitment

The first equation only considers the degree of commitment. In (6.5) institutions are neglected. It has the following form:

$$\ln ACPI = \beta_0 + \beta_1 C + \beta_2 SEIGN + \beta_3 PostBW + \varepsilon \quad (6.5),$$

---

11 We are unable to run the standard test, a Granger causality test, since we do not have a time series.

where $\varepsilon \sim \text{ND}(0,\sigma_\varepsilon^2)$. In addition to *ACPI*, we also take *WCPI* as the dependent variable. Both are used in logarithmic form. Whether *ACPI* or *WCPI* is the dependent variable does not make a great difference for the parameters and test statistics. In general, *ACPI* is explained a little better than *WCPI*. Therefore, we mainly take recourse to *ACPI* and only occasionally show both estimations.[12] The results of different estimations are reported in *Table 6.4*.

The impact of the index of commitment on inflation is shown in estimations 1 through 4. The differences between the specifications are relatively small. Hence, in the following estimations (7 through 12), we concentrate on two specifications, namely C_{uw} and C_{w2}. Estimations 5 and 6 show that even without the consideration of commitment, inflation can be explained by the reliance on seigniorage and the acknowledgement of *PostBW*. The first hypothesis about the determinants of the average inflation after monetary reforms as expressed in (6.5) is tested via estimations 7 through 12. It cannot be rejected. The index of commitment regardless of the chosen weighting (*uw* or *w*2) and seigniorage show the expected sign and are significant on the 1 per cent level. The higher the degree of commitment, the lower the average inflation. The politically optimal inflation is positively correlated with monetary seigniorage. It makes no substantial difference whether the regressors are estimated in logarithmic form or not. The post-reform rate of inflation as the dependent variable is explained similarly well. Thus, in the subsequent subsections we only report the semi-log estimations of variants 2 and 3.

The sign of β_3, the coefficient for *PostBW*, is positive. This evidence can be interpreted as follows: the Bretton Woods system with its fixed exchange rate exerted a disciplinary pressure on governments, in particular in those countries that had a fixed dollar exchange rate. Higher inflation than in the USA regularly forced these countries to devalue their currency towards the US dollar. This certainly had disciplinary effects on developing countries. After 1973, the exchange rates became flexible. It also became easier to produce high inflation rates heavily without the external anchor. The increasing capital mobility related to the post-Bretton Woods era has not become a similarly disciplining institution. Furthermore, the reform countries were subject to supply shocks after 1973. *PostBW* does not separate between these two effects. This dummy has a lower impact than commitment and seigniorage.

12 This holds also for variants 2 and 3.

Table 6.4 Regression Results for Variant 1

Estimation	1	2	3	4	5	6
Dependent	*lnACPI*	*lnACPI*	*lnACPI*	*lnACPI*	*lnACPI*	*lnWCPI*
Intercept	7.652***	6.793***	6.325***	6.097***	0.582	0.291
C_{uw}	-7.434***					
C_{w1}		-5.697***				
C_{w2}			-5.092***			
C_{w3}				-4.675***		
SEIGN					8.297***	10.969***
PostBW					2.289***	2.736***
R^2	0.359	0.274	0.276	0.244	0.548	0.535
R^2adj	0.335	0.247	0.250	0.216	0.513	0.499
F-stat.	15.095	10.295	10.308	8.709	15.744	14.948
N	29	29	29	29	29	29
Intercept	3.953***	2.911***	2.078**	1.714**	4.063	2.859***
C_{uw}	-5.944***				-6.653***	
C_{w2}		-4.702***				-5.186***
lnC_{uw}			-2.56***	-2.323***		
lnC_w						
SEIGN	6.229***	6.377***			8.654***	8.851***
lnSEIGN			1.005***	0.982***		
PostBW	2.353***	2.677***	2.48***	2.868***	2.807***	3.164***
R^2	0.758	0.763	0.718	0.75	0.694	0.693
R^2adj	0.729	0.735	0.684	0.72	0.657	0.656
F-stat.	26.12	26.87	21.12	24.97	18.88	18.8
N	29	29	29	29	29	29

Notes: *, **,***: significant at 10 per cent level, 5 per cent level, 1 per cent level, respectively. For an explanation of the variables see Appendix 2, sections I through IV. The data can be found in Appendices 3 and 4.

Source: See Appendix 2, section V.

The multivariate regressions (estimations 7 through 12) explain the post-reform inflation rate better than univariate or bivariate regressions (estimations 1 through 6). The coefficient of determination R^2 shows how much of the variation of the dependent variable can be explained by variations of the regressors. Naturally, it rises with the growing number of independent variables, no matter whether or not they are theoretically related to the dependent variable. To make it a meaningful statistic, it has to be corrected for the degrees of freedom in the respective equation (R^2adj). Given that the degree of freedom diminishes when adding more independent variables, the improvement of R^2adj after including all three independent is remarkable (estimations 7ff).

b) Specification 2: institutions matter

So far, we cannot reject the hypothesis that commitment matters for the success of monetary reforms. The second hypothesis to test is that institutions are also relevant. Equation (6.6) adds in institutional factors in the specification's independent variables.

$$\begin{aligned}&\ln ACPI = \beta_0 + \beta_1 C + \beta_2 SEIGN + \beta_3 PostBW + \\ &[\beta_4 \beta_5 \beta_6 \beta_7 \beta_8 \beta_9][PS2\ FS1\ LM73\ OP4\ POI\ RC]^T + \varepsilon\end{aligned} \quad (6.6).$$

The estimation results from various forms of (6.6) are reported in *Table 6.5*. To incorporate all six institutional factors is meaningless. There are ten independent variables and 23 observations. In addition, *LM* and *LM*73 are insignificant and do not have the predicted sign. Thus, we report of the other institutional factors in different estimations.

In equation 13, four institutional factors are regressed on inflation. Although only *FS*1 is significant, the institutional setting as a whole is also significant. We have done the Wald-test, producing an χ^2-statistic of 25.6. The null hypothesis of this test is that the factors *PS*2, *FS*1, *OP*4 and *POI* taken together have no influence on the outcome of the dependent variable. This hypothesis can be rejected. Estimations 14 and 15 show that political stability, fiscal stability and properties of the reserve currency have the correct sign and are significant. *EF* and *EF*2000 as a comprehensive alternative to the institutional setting have the expected negative sign and are significant (estimations 16 through 18). High economic freedom causes inflation to be politically costly. In combination with a high degree of commitment, the political costs of inflation even rise. Given their rather high coefficient of correlation, it is not astonishing that C_{uw} and C_{w2} are less significant than in estimation 13 through 15.[13] It has been impossible to run a common regression with *PostBW* since all reforms covered by *EF* and *EF*2000 took place in the post-Bretton Woods era. Adding *PostBW* would yield no additional information.

---

13 The correlation coefficient of *C* and *EF* is 0.584. In estimations of *EF* and *EF*2000 without *C* (not reported here), R^2adj is only slightly lower than in estimations 16 through 18.

Table 6.5 Regression Results for Variant 2

Estimation	13	14	15	16	17	18
Dependent	*lnACPI*	*lnACPI*	*lnACPI*	*lnACPI*	*lnACPI*	*lnACPI*
Intercept	6.012***	6.335***	6.428***	6.79***	7.617***	7.183***
C_{uw}	-4.189***	-4.515***		-4.019**	-3.088*	
C_{w2}			-3.607***			-2.394*
PS2	-0.992	-1.218*	-0.985			
FS1	-3.516**	-4.273***	-3.595***			
OP4	-5.91E-05					
POI	-0.69					
RC			-2.384**			
EF				-3.242**		
EF2000					-4.476***	-4.43***
SEIGN	5.576***	6.016***	5.635***	6.374***	4.43***	4.567***
PostBW	2.343***	2.314***	1.785***			
R^2	0.837	0.827	0.851	0.783	0.799	0.794
R^2adj	0.783	0.789	0.795	0.745	0.77	0.765
F-stat.	15.42	21.92	15.19	20.473	27.84	27.04
N	29	29	23	21	25	25

Notes: *, **,***:significant at 10 per cent level, 5 per cent level, 1 per cent level, respectively. For an explanation of the variables see Appendix 2, sections I through IV. The data can be found in Appendices 3 and 4.

Source: See Appendix 2, section V.

c) Specification 3: ex-ante proxy for credibility also relevant

Still, (6.6) does not give evidence for the ex-ante credibility of monetary reforms. The impact of credibility is estimated in equation (6.7) and reported in *Table 6.6*.

$$\ln ACPI = \beta_0 + \beta_1 (1/(C - \frac{\sum_{i=1}^{n} IF_n}{n})^2) + \beta_2 SEIGN + \beta_3 PostBW + \varepsilon ,$$

$$\text{with} \quad IF = \frac{\sum_{i=1}^{n} IF_n}{n} \qquad (6.7).$$

The squared difference between commitment and the average outcome of the institutional factors emphasises great differences and diminishes small ones. Unless marked differently, the institutional factors are used in the following specifications: *PS*1, *FS*1, *LM*73, *OP*3, *POI*. The estimation results are reported in *Table 6.6*. It turns out that the proxy for credibility based on the weighted index of commitment C_{w2} (estimations 21 and 23) has a more significant impact on inflation than the one based on the unweighted index (estimations 19 and 20). The significance level and the coefficient of determination are higher in the latter case. Estimation 22 shows that the absolute value of the difference of C_{w2} and *IF* yields the highest ß-value. In general, the theoretical hypothesis cannot be rejected: the higher the ex-ante credibility of a monetary reform is, the lower the politically optimal inflation rate will be. However, the coefficient of credibility has a very low value. The impact of an absolute increase in credibility on the relative decrease in inflation is almost negligible. Notwithstanding this unsatisfactory result, we conclude that the theoretical considerations cannot be rejected on the grounds of these estimations.

The estimation results reported in *Table 6.6* make clear that the construction and weighting of the index of commitment is of crucial importance. The proxies for credibility which are based upon C_{w1}, and C_{w3} did not show the expected sign (not reported in *Table 6.6*).

Table 6.6 Regression Results for Variant 3

Estimation	19[1]	20[2]	21	22	23
Dependent	*lnACPI*	*lnWCPI*	*lnACPI*	*lnACPI*	*lnWCPI*
Intercept	0.05	0.472	0.543	0.527	0.239
$1/(C_{uw}-IF)^2$	-6.69E-05	-2.98E-06			
$1/(C_{w2}-IF)^2$			-7.34E-06***		9.63E-06***
$1/\lvert C_{w2}-IF\rvert$				-0.003***	
SEIGN	13.207***	10.893***	8.655***	9.053***	11.439**
PostBW	2.901***	2.577***	2.43***	2.422***	2.921***
R^2	0.569	0.537	0.605	0.595	0.594
R^2adj	0.518	0.482	0.557	0.547	0.545
F-stat.	11.02	9.777	12.74	12.26	12.185
N	29	29	29	29	29

Notes: [1]: *LM* instead of *LM*73 used in $1/(C_{uw}-IF)^2$; [2]: no use of *LM* or *LM*73 in $1/(C_{uw}-IF)^2$.

*, **,***: significant at 10 per cent level, 5 per cent level, 1 per cent level, respectively. For an explanation of the variables see Appendix 2, sections I through IV. The data can be found in Appendices 3 and 4.

Source: See Appendix 2, section V.

This is different with the ex-ante proxies for credibility based upon C_{w2}. It contributes significantly to the explanation of the politically optimal inflation after a monetary reform. Changing the weight to C_{uw} shows another interesting feature. Only if the proxy for labour market flexibility is either dropped or changed into *LM*, the regressor is significant. To summarise: the significance of the proxy of credibility is very sensitive with respect to the specification of (a) the degree of commitment and of (b) the institutional setting, *IF*. Estimation 22 shows that the proxy is significant when well specified regardless of whether it is used in quadratic or in absolute form (see also equation (6.3)). In all estimations, R^2adj is smaller than in variants 1 and 2. Moreover, the magnitude of the influence of credibility on inflation is relatively small as compared to the influence of commitment alone (*Table 6.4)*. The impact of commitment estimated alone is greater than the impact of credibility as defined here.

IV. DISCUSSION OF THE RESULTS

The estimations of equations (6.5) through (6.7) obtain very promising results. Monetary commitment as well as some institutional features can prevent governments from inflating heavily, as long as the government is willing to forgo the money press to finance its budget. In addition, international exchange rate co-ordination makes inflation politically costly. Although the impact of the explanatory variables on post-reform inflation differs, the econometric analysis confirms the theoretical considerations. The theoretical model cannot be rejected on these grounds.

The most important independent variable is monetary commitment. It has a great impact on the inflation rate: a change in the degree of commitment of 1 per cent *ceteris paribus* leads to a reduction in the politically optimal inflation rate of more than 4 per cent. This holds for any of *C*'s four specifications. Hence, the design of the monetary regime surely matters for the success of the reform. Moreover, the result shows that it is necessary to construct a comprehensive measure of commitment. Different to the index of CBI, the index of commitment is significantly correlated negatively with inflation.

A very relevant explanatory variable is *SEIGN*. This variable has proven significant regardless of the specification. This upshot is not new, rather, it can be regarded as being another confirmation of the generally accepted insight that solving fiscal problems via money growth causes inflation. The strict separation of fiscal and monetary policy is certainly one important prerequisite for the success of a monetary reform. If it is possible to reduce *SEIGN*, the post-reform inflation rate is very likely to drop. For instance in Argentina 1991 – a successful reform in the sample – the outcome of the variable changes considerably after the monetary reform, e.g. from a value higher than 0.5 prior to 1990 to a value of approximately 0.1 thereafter (Appendix 4).

Another regressor of crucial importance is *PostBW*. The probability of a monetary reform to fail rises dramatically when price shocks occur and when the disciplining structure of the Bretton Woods system vanishes. The international attitude to inflation is influential on policymakers' decision to create stability. That does not necessarily mean that freedom of capital transaction which started after the end of Bretton Woods does not discipline governments either, producing a negative correlation between inflation and *PostBW*. However, since the sample contains countries with extremely poor monetary performance, the highly significant positive correlation between *PostBW* and inflation makes sense economically. It is also very interesting from the policymaker's point of view.

With the exception of the proxy for labour market flexibility, the institutional factors contribute to the explanation of the politically optimal inflation rate. However, the strength and significance of their contribution is remarkably lower than those of commitment, seigniorage and international discipline. Nevertheless, openness of the country, political stability, public opposition to inflation and a properly chosen reserve currency can contribute to a low post-reform inflation rate. Fiscal stability is a significant determinant of low post-reform inflation. The other exception is *EF* (and *EF*2000 respectively), the index of economic freedom. It has a strong and significant negative impact on the politically optimal inflation.

The low performance of institutional factors in general can have two explanations. The first explanation is that the institutional setting may not be important economically: if this is true, the organisation of the monetary regime itself (*C*) is more much relevant for the success of the reform although they are restrictions for the monetary policy. Moreover, one basic restriction is covered by *SEIGN*. This would mean that fiscal stability as defined in Appendix 2 is not relevant. However, *SEIGN* is not correlated with the institutional factors, in particular with fiscal stability.[14] Thus, we regard this explanation as being misleading.

The second and more plausible explanation for the rather low significance is that the composition of the variables for institutional factors (except for the index of economic freedom) suffers from the data shortcomings and the diversity of the sample; especially labour market flexibility is a case in point.

[14] The correlation between *SEIGN* and *FS*1 is 0.1556.

It has turned out to be impossible to compose a proper indicator. The finally chosen gross shift in per cent of the work force is calculated for the same period for all reform countries and does not take into consideration the individual point in time of each monetary reform.

Finally, the proxy for credibility can add to the explanation of post-reform inflation. This is a very promising outcome since it may eventually enable monetary reformers to measure the credibility of a planned monetary reform. Thus, the theoretically most challenging specification of the econometric model cannot be rejected. However, the proxy for credibility is a very sensitive variable; changing the weights in C or in $\sum F_i/n$ can even lead to a changing sign of the parameter, let alone the loss in significance. Currently, the data does not allow for better results, a problem that regularly occurs in econometric analyses, particularly if the variables are constructed.[15] Therefore, to be definitely seen as a reliable ex-ante measure of credibility, the proxy needs to be based on better data. To draw a conclusion with respect to this variable, the result gives a first indication of how credibility can be applied as an ex-ante concept in a post-reform model.

V. POLICY SIMULATION BASED ON THE PARAMETERS

In this final section, we discuss the usefulness of these findings for policymakers, since the eventual aim of this study is to draw lessons for policy options: how can a failure of monetary reforms be avoided in the future? For a monetary reform to be successful, three elements have turned out to be crucial: first, the legal monetary regime established by the government can induce the monetary policymaker to care for (relative) price stability. Second, institutions certainly restrict the policymaker's discretion to use monetary policy for other economic policy goals. However, there is a need for further research, especially for better data and as a consequence improved institutional variables.[16] Third, a monetary reform undoubtedly does not succeed if the government is unable or unwilling to generate

15 The following quote points to this very aptly: 'Econometric theory is like an exquisitely balanced French recipe, spelling out precisely with how many turns to mix the sauce, how many carats of spice to add, and for how many milliseconds to bake the mixture at exactly 474 degrees of temperature. But when the statistical cook turns to raw materials, he finds that hearts of cactus fruits are unavailable, so he substitutes chunks of cantaloupe; where the recipe calls for vermicelli he uses shredded wheat; and he substitutes green garment dye for curry, ping-pong balls for turtle's eggs, and, for Chalifougnac vintage 1883, a can of turpentine' (Valavanis 1959, p. 83)

16 It has also become clear that case studies are needed to overcome the aggregation problem caused by the diversity of reforms in the sample.

revenues from other sources than the money press. The model provides another lesson for reformers: international co-operation can be helpful as a disciplinary factor. However, since it is impossible for potential reformers to recreate the Bretton Woods system, it is difficult to take this lesson explicitly into account.

Under the assumptions that the econometric model is correctly specified for the sample and also holds for other countries with similar monetary problems, it can be used for a policy simulation (Hansen 1993, pp. 83–89). It can be simulated which degree of commitment is optimal for a country that actually experiences high inflation rates. Given the rather unsatisfactory estimations of variant 3 (*Table 6.6*), we show how a policy simulation for variant 2 can work.

In the course a of monctary reform the institutional setting is not necessarily strictly exogenous. It can also be subject to reform. In this case, the monetary reformer has to make a projection for the institutional factors. Then the procedure of a policy simulation is as follows: given the – observed or forecast – institutional setting, a certain projection for *SEIGN*, the value '1' for *PostBW* and a projection of the politically and economically desired average inflation rate for the next five years[17] as well as the estimated parameter values $\hat{\beta}$, the policymaker can calculate an optimal degree of commitment C^*_{uw}. The result of the calculation can be transformed in a certain monetary regime. Its simplest form is shown in equation (6.8).

$$C^*_{uw} = \frac{-\pi^* + \hat{\beta}_0 + \hat{\beta}_2 SEIGN + \hat{\beta}_3 PostBW +}{\hat{\beta}_1}$$
$$\frac{\left[\hat{\beta}_4 \hat{\beta}_5 \hat{\beta}_7 \hat{\beta}_8 \hat{\beta}_9\right]\left[PS2\ \ FS3\ \ OP4\ \ POI\ \ RC\right]^T}{\hat{\beta}_1} \qquad (6.8).$$

Such a policy simulation is certainly no guarantee for the success of a monetary reform. It undoubtedly provides many degrees of freedom for governments that plan a monetary reform. For there is no manual for the choice of the estimation that will be used for the parameter values $\hat{\beta}$. Moreover, a government can be tempted to choose very optimistic projections of seigniorage, fiscal policy etc. To be useful, a policy simulation has to be carried out very carefully and - ideally - by an independent institution. One can even imagine commissioning the task to a foreign agency

17 The variable π^* in equations (6.8) and (6.9) is the logarithmic value of the desired inflation rate.

or to an IO. This would possibly raise the credibility and independence of the calculation. At least every assumption should be made transparent and public. Some discretion can be avoided by using *EF* or *EF*2000 in (6.9). Since they are calculated on the basis of the index for economic freedom by Gwartney and Lawson (1997) or Gwartney, Lawson and Samida (2000), they are external criteria.

$$C_{uw}^{*} = \frac{-\pi^{*} + \hat{\beta}_0 + \hat{\beta}_2 SEIGN + \hat{\beta}_3 PostBW + \hat{\beta}_{10} EF2000}{\hat{\beta}_1} \quad (6.9).$$

In Chapter 8 of this study, we make use of this instrument when discussing potential monetary reform countries. We take into account the fact that the simulation with equation (6.8) and (6.9) can produce somewhat arbitrary results. Moreover, economic policy is not a purely technical endeavour which is comparable to solving an equation. Reformers and policymakers have to take into account detailed institutional circumstances of the country which cannot be adequately covered by the institutional factors defined in this study, even if better data were available. The situation in reality is much more complex than suggested by any model. Thus, a policy simulation based on the econometric model can at best be a support for deeper analysis of the economic situation in a potential reform country. To derive a policy conclusion, another source of the analysis is to look at case studies. This is done in the following chapter.

7. Successful and Unsuccessful Monetary Reforms: The Case Studies

I. THE GOAL OF DISCUSSING CASES

In this chapter, the theoretical considerations are further tested empirically via case studies. They add evidence to the econometric analysis which has proven the relevance of commitment and institutions as well as the importance of refraining from the monetisation of budget deficits for the success of monetary reforms. The cases discussed here emphasise these findings. Whereas the econometric tests unambiguously clarify the general features of a successful monetary reform, the cases are assessed to explain institutional details. This is particularly important given the fact that we intend to derive some lessons for economic policymaking. On its own, none of the two approaches can give sufficient orientation for the monetary reformer. Taken together, econometric analysis and case studies form the basis for policy options of those countries that are still in monetary difficulties.

Case studies certainly have one disadvantage when compared to econometric models. They lack analytical precision and, therefore, '...may be regarded as story telling informed by theory' (Little et al. 1993, p. 2). However, they can illustrate the interdependence of components of economic order in deeper detail than the econometric analysis (Bergsten and Williamson 1994, p. 4). Monetary policymakers and reformers do not operate in isolation from politics. They have to react to political pressures and economic problems. They also have to take into account the institutional constraints of a successful monetary reform. If the institutional setting is not considered adequately, the monetary problems can even be aggravated by a reform which introduces an inappropriate monetary regime. It is also important to note that the individual institutional factors do not play an equally important role in each reform country. On the contrary, the institutional constraints to reform differ considerably between the countries analysed in this chapter. This cannot be revealed in an econometric analysis, but will be clarified in the case studies. Twelve cases of monetary reform which cover every theoretical aspect have been selected for the analysis of this chapter. They show the varying impact of institutions and other determinants of success of the reforms.

At any rate, the case studies are not meant to be narratives. Although there are many interesting stories to be told in the context of the monetary reforms presented in this chapter, we are abstaining from this. The cases have been analysed frequently in the literature. A large part of the evidence presented here is based on very competent and detailed reports made by economists and economic historians. These longer accounts are quoted in the text.[1] Since our goal is both to assess some monetary reforms against the background of the theoretical considerations as well as to strengthen the results of the econometric analysis, we concentrate on these issues.[2]

The analysis is divided into two parts. The following section is dedicated to a short introduction into a dozen monetary reforms in this century. This introduction is necessary to give a comprehensive overview on the reform cases. We give an account of what led to the monetary reform and how it was pursued. Thus, this section has to be descriptive in parts to be informative enough for the analytical objective of the chapter. We will be as brief as possible. In the three subsequent sections we consider the fact that not all determinants of success of a monetary regime which have been tested empirically in Chapter 6 are equally important for every reform. The particular relevance of monetary commitment (7.III), the institutional setting (7.IV) and other factors (7.V) for single reform cases are shown. Common lessons from the empirical analysis are drawn in the final section.

---

1 For instance, a huge body of literature about the German monetary reform in 1948 exists of which a selection is mentioned without claiming that other contributions are less important or interesting. The contributions in the volume edited by the Deutsche Bundesbank (1998), especially the papers by James (1998), Buchheim (1998) and Neumann (1998), are particularly interesting from a contemporary perspective. The book by Marsh (1992) is full of interesting stories; however not exclusively analytic. Older perspectives are taken in the little volume edited by Klump (1989) as well as in the symposium in the *Zeitschrift für die gesamte Staatswissenschaft*, nowadays called *JITE*, Vol. 135 (Sauermann (1979), Wandel (1979), Domes and Wolffsohn (1979) as well as Pfleiderer (1979) who was a member of the Conclave of Rothwesten). For an early analytical assessment of the German post-war situation see Wallich (1955).

2 All figures reported here are calculated from the sources listed in Appendix 2, section V. Inflation in this chapter is always consumer price inflation (CPI).

II. MONETARY REFORMS DISTINGUISHED BY THEIR SUCCESS

The monetary reforms chosen for this chapter can be distinguished into three groups. First, there are highly successful reforms that established credible monetary regimes. Three examples are introduced here: Germany in 1948, Argentina in 1991 and Estonia in 1992. Details about the reforms can be found in *Table 7.1*. The assessment of whether or not a reform is very successful cannot only be based on the average inflation rate in the years after the reform. Other criteria like the sustainability of stability and other institutional features of the economic order are also important. In other words, the credibility of a monetary reform cannot exclusively be judged on the basis of the post-reform inflation rate (Chapter 4, section V). Taking this into account, there is a second group consisting of reforms which can be regarded as having been moderately successful such as Germany in 1923/24, Hungary in 1924, Israel in 1985, Lithuania in 1994 and Poland in 1995 (*Table 7.2*). The distinction of the first and second group is not simple. For instance, it may be asked why the reforms in Estonia in 1992 and Lithuania in 1994, leading to similar monetary regimes with similar post-reform inflation rates, are not assessed within the same group. As will be proven in this chapter, there are substantial differences. The distinction between these two groups and the third one is less difficult. It contains complete, and easily to identify, failures as the reform attempts in Paraguay in 1943/44, Greece in 1944, the Plan Austral in Argentina in 1985 and Brazil in 1986 (*Table 7.3*).

a) Highly credible reforms

In *Table 7.1*, the successful monetary reforms are summarised. In these three cases, the average post-reform inflation rate was low or in the case of Estonia strongly declining in the first five years after the reform. Other elements of the economic order were consistent with the degree of monetary commitment, and in all cases, the governments abstained from the money press to finance their budget.

To begin with, the *German* monetary reform of 1948 was a complete success. During World War II, the Nazi regime financed its expenditures via monetisation. The monetary base grew very fast; prices however did not rise as rapidly since they were entirely controlled by the regime. The inflation during the war was a repressed one. In 1945, a consistent system of relative prices in Germany hardly existed (James 1998, pp. 76–83). The monetary overhang was high (Buchheim 1998, pp. 96f.). Until mid-1948, monetary policy was not very effective. The situation was worsened by the industrial slack. The incentive to produce was very low, not least since price controls remained in effect. Thus, most of the economic activity took place in the shadow economy (Giersch, Paqué and Schmieding 1992, p. 21; Buchheim 1998).

Table 7.1 Success Stories at a Glance

	Germany 1948	Argentina 1991	Estonia 1992
Annual pre-reform inflation: t-3	n.a.*	343.00	n.a.*
t-2	n.a.*	3,079.80	n.a.*
t-1	6.35	2,314.00	210.60
Av. post-reform inflation (t to t+5)	1.00	8.30	37.63
Monetary regime	CB, fixed ER	CBS	CBS
C_{uw} (if available)	0.707	0.798	0.787
Elements of economic order: *PS*	high	medium	high
FS	high	medium	medium
LM	flexible	inflexible	flexible
OP	increasing	high	high
POI	high	high	n.a.
RC	consistent	consistent	consistent
Reliance on seigniorage	very low	very low	very low
External factors	foreign occupation	reluctant help by IMF	insignificant
Success?	full	full	full

Notes: *: Prices were administered.

Source: See Appendix 2, section V.

In spring 1948, the 'Bank deutscher Länder' as an independent central bank was founded as the top level in the two-tier system which had not been destroyed by the allied forces. The 'Landeszentralbanken' remained autonomous. The members of the system's executive board (Zentralbankrat) could not be appointed by the German authorities. The D-Mark was introduced, and the central bank was not allowed to grant credit to the government.[3] In addition, an accompanying economic reform was made in

3 This was criticised by Pedersen (1949) who also argued that following the quantity equation would be a severe mistake and would stop economic recovery.

June 1948. The inflation rate could be reduced to a very low level and remained that low for a long time. The German monetary reform of 1948 is a good example of the relevance of a consistent and compatible reform package in case of complete economic disorder. Commitment and institutions matter: without the accompanying changes of the economic order, the monetary reform would certainly not have had the immediate success it had.

In *Argentina*, the failure of the Plan Austral (see below) led to a hyperinflation in 1989 and 1990. In 1989, a new, Peronist government was appointed and was not necessarily expected to carry out an orthodox stabilisation programme. The macroeconomic situation, however, did not improve, and after another two years the Menem administration in early 1991 decided to make a comprehensive liberal economic reform, the core of which was the introduction of a currency board.[4] A new currency, the Peso, was introduced on April 1, 1991, and the exchange rate towards the US dollar as reserve currency was fixed after a two-month period of floating (Mastroberardino 1994, p. 187), and full convertibility was maintained. The monetary base had to be backed with foreign exchange; however about one third of the backing could consist of BONEX, the US dollar denominated governmental bond. There were no minimum reserve requirements for banks. The central bank was not allowed to give credit to the government and it was not expected to act as a lender of last resort for participants in the financial markets (Bennett 1994, pp. 15f). The Argentine peso was not the only currency to circulate, the US dollar also became legal tender. This certainly reflected a high dollarisation of the Argentine economy before the reform package was introduced. To sum up, the new monetary regime had a very high degree of commitment; the value of C_{uw} is 0.798. Inflation was reduced rather quickly. In 1998 almost price stability was reached.

The story of the *Estonian* monetary reform is somewhat different to Germany and Argentina: there was no long-term experience with inflation and the battle against it in the country. Estonia gained independence from the Soviet Union in 1991. It did not introduce its own currency; the Russian rouble remained legal tender. Subsequently, Estonia did not manage the transition from administered prices to free relative prices very well. Instead of a pure adjustment inflation, Estonia experienced very high monthly inflation rates (up to 30 per cent) in the first half of 1992. Thus, the government started planning a stabilising reform in March 1991 (Buch 1993, p. 446). In June 1992 this reform was made public and carried out by

4 It is worth mentioning that Argentina is not the only example of a rather leftish government pursuing a liberal and stability-oriented economic policy. For a theoretical explanation see Cukierman and Tommasi (1998).

establishing a currency board system[5] with the introduction of a new currency, the Estonian crown. The D-Mark became the reserve medium, the exchange rate being 8 crowns for 1 D-Mark. Full convertibility was guaranteed. The choice of the D-Mark was not self-evident since the most important trading partners of Estonian firms were located in Finland and Sweden. As these countries had pegged their currencies to the D-Mark, it seemed wise to choose this as the reserve currency. The monetary base had to be backed to a 100 per cent by foreign exchange. The initial reserves were easily available because of a more than 50-year-old stock of gold deposited in the Bank of England, Sweden and Switzerland (Kallas and Sörg 1993).

The inflationary performance of Estonia after the monetary reform was not particularly satisfactory. It was not before 1998 that the inflation rate could be brought below 10 per cent. Part of this inertia can be explained by the failure to free the prices of non-tradables. Another reason is certainly the fact that economic growth in Estonia was faster than the growth in the reserve country, Germany and other industrialised countries (Banerjee et al. 1995, p. 10). To summarise, inflation in Estonia was higher than one could expect, but for good reason.[6] Estonia is another case in point for the basic hypothesis of this study, namely that commitment and the institutional setting in a country have to be compatible to conduct a successful monetary reform after a period of high and volatile inflation rates.

b) Moderate successes

In this subsection, five monetary reforms are introduced which reduced inflation remarkably but which were not as successful as those discussed above. Although inflation decreased after the reforms, they were not likely to either reduce the inflation rate to a value below 10 per cent or to make the process of disinflation irrevocable. These problems were in some cases caused mainly by exogenous factors and in others by domestic factors, in particular by incompatibility of the economic order with the monetary regime. *Table 7.2* gives a summary of the cases.

The reforms have some common properties. First, the degree of monetary commitment is on average lower than in the reforms introduced above. Furthermore, the institutional factors are not consistent with the monetary regime to the same extent as above. In addition, the governments were not

---

5 For a detailed description of the institutional arrangement of the Estonian CBS see Bennett (1993).

6 In unofficial statements, Estonian central bankers emphasised another argument for the success of their monetary policy. In their opinion, the fact that in the mid-1990s short-term interest rates were only half of the annual inflation rate documented that the official inflation rate overstated the loss in purchasing power. However, it has to be questionend whether or not the official interest rates reflect the true rates.

able to become completely independent of monetary policy for other policy areas. Especially in Israel after 1985 and Poland after 1995, the governments had difficulties financing their budget without the help of fresh money. As a consequence, inflation in Israel and Poland remained rather high after the reform.

Table 7.2 Moderate Successes at a Glance

	Germany 1923/24	Hungary 1924	Israel 1985	Lithuania 1994	Poland 1995
Annual pre-reform inflation (in per cent): t-3	233.5[1]	314.3[2]	120.4	224.7	43.0
t-2	12,574,6	1,543.7	145.6	1,021.0	35.3
t-1	2.3E11	702.3	373.8	410.4	32.2
Av. post-reform inflation (t to t+5)	4.4[4]	n.a.	23.8	30.4[3]	15.9[4]
Monetary regime	CB, fixed ER	CB, fixed ER	CB, fixed ER	CBS	CB, crawling peg
C_{uw} (if available)	0.6 to 0.7	n.a.	0.503	0.715	n.a.
Elements of economic order: *PS*	low	very low	high	high	high
FS	high	high	low	low	low
LM	high	n.a.	low	medium	low
OP	medium	n.a.	high	high	high
POI	high	n.a.	low	n.a.	n.a.
RC	high	n.a.	high	medium	high
Reliance on seigniorage	low	low	high	low	medium
External factors	help	help	help	no	IMF help
Success?	medium	medium	medium	medium	medium

Notes:[1]: starting in the third quarter of 1921; [2]: starting August 1921; [3]: *t* to *t+3*; [4]: *t* to *t+4*.

Source: Sargent (1982, p. 62) and Vaubel (1983, p. 13) as well as Statistisches Reichsamt (a, various issues) for inflation data in Hungary and Germany, respectively. See also Appendix 2, section V.

The *German* hyperinflation , which started in the fourth quarter of 1922 and ended in mid-1924, can only be correctly analysed in the context of World War I and the post-war institutional setting in Europe.[7] The hyperinflation was fuelled by a steady and immense increase in the money supply during the decade between 1914 and 1923.[8] Eucken (1923) was the first to show the relation between money growth and inflation. Demand for money decreased, as did the money base in real terms (Holtfrerich 1980, pp. 183–190). Inflation accelerated and reached an annual rate of 12,675 per cent in the second quarter of 1923 and $5.9*10^6$ per cent in the third quarter of 1923, respectively. It reached its peak in the first quarter of 1924 with approximately $530*10^6$ per cent (Vaubel 1983, p. 13). As a consequence, dollarisation also rose. Moreover, besides the D-Mark, about 2,000 kinds of tender were produced both legally and illegally (Yeager et al. 1981, p. 57). In November 1923, the Rentenmark became legal tender, the exchange rate towards the US dollar was fixed at the pre-war level of 4.2 Rentenmark for 1 US dollar. The Rentenmark was issued by the Rentenbank and backed with land (Vaubel, 1983, pp. 8f). The D-Mark remained legal tender and the exchange rate was 1 billion D-Marks for 1 Rentenmark. The Rentenbank's credit to the government was strictly limited. The Rentenmark was replaced by the Reichsmark in 1924[9] as legal tender under the gold standard . The Bankgesetz of August 30, 1924 (central bank law) abolished loans to the government. It also put the Reichsbank under foreign scrutiny by the Dawes committee. This date marks the end of a process of monetary reform in Germany. It was supported externally by the Dawes Plan which included a 200 million US-dollar loan to the German government to build up foreign reserves. The reparation schedule was also altered in favour of Germany (Sargent 1982, p. 84). The degree of commitment of the monetary regime was rather high. Not all criteria for measuring the degree could be found, but the value of C_{uw} was between 0.6 and 0.7.

Similar to Germany in the 1920s, *Hungary* experienced a hyperinflation as a result of the post-war institutional arrangements. As being a loser of war, Hungary lost a substantial part of its territory and population and was forced to pay reparations. Unfortunately neither a total sum of separation nor a

---

7 For a comprehensive and detailed analysis of the German hyperinflation see Holtfrerich (1980).

8 In particular, three reasons were responsible for the enormous increase in the money supply starting during the war. First, the war was mainly financed by means of the money press (James 1998, p. 47); second, Germany, since it lost the war, had to carry the burden of reparation which as such was not a cause for inflation (Vaubel 1983, pp. 1f; Eucken 1923); third, also due to the war and the post-war situation, welfare expenditure increased (Yeager et al. 1981, p. 56).

9 For a lively description about the weeks after the introduction of the Rentenmark see Yeager et al. (1981, pp. 58-65).

schedule for it were specified. This omission was similar to a 100 per cent marginal tax. Thus, there was a strong disincentive both for the government to stabilise the economy and for the population to engage in economic activities, in particular in investment directed into the future (Yeager et al. 1981, pp. 52f). Given this incentive structure, Hungarian inflation started to accelerate in 1921;in the second half of this year the wholesale price index approximately doubled; in 1922 it quadrupled; and by the end of 1923 it had attained almost the twentyfold level compared with the beginning of that year. By the end of February 1924, inflation reached its highest rate: the price level was 1.8 times as high as by the end of January (Sargent 1982, p. 62).

There were two reasons worth mentioning for this inflationary process: first, the public budget deficits from 1919 to 1924 were high, mainly due to the reparations, losses of state-run enterprises and a by far too large staff of civil servants (Yeager et al. 1981, p. 53). They were financed by monetisation through the central bank called State Note Institute. Moreover, this institute gave credits at extremely low interest rates to private enterprises and persons. According to Sargent (1982, pp. 58–61), these loans contributed more to inflation than did the monetisation of public budget deficits. This is very much different to all other cases of high inflation discussed in this chapter and may be caused by the absurd economic incentive structure as well as by the very unstable political situation in the country.

The core elements of the monetary regime were the following: in June 1924, an independent central bank, the Hungarian National Bank, replaced the State Note Institute and assumed its assets and liabilities.[10] A new currency was not introduced.[11] Newly issued paper money and deposits had to be backed to 100 per cent with the British pound. The Hungarian krone was pegged to the British pound with a fixed exchange rate. Most importantly, the National Bank was not allowed to give credit to the government. The League of Nations controlled the monetary policy and gave a 250 million gold kronen loan to support the reform contingently (Sargent 1982, pp. 61–64). The subsequent period of low inflation did not last very long. Only a few years later, the pengö was devalued and foreign exchange controls were introduced again in 1931. In 1938, inflation rose again (Pick 1955, p. 109).

Israel has a long tradition of inflationary monetary policy. Since the beginning of the 1970s, the annual inflation rate has been on the two-digit

---

10 A few months earlier, a unit of credit and account, the thrift-Krone was introduced which was supposed to be stable towards foreign exchange and, thereby, keep the real value of credits and loans constant. It was not a compulsory, but a legal tender. With the introduction of the Hungarian National Bank, it was abandoned. Thus, an assessment of its effects is impossible. See Ecker (1933).

11 This happened in 1925 when the pengö replaced the krone, but only for the convenience of a greater monetary unit (Yeager et al. 1981, p. 55).

level. In 1980, a reform was made, but completely failed. In subsequent years, the inflation rate increased above 100 per cent per annum. The situation grew particularly bad in 1984 when the annual inflation rate exceeded 370 per cent. The reason why the public accepted such an inflationary level was indexation of nearly all prices and wages (Cukierman 1990, p. 49). Indexation reduces public opposition to inflation. Nevertheless, the government already began in 1984 to combat inflation through tripartite package deals with trade unions and employers' organisations. These deals were not credible (Bruno and Piterman 1990, pp. 5f). A second problem of the Israeli economy was the persistent deficit in the current account which was not caused by intertemporal decisionmaking. Accompanying these difficulties, the public budget deficit rose, partly as cause of the inflation and partly fuelled by the latter through the Oliveira-Tanzi effect, i.e. increasing tax revenues after the stabilisation (Cukierman 1990, pp. 49f). The public deficit also contributed to the current account deficit.

In July 1985, a comprehensive stabilisation programme was launched which included monetary and fiscal policies as well as price and wage controls (Bruno and Piterman 1990, pp. 6–9). The monetary regime was changed in that a nominal anchor was introduced. After a devaluation of 25 per cent, the Shekel was pegged to the US dollar. The system of multiple exchange rates was only partially given up. The system of accounts indexed to the exchange rate (PATNAM) was abolished.[12] The US government also supported the programme by adding 750 billion US dollars to its annual foreign aid to Israel (Cukierman 1990, p. 54). Other changes, e.g. in the central bank statute or law were not reported. Nonetheless, the degree of commitment was raised by the reform. Inflation could be reduced fairly rapidly, but not below an annual rate of 20 per cent.

After the disintegration of the former Soviet Union, *Lithuania* had to bear high inflation, even higher than Estonia. Concerning monetary policy, the Lithuanian government tested a number of regimes, before it finally introduced a currency board in April 1994. Prior to that date, monetary policy was unsustainable and incredible. The annual inflation rate in 1992 was 1,021 per cent. In September 1992, the Russian rouble was replaced by the talon. Despite the introduction of a new currency, consumer prices still rose very fast. In summer 1993, the talon was substituted by the litas. This new currency was pegged to a currency basket before it was finally pegged to the US dollar in April 1994 when the currency board (still called Bank of Lithuania) was established. This event marks the moment of the monetary

---

12 Cukierman (1992, pp. 448f) shows that PATNAM had significantly reduced the CBI of the Bank of Israel since it had to increase the money supply each time the shekel devalued towards the US dollar.

reform. However, the currency board system was not orthodox which can be demonstrated by two elements: first, the board did not guarantee convertibility, in particular for foreigners. Neither the Bank of Lithuania nor other banks are obliged to exchange litas offered by foreigners into US dollar (DEG 1996).[13] Second, the board was allowed to act as lender of last resort (Bank of Lithuania 1996, p. 12) which it did during the banking crisis in 1996 (Freytag 1998a, p. 14). As part of the monetary reform, fiscal and monetary policy were separated. Prior to the reform, budget deficits could easily be monetised. Despite the heterodox character of the CBS, the formal degree of commitment was high (C_{uw} = 0.715). Inflation decreased to an average of approximately 30 per cent in five years after the reform.

After 1989, the fight against inflation in *Poland* was part of an overall economic reform. However, in the first few years it did not succeed in combating inflation. After annual inflation rates of 244.6 per cent in 1989 and 555 per cent in 1990, inflation could be reduced to a two-digit level. In 1994, it was 32.2 per cent (IMFa and IMFc). Although there was progress, the government decided to make a monetary reform. In May 1995, Poland revalued the zloty in two respects: 1 new zloty was equal to 10,000 old zloty, and the zloty was appreciated by 3 per cent to reduce expectations to further appreciation (Gomulka 1998, p. 391). Poland also introduced a crawling peg with a band of ± 7 per cent (after February 1998 ± 10 per cent) *vis-à-vis* a currency basket, consisting of the US dollar (45 per cent), the D-Mark (35 per cent), the British pound (10 per cent), the Swiss and the French franc (5 per cent each). It started with a crawl of 1.2 per cent monthly in 1995 which was gradually diminished to 0.8 per cent later on. The zloty did not obtain full convertibility (Tkaczynski and Mühlbauer 1998, p. 185). The National Bank of Poland (NBP) was granted formal independence (Ugolini 1996), yet the degree of commitment was low. Until October 1998 the NBP was allowed to directly lend money to the government. Also exchange rate policy was not within the range of competencies of the NBP. The annual inflation rate dropped to below 10 per cent in 1999, but started to rise again thereafter.

c) Complete failures

In history, monetary reforms often failed. A few of these failures are discussed in this section. *Table 7.3* shows at a glance the chosen degree of commitment and its compatibility with other elements of economic order in four reform countries. Again, one can find common properties of the reforms. Apart from Paraguay, the degree of legal commitment in the reform countries is low. Moreover, the reliance on the money press is – again with the exception of Paraguay – very high. These two properties are sufficient to turn

---

[13] However, no case has been reported yet where the exchange was denied.

the reforms into a failure. Neither did institutional factors coincide with the degree of monetary commitment, in particular in Paraguay.

Beginning with the Great War (1865–1870), *Paraguay* was involved in almost a century of turmoil including a second war and many coups. This period climaxed in a six months civil war during 1947. The situation did not calm down afterwards. In 1949, a civil government took office which ended with the coup by Alfredo Stroessner. As for monetary policy, in the 70 years following the Great War, at least ten reform attempts were made which did not bring a stable currency for Paraguay (Triffin 1946, pp. 2–16). In 1942 the government asked the Federal Reserve System for assistance. A team of experts went to Asunción to advise the government. These efforts resulted in a totally new monetary conception. The monetary regime now consisted of a modern central bank law (1943) and a general banking law (1944). A new currency, the guarani, was introduced which was to be pegged to a composite exchange standard which was not fully defined from the start. Obviously, the US dollar was the actual reserve currency (Pick 1955, pp. 166–168). The central bank which also served as an ordinary bank had the task of issuing money. The relations between government and the central bank were not clear; the government was able to get credit directly (Triffin 1946, pp. 16–25). Apart from this, the increase in central bank independence was high which can be documented by a high degree of legal commitment (C_{uw} = 0.695). The reform eventually failed due to the political instability. The price level could be kept stable only until 1947. Afterwards, annual inflation rates were very volatile and exceeded 100 per cent (Yeager et al. 1981, p. 119).

As was the case in all countries occupied by the German army during World War II, *Greece* suffered from heavy inflation caused by the exploitation by the occupiers. In order to meet the German demand for goods and services, the issuing of money and credit expansion were higher than required in order to be compatible with stability (Klopstock 1946, pp. 580–583).[14] When Greece was liberated in 1944, consumer prices had increased sharply as compared to the situation before the war (Grotius 1949, p. 294). In November 1944, a monetary reform was implemented under the guidance of the British administration. A new currency was introduced with a conversion rate of 50 billion old drachma to 1 new drachma, and the exchange rates towards the British pound and the US dollar, respectively, were fixed, as well as the exchange rate of the gold sovereign. Fiscal and monetary policies were not separated, leaving the government in a situation where it felt the need to monetise its deficits (Makinen 1984, p. 1068).

---

14 For more details see Freris (1986, pp. 114-120) as well as Delivanis and Cleveland (1949, part I). For a more general analysis of the political and economic situation in Greece see Hadziiossif (1987).

Nominal wages were centrally set in November 1944 (and again February 1945) on a high level, incompatible with productivity and demand and supply on the labour market (Grotius 1949, pp. 289f).

Table 7.3 Complete Failures at a Glance

	Paraguay 1943/44	Greece 1944	Argentina 1985	Brazil 1986
Annual pre-reform inflation:				
t-3	10.9	15[1]	164.8	135.0
t-2	20.9	n.a.	343.8	192.1
t-1	30.8	n.a.	626.7	226.0
Av. post-reform inflation: (t to t+5)	70.2[3]	181.4[1,2]	577.6	1,310.7
Monetary regime	CB, fixed ER	CB, fixed ER	CB, fixed ER	CB, fixed ER
C_{uw} (if available)	0.695	n.a.	0.462	0.346
Elements of economic order:				
PS	very low	very low	low	low
FS	medium	low	low	low
LM	n.a.	very low	inflexible	inflexible
OP	n.a.	n.a.	low	low
POI	n.a.	n.a.	very low	very low
RC	high	n.a.	high	high
Reliance on seigniorage	medium	very high	very high	very high
External factors	US help	British help	no	no
Success?	no	no	no	no

Notes: [1]: information based on a telephone call with the National Bank of Greece on October 6, 1999; [2]: 1945-1948; [3]: 1950-1954.

Source: See Appendix 2, section V. Post-reform inflation rates in Paraguay were sent to the author by the Central Bank of Paraguay.

The monetary reform itself was not characterised by a high degree of commitment, although external help played a major role, even in the following years. In addition, the institutional setting considerably opposed a credible monetary policy regime. Directly after the war, a civil war started that lasted until 1949 (*The Enzyclopedia Americana 1973*, Vol. 13, p. 378). The labour market was totally inflexible; wages were centrally set. In addition, the government heavily relied on seigniorage to cover its expenditure; in the fiscal year 1946/47 only 30 per cent of the expenditure were covered by taxes (Grotius 1949, p. 292).

Soon after the reform, the monetary base had reached the threefold of its origin in November 1944. Two-thirds were due to monetisation; an additional sixth by the needs of the British troops. Unfortunately, the exchange rates were miscalculated with the consequence that the gold sovereign was cheaper in Greece than abroad which caused arbitrage and fuelled inflation (ibid., pp. 289f). In June 1945, the reform was acknowledged as a failure, and a second attempt was made which also failed. A third attempt in January 1946 backed by foreign (British and US) loans and transfers brought a short but unsustainable relief (Makinen 1984, pp. 1069f). A successful reform was finally made in 1954.

In *Argentina*, for a decade between 1976 until 1985, there was virtually no real economic growth, and the annual inflation rate permanently exceeded 100 per cent (Freytag 1998b, p. 393). In 1985, the situation deteriorated further; the annual inflation rate which had been 626.7 per cent in 1984 was still rising. Real GDP was decreasing (by an annual rate of 6.6 per cent). The public budget deficit was ballooning and the burden of foreign debt became virtually unbearable (Fischer, Hiemenz and Trapp 1985, pp. 13–19; Machinea and Fanelli 1990, pp. 111–120). The main cause of inflation was the monetisation of public budget deficits. Fiscal problems shook the Argentine economy from the early 1960s until 1989 (Little et al. 1993, pp. 191f).

Thus, in June 1985, the government announced a monetary reform, the so-called Plan Austral. The government tried to tackle both the monetary and fiscal problems. Concerning the monetary part of the reform package, a new currency, the austral was to replace the peso (1 austral = 1,000 pesos). Additional changes in the central bank law were not planned. Especially, there was no ban of government bond purchases by the central bank. The independence of the central bank remained low. After an initial devaluation of 15 per cent *vis-à-vis* the US dollar, the austral was pegged to the latter (1 US dollar = 0.80 austral). Partial convertibility was introduced. Nevertheless, the overall degree of commitment still was rather low (C_{uw} = 0.462). The package deviated sharply from a reform proposal made by a team of foreign experts who emphasised the interdependence of economic order (Fischer, Hiemenz and Trapp, 1985, pp. 70–76). The reform failed as the government was unable to stop the monetisation of budget deficits. A number of small, but economically senseless reform trials followed in the subsequent two years.

The *Brazilian* cruzado Plan in February 1986 was similar to the Argentine Plan Austral some months earlier, concerning both the reform package and its definite failure some years later. Pre-reform annual inflation rates had steadily increased and reached a three-digit level, yet they were below the Argentine rates (*Table 7.3*). Especially in the last two years prior to the reform, the accelerating annual inflation rates had been caused by huge public budget deficits which had been monetised. Due to high GDP growth rates in the 1970s, Brazil had been able to finance such deficits on the capital markets. A recession and the debt crisis in the early 1980s forced the government to rely increasingly on seigniorage, as it was not willing to reduce public spending (Cardoso 1991). In 1985, *SEIGN* as calculated in equation (A.8) was 0.30.

In February 1986, the prospects for a monetary reform were good because from 1984 on Brazil had recovered from a recession and GDP growth was about 7.0 per cent. The reform effects can be called disappointing: strictly speaking, the monetary component of the plan did not deserve to be called monetary reform. First, the system of administered prices was not given up. A new currency, the cruzado, was introduced that equalled 1,000 old cruzeiros (Fischer 1986). Another new element was an exchange rate peg to the US dollar. The crawling peg was given up, but not so the system of multiple exchange rates. The low degree of independence of the central bank remained unchanged. Especially the government was still allowed to borrow from the central bank and monetise its deficits. The degree of commitment was correspondingly low (C_{uw} = 0.346). Consequently, this reform failed as well.

III. THE IMPORTANCE OF COMMITMENT HIGHLIGHTED

There is one common pattern of all monetary reforms discussed in the foregoing section, regardless of whether or not they were successful. First, expressed in a comprehensive measure, commitment contributes to the success of the reform. If the discretionary power left to the government is extremely limited, the reform will more likely turn into a success. Similarly if the government is not willing to commit to a rule-bound monetary regime, it will be unlikely that the reform will be successful. A few examples will clarify the point.

First, we take a closer look at the elements of commitment in *Germany* 1948. The monetary reform had three constitutive elements (Giersch, Paqué and Schmieding 1992, pp. 36f). First, a new currency was introduced on June 20, 1948. The Reichsmark was replaced by the D-Mark. Thus the monetary overhang was eliminated by an exchange scheme that converted all private cash balances and bank deposits by a factor of ten to one or even greater for higher deposits into the D-Mark. Second, both public and private debt was consolidated. Third, and mostly important, the 'Bank deutscher Länder' remained independent from the government. In addition to this requirement, the German authorities were not allowed to run huge public budget deficits. Furthermore, the D-Mark was pegged to the US dollar. The monetary regime established by the reform reached a high degree of commitment. The value of C_{uw} is 0.707 which is far above the average but not the highest value among all monetary regimes.[15] As a consequence of the monetary reform, the price level remained almost stable for a number of years.

After that, we assess the effects of the currency board system in *Argentina* after April 1, 1991. Monetary policy became credible in due course. The annual inflation rate could be reduced very quickly, and the consumer price level stayed almost constant from 1995 to 1998, the latest date available for this study (IMFb, May 1999). In addition, the new monetary regime induced an instant reversal of capital flows. Since 1992 net capital inflows could be observed. The currency board with its high degree of commitment was even strong enough to survive the Mexican peso crisis in late 1994/early 1995 and the crisis in Brazil in January 1999. In both cases, there were rather small contagion effects (Hanke 1996).[16] After the crises in both Latin American countries, international investors transferred their capital into other investments. As a consequence, the – exogenously determined - monetary base decreased. Since wages and prices were not fully flexible, unemployment rose and Argentina suffered from a recession.[17] However, the monetary regime proved sustainable. In the more recent crisis, the Argentine government reacted by announcing an even stronger commitment, namely dollarisation. This announcement proves the determination and commitment of the government and is likely to stabilise expectations.[18]

---

15 In terms of Cukierman's index of CBI, the Bundesbank was the second most independent central bank in the world before the establishment of the ECB which is even more independent than the Swiss National Bank (Cukierman 1992, p. 381; own calculations).

16 The Argentine experience is in line with the result of an IMF study on international financial contagion (IMFa, May 1999, pp. 66–87). A proper set of institutions is likely to protect a country from contagion.

17 For a more detailed analysis see Freytag (1998b, pp. 394f).

18 It remains an open question whether the government meant this proposal seriously or whether it was only made to reassure the public of its determination to stick to rule-based monetary policy at any rate. See also section 8.VI.

In these cases, commitment was strong and accompanied by other components of economic order. In other instances, the monetary commitment was not as strong. The low degree of commitment coincided with a failure of the monetary reform in *Argentina* in 1985 and in *Brazil* in 1986. In both cases, the central bank law did not abolish direct loans to the government. This was certainly crucial for the failure. Other shortcomings of the economic order added to it.

In addition, the example of *Paraguay* shows that high commitment as such is not sufficient for the success of the monetary reform. Although the degree of formal commitment was high, the reform in Paraguay failed. Obviously, the reform was not compatible with the institutional setting. In particular, the political stability in the country was too low (see below).

IV. THE RELEVANCE OF INSTITUTIONS

Without the acknowledgement of the institutional setting, the analysis would remain incomplete. As shown above, commitment alone is not sufficient to guarantee a successful reform. For this, the institutional setting has to be in line with the degree of commitment. The three complete successes among the cases make this very clear. Therefore, we first discuss the impact of the overall institutional setting on the fate of the monetary regime. After that, the impact of individual factors, namely political stability, fiscal stability, the labour market regime and the choice of the reserve currency on the reform's success is illustrated. The impact of the public attitude to inflation on the reforms is rather uniform and does not reveal any differences across the 12 reforms discussed here. We exemplify it by comparing the two reforms made in Argentina. In 1985, the public was used to three-digit level inflation rates per year which were cushioned by indexation. Inflation was more or less accepted. In 1991, after two years of four-digit annual inflation rates, price stability became more desirable. The negative experience caused the Argentine public to be more critical with respect to inflation. In other countries, the impact of the public attitude to inflation is roughly the same. Hence, it is not necessary to analyse its impact in more detail. The econometric results can be assessed as being sufficient in this respect.

a) The overall institutional setting

In *Germany* in 1948, the monetary reform was carried out parallel to an economic reform. Prices were freed, and the rationing of goods was lifted by Ludwig Erhard. As a consequence, the supply of goods increased almost immediately delay and the shadow economy drained.[19] In the following years, the German economy was also opened unilaterally to international competition (Giersch, Paqué and Schmieding 1992, pp. 106–116; Buchheim 1990). These reforms helped considerably with gaining credibility and stabilising the economy. Political stability can be regarded as having been high and guaranteed by the allied powers. Fiscal stability started to rise. The public budget was nearly balanced, in some years it even reached a surplus. The labour market regime was endogenous rather than exogenous in the German situation. We judge its flexibility as being high since it took a rather long time for the traditionally strong interest groups to form themselves again. They did not impede the stabilisation process significantly. Public opposition to inflation was certainly high after two bad experiences with inflation within one generation. The institutional factors were in line with the high commitment to stability of the reform.

The development in *Argentina* can be judged comparably. Before 1991, for a long time there had not been a consistent economic order in Argentina. Consequently, reform attempts prior to this year had failed. Therefore, to create stability and credibility, the convertibility plan had to be accompanied by an assortment of other reform efforts. First, political stability in Argentina can be regarded as being on the rise. In 1991, the democracy had met its first contest. The change in government through elections took place peacefully. Coups had not happened since the end of the military regime in 1983. Besides the monetary reform, other steps to improve the economic order were taken. Argentina liberalised its foreign trade immensely. Import tariffs as well as quotas were reduced and domestic relative prices were adjusted to the world markets' relative prices. Apart from the positive effects on the price level, the resource allocation could be improved by the increase of competition. As a good means to stabilise expectations, indexation was forbidden. By such a measure, the public opposition to inflation could be increased which in the long run makes it more difficult to abuse monetary policy. Before 1991, wages, prices, taxes and debts had been indexed which had led to a perception that inflation was economically less harmful than it actually was. Nevertheless, there were weaknesses in the reform programme which did not immediately turn out to be problematic, but caused difficulties in the medium run. The privatised enterprises were mostly former state

---

[19] Lutz (1949, p. 132) emphasises the relevance of the end of the controls for the success of the whole undertaking.

monopolists. Without an appropriate regulation the transition from monopoly to increased competition is difficult to handle. Argentina made no serious efforts to regulate the new private monopolies, especially utilities (Gerchunoff 1993) which led to price increases. In addition, the labour market was not deregulated. Wage increases were decided politically which caused unemployment to rise during the Mexican peso crisis. To summarise, the institutional setting was almost, but not perfectly in line with the monetary regime.[20]

In *Estonia*, the strong commitment (C_{uw} = 0.787) also had to be made compatible with other institutions in the country. The institutional setting had to be introduced. The monetary reform was accompanied by reforms in other fields. As regards political stability, there seemed to be a broad consensus among the population to rely on democracy and a free market economy. The political system proved to be stable after reaching independence. Fiscal and monetary policy were clearly separated. The Eesti Pank was not allowed to give credit to the government (Schrader and Laaser 1994, p. 85). As regards public expenditures, subsidies were reduced remarkably. The public budget was – with the exception of 1992 – in surplus from 1991 to 1997. Fiscal stability, therefore, can be regarded as being high. The labour market was made more flexible, wages were to be negotiated on firm level rather than on trade union and employers' organisation level (Sepp 1996, p. 21).[21] At the same time, the foreign trade regime was almost completely liberalised. Only a few products (e.g. cars and furs) were subject to moderate tariffs. Thus, the world markets' price relations were put into effect for Estonia which made it one of the most open countries in the world. Estonia's foreign trade increased remarkably. However, there was one shortcoming. Many prices, mainly of non-tradables (e.g. energy, rents, fuel, water and basic food) were not freed; they were kept low and the government intended to adjust them gradually. This led to a continuous real appreciation and fuelled the rising price level (Freytag 1998a, p. 12f).[22] Another reason for the author's judgement of the Estonian reform package being a success is that the reserve currency was well chosen (see below).

In contrast to Estonia, institutional factors were not very compatible with the high degree of commitment in *Lithuania*. Political stability was similarly

---

20 Schweickert (2000) compares the Argentine reform to the Mexican stabilisation programme in 1987 (*Tables 4* and *5*) which also was backed by a nominal anchor and comes to similar conclusions.

21 Yet, a judgement on the degree of opposition against inflation in 1992 seems to be too difficult to make. The value of *POI2* is 0.347 which is below the average of the sample of 29 reforms (Appendix 4).

22 It has been correctly argued that the crown was undervalued in real terms (Buch 1993, p. 451). Thus, the inflationary pressure in the first few years after the reform did not impede the competition position of Estonian firms.

high. Lithuania and Estonia had a comparable political development after they gained independence. Fiscal stability, however was lower than in Estonia. On average, the Lithuanian government ran a small budget deficit. Although wages in Lithuania were subject to free negotiation, this held only for a small fraction of jobs, namely in the private sector, which was smaller than in Estonia. Openness of the country was also smaller and trade policy more restrictive (Schrader and Laaser 1994, pp. 131–138). Moreover, the choice of the reserve currency was not as good as in Estonia (see below). As in Estonia, a reliable assessment of public opposition to inflation in the year of the monetary reform is impossible.

Finally, there is an example of an institutional setting being completely averse to stability. In 1986, *Brazil* suffered from various institutional shortcomings which contributed to the failure of the monetary reform. Political stability in the newly democratic country was low; fiscal stability did not improve. The labour market grew increasingly inflexible as compared to the status-quo ante. Brazil was not an open country, a fact that had a negative effect on competition. Finally, despite high losses through inflation for the people, the previous system of indexation had lowered public opposition to inflation.

b) Political stability

Two reforms discussed here failed due to political instability. In *Greece*, political instability was accompanied by a low degree of commitment, which makes it difficult to distinguish the relative impact of both factors, respectively. In *Paraguay*, the distinction is easier. The main reason for this failure was the extremely low political stability regardless of other institutional factors and the high degree of legal commitment. Even the fact that the reform was supported by external help did not avoid the eventual failure. The civil war that struck Paraguay during the 1940s and early 1950s was an obstacle to stability. This argument is emphasised by the fact that the government did not receive excessive credit by the central bank. On the contrary, the central bank gave considerable credit to private agents and thereby contributed to higher inflation (Ahrensdorf 1959/60, pp. 280–282). The government seemed to be rather weak. Only after a fortunate military coup induced a strong government in 1954[23] was a successful reform made in 1956, again with international help (by the IMF). The Paraguayan experience permits the conclusion that political stability is of utmost relevance for the success of a monetary reform.

23 The use of the word strong in this context does not imply any positive judgement about that government as regards other political issues.

c) Fiscal stability

Fiscal policy can also contribute to the success of a monetary reform. In the cases of successful reforms, fiscal policy was sustainable; public budget deficits could be kept small. In some of the cases of complete failure, high deficits occurred which were mainly financed via the money press. But even if monetisation of deficits does not play a role, a lack of fiscal stability can be an obstacle to the long-term success of the new monetary regime. Since fiscal deficits can be financed on international capital markets, they do not *per se* endanger the monetary reform. Moreover, the problems may not appear immediately.

However, public expectations can react very sensitively to growing fiscal deficits, especially given the experience in the recent past that was characterised by hyperinflation caused by monetisation. Bearing this in mind, public deficits, which either remain high or grow again a certain time after the reform, may cause new inflationary pressure in that they induce pressure on the monetary authority to finance at least parts of the deficit. The situation observed in *Poland* in 1999 can be interpreted in this way: as the government was unable to meet its fiscal objective, the central bank commented on this very sharply trying to exert pressure on the government to care for a balanced budget. The traditionally low fiscal stability in Poland gave rise to the expectation that the government may be tempted to monetise deficits again.

In *Germany*, the 1923 reform package was not likely to allow for a balanced budget and sustainability in the following years, although the government began to lower public expenditure. The reduction of the number of public sector employees was most important and resulted in the dismissal of 400,000 employees until April 1924. In addition public sector salaries and public investment were cut, subsidies as well as cultural expenditures were lowered and taxes were raised. In the fiscal year 1924/25, there was a surplus in the public budget (Franco 1990, p. 183). Obviously, the Oliveira–Tanzi effect was responsible for the positive fiscal development. Franco (1990) also has made the point that the fiscal reform in the 1920s in Germany (as was the case in Hungary at that time) was not sustainable in that it provided no mechanism to reduce expenditures. It was clear that some of the cuts had to be taken back later, especially those concerning the number and payment of civil servants. To drop public investment cannot be a means to gain sustainable fiscal stability. The public deficit in Germany rose again beginning in the fiscal year 1926/27 (2.3 per cent of GNP) and peaked with 4 per cent of GNP in 1928/29 (James 1986, p. 52). The rather poor interaction of the components of the economic order did not allow for a full success of this reform.

d) The labour market regime

The labour market regime was also a serious constraint for monetary reformers in the cases discussed here. For instance in *Brazil* in 1986, the core of the package to combat inflation consisted of a nearly complete price freeze and a disindexation.[24] Wages were not totally frozen; an automatic adjustment was to be made every time the annual inflation rate exceeded 20 per cent. Given the price stop, this element squeezed entrepreneurial profits (Fischer 1986, pp. 6–11). Hence, it is not surprising that the reform did not work. Only in 1986, particularly in the first half of 1986, the internal value of the Cruzado could be stabilised. Inflation sped up again in 1987 and reached an annual level of over 30,000 per cent in 1990. In addition it became more volatile than before (Kiguel and Liviatan 1991, p. 225). In this case, the labour market organisation was an important reason to turn the monetary reform into a failure.

The *Israeli* heterodox stabilisation programme succeeded in bringing down inflation at once to a level between 15 and 20 per cent per annum. Nevertheless, it also clarified the fact that it seems impossible to reach a truly low inflation rate (1–3 per cent per annum) if the single elements of economic order are not compatible. It has to be seriously questioned whether the labour market regime would have allowed for a consequent stabilisation. Traditionally, the labour market in Israel was very corporatist; unionisation was widespread, and the government was a large employer (Cukierman 1990, p. 81). Wages were agreed on centrally in tripartite negotiations between the government, the labour union and employers' associations. Thus, there was little labour market flexibility. With this little flexibility, the monetary policy was forced to take employment into account. An austere stabilisation policy would have led to rising unemployment with the probable consequence of the eventual failure of the reform, for it seemed to be very unlikely that the labour market structure could be opened at short notice. Given the low public opposition to inflation in Israel, this mild monetary rule-binding could be justified, albeit at the expense of price stability. To put it the other way round, it is not self-evident that stronger commitment in Israel would have led to on average lower annual inflation rates. In the meantime, Israel made some efforts to structurally adjust in the early 1990s when the overall economic situation improved (Bruno 1993, pp. 147–155). However, as long as it does not overcome the structural problems on the labour market, there will be no way to solve the trade-off between absolute price stability and full employment.

[24] Like in Argentina a year before, the disindexation included governmental bonds and, therefore, threatened to have strong redistributional properties at the expense of savers.

e) Choice of the reserve currency

The relevance of the choice of the reserve currency can be assessed very well when comparing the *Estonian* with the *Lithuanian* currency board. Two aspects are relevant. First, both countries imported stability, albeit less than generally expected and experienced in prior currency board systems (like Argentina a year before or like Hong Kong in 1983). Second, the choice of the D-Mark as reserve currency protected Estonia from external shocks,[25] whereas Lithuania was imposed to one due to its reliance on the US dollar. The reason for this asymmetry is as follows.

Most competitors of Estonian firms are located in the D-Mark area (Statistisches Bundesamt 1994b, pp. 83–97). Fluctuations of the D-Mark rate did not affect the Estonian economy considerably (Freytag 1998a). This was different in Lithuania. The US dollar did not meet two out of three properties identified as prerequisites for protection against external shocks for Lithuania: the USA was a minor trade partner of Lithuania; less than 1 per cent of its foreign trade took place with US firms and consumers. In addition, most competitors of Lithuanian firms came from countries that pegged their currencies to other European currencies. Indeed, Lithuania was subject to a negative external shock in the first half of 1997, when the US dollar appreciated against the D-Mark and other European currencies for reasons beyond Lithuanian responsibility. Accordingly, the Litas also appreciated against these currencies. Although a causal relationship cannot be verified, it has to be noticed that following the dollar appreciation, the Lithuanian trade deficit increased and foreign reserves as well as the monetary base decreased. This caused adjustment costs which were borne by the Lithuanian enterprises (ibid. pp. 14–17). Thus, the Estonian currency board was better protected from external shocks than the Lithuanian one.

---

25 For an empirical assessment, see Sepp and Randveer (2001, pp. 13f).

V. OTHER CONSTRAINTS TO MONETARY REFORMS

a) Seigniorage as a major cause for failure

In the cases which were identified as being successful, seigniorage did not play a role in the budget. In examples of failure, the inability or unwillingness of the government to abstain from the money press often was crucial for the disappointing outcome. This can be very well illustrated by indicating the two *Argentine* cases. The Plan Austral did not prevent the government from monetesing budget deficits which among others led to annual inflation of higher than 1,000 per cent.

In the convertibility law in 1991, the most urgent task was to provide a balanced budget or at least an orderly financing of fiscal deficits on the international capital markets. As a consequence, Argentina started a privatisation programme which indeed led to a balanced budget in 1992 and – compared to the 1980s – to modest fiscal deficits thereafter. There were two potential sources of revenue: the privatisation turnover and the saved resources since the state no longer had to cover huge losses of the enterprises not in private property. After the privatisation revenue ran dry, the deficit started rising again. This time, however, the deficit was financed through the emission of bonds denominated in foreign currencies and bearing a market interest. Thus an important step was made as regards the abuse of monetary policy for fiscal needs. The weight that the government gave to seigniorage (*SEIGN*) as a source of revenue obviously declined rapidly. Money growth as a share of total revenues plus money growth went down from 50 per cent in 1990 to 7 per cent in 1994 and even 1 per cent in 1995. It slightly increased again afterwards.

b) External factors and the success of the reform

Many monetary reforms discussed here have been supported by external help. Some of them failed, others succeeded. There is no clear-cut relationship between external help and the success of a reform. In this subsection, two examples for effective foreign help and three cases of unproductive attempts are analysed.

In 1948, foreign help proved important in *Germany*. It is difficult to assess whether the monetary reform would have had a chance had it not been introduced and implemented by external forces. In Germany itself, there was a strong – albeit not overwhelming – academic and political opposition against a liberal, rule-based economic policy which included monetary policy (Giersch, Paqué and Schmieding 1992, pp. 32–36). The sudden success of the reform certainly helped to overcome this opposition.

Another example for beneficial foreign assistance is *Hungary* in 1924. The monetary reform was virtually forced on the Hungarian government by the League of Nations and, therefore, strongly backed externally. In July 1923, Hungary accepted the political order in the region. Only then its neighbours agreed on international assistance for Hungary, which was given in March 1924 by the League of Nations, who fixed and scheduled the Hungarian reparation payments on a bearable level. This paved the way for a fiscal and monetary reform which was planned and supervised by a delegation of the League. The external commitment made the reform relatively credible in the short run. Whether this credibility lasted for long, must be doubted.

In other instances, foreign help proved pointless. The *Argentine* government announced the Plan Austral as being the full application of a blueprint of foreign experts (Fischer, Hiemenz and Trapp 1985, pp. 70–86; Donges 1985). This, however, was certainly not the case as a comparison of this blueprint and the reality reveals. Obviously, the government tried to raise credibility of the programme by pointing at external help. It had allies among Argentine economists who seemed to be involved in the reform process. Even in 1988, the programme was celebrated by Argentine economists as being consistent and well suited to bring down inflation sharply.[26] Nevertheless, the Plan Austral was at best suited to reduce inflation in the short run (Heymann 1991, p. 124). It was not the appropriate means to solve structural problems that had been responsible for the high inflation rates in the recent past. Thus, the foreign advice was only used as a scapegoat and to borrow credibility without being taken seriously by the government.[27]

Besides Argentina, there were other examples of the ineffectiveness of foreign help. *Paraguay* and *Greece* both reformed their monetary regime with the help of external advisers. Nevertheless, both reforms failed as well. The lesson to be learned from these experiences is that monetary reform needs to be underpinned by domestic commitment and ability to stick to commitment. As successful reforms have shown, external assistance can support a reform package characterised by strong commitment very well via the application of the 'dirty-work' strategy (Chapter 4, subsection II.e). However, if the domestic government is unwilling or unable to stick to the announced monetary policy, the commitment is incredible and the

---

26 See Machinea and Fanelli (1990), Canavese and di Tella (1990) and slightly less enthusiastic Heymann (1991).

27 The authors made this clear in their study (Fischer, Hiemenz and Trapp 1985, p. IX).

stabilisation efforts are useless. This holds regardless of whether the monetary regime as such is well-suited and makes sense economically (Paraguay) or it is incredible from the very beginning (Argentina 1985 and Greece).

External help is not always a pure blessing for its recipient. Sometimes, external advice, e.g. by IOs, proved not very well suited in that it opted for less commitment than the government actually desired. Two examples briefly illustrate this point. The *Polish* monetary reform in 1995 was supported by several IMF and World Bank programmes (Gomulka 1995). Gomulka implicitly criticises these institutions for being only interested in short-term macroeconomic performance, rather than in a long-term, rule-bound policy. This critique is also made by Cavallo and Cottani (1997) who complained about the IMF's low interest in strong commitment during the preparations of the 1991 reform in Argentina.[28]

c) Financial market regulation does not come first

Both the *Estonian* and 1991 *Argentine* reform packages show that financial market regulation is not a prerequisite for success, but has to be introduced in due course. In 1995, a banking crisis occurred in Argentina in the aftermath of the Mexican peso crisis. It led to a declining number of banks in the country and shrinking liquidity (Marengo and Vilar 2000). Thus, in 1996 the banking regulation was tightened. It contains three prominent elements: a new surveillance system, deposit insurance with foreign participation, and privatisation of provincial state banks, also with foreign participation (*The Economist* 1997). Especially, the authorisation of foreign banks can help with generally making the sector more competitive. Despite the lack of financial market regulation, in both the Mexican and Brazilian crisis, the monetary regime proved to be credible.

Similarly, in Estonia the banking regulation was very weak. The Estonian banking system consequently experienced two crises, one in 1992/93 and one in 1998. As a consequence of these crises, the banking sector consolidated: whereas in 1994, 21 domestic banks were authorised, in June 1999 only five domestic and six foreign banks remained in Estonia. Many banks merged, others went bankrupt. To overcome the problems of the banking sector, Estonia introduced 'rules for good banking' in 1996 (Sörg 1999). In addition, the Eesti Pank tried to attract foreign investment in the banking industry (Bonin et al. 1998, p. 95).

Thus, the relations between the quality of the financial market regulation and the success of a monetary reform are rather lose. Two general – opposing – conclusions can be drawn: on the one hand, a well-functioning and properly

[28] See also section 4.II.

regulated financial sector helps to overcome the problems at hand. When crises in the sector causing liquidity problems can be avoided the central bank is not forced to act as lender of last resort. Monetary policy is more predictable than in case of a crisis. On the other hand, it seems that even an inappropriate regulation of the financial sector cannot impede the stabilisation efforts too much, as has been indicated in the two cases mentioned above. At least in the short run, the success of monetary reforms does not depend on the regulation and performance of domestic financial markets. A methodical argument strengthens this point. Indirectly, financial regulation is incorporated into the analysis, namely as one criterion of the index of commitment. A lack of regulation indicates a relatively low degree of legal commitment which *ceteris paribus* causes the monetary reform to be less successful than otherwise.

VI. LESSONS TO BE LEARNT FROM CASE STUDIES

This chapter has presented a discussion of 12 monetary reforms which took place in three continents and over a time span of more than 70 years. These properties could make sure that the circumstances of the reforms differed widely among the cases. Thus, the case studies presented here are very useful from several perspectives.

a) Different empirical approaches are justified: a methodical clarification

The first point to mention is a methodical one. Both economic theory and econometric calculation are sometimes accused of being misleading because they do not take into account institutional details and because they claim to identify regularities which in reality cannot be recognised. Reality is said to be much too complex to be covered by formal analysis and applied statistical theory (e.g. Lawson 1997). Instead, following this opinion, every economic event should be analysed individually without a theoretical framework. Apart from the fact that this view has serious weaknesses by itself,[29] the theory presented in this study explicitly takes into account institutional details when assessing monetary reforms. In particular, it is the goal of this study to show the relevance of formal and informal institutions by incorporating these into a macroeconomic framework.

---

[29] See Backhouse (1998) whose critique is especially directed towards Lawson (1997). For a recent substantial critique of the historical school see Leipold (1998) in his essay on the great antinomy in economics.

Nevertheless, it has to be admitted that an econometric cross-sectional analysis of approximately 30 very divergent monetary reforms has its shortcomings which diminishes the reliability of its results (Chapter 6, section IV). The institutional setting in different countries is very difficult to compare and, as a consequence, can hardly be measured consistently. It can be questioned whether the estimated parameters meant to describe and show a valid correlation between variables hold regardless of time and region. Bearing this in mind, the shortcomings in the results of Chapter 6 can be interpreted in two ways: either there are measurement problems or the theory is weak. As long as one is willing to follow the theoretical reasoning, i.e. one assumes problems in measuring institutions; one has to look for further evidence via case studies.

Indeed, the case studies show the relevance of the theoretical considerations and, thereby, confirm the econometric findings. Each case adequately takes into consideration the historical circumstances of the reform. Hence, this chapter allows for a differentiation in that not all determinants of a reform's success, which are identified as being relevant in Chapter 6, are equally important for all countries. Instead, their influence varies across them. In addition, some factors seem to be more relevant than others which was also a result of Chapter 6. To sort out the details is one major advantage of the case studies. Moreover, the case studies allow for differentiated policy conclusions. The shortcoming of case studies is that they do not enable the researcher to isolate the systematic effects of different exogenous variables (e.g. Killick 1995). Thus, applying both methods is justified. To summarise, econometric estimations and case studies jointly make clear that inflation can be combated the better, the more monetary commitment and institutional features in the country are compatible.

b) Ex-ante credibility difficult to measure

Both the cases and the econometric analysis have revealed the importance of the extent to which the monetary regime fitted other components of economic order as well as other constraints: it separated full successes from moderate winners. The most successful monetary reforms were those which were fully compatible with the institutional setting. The compatibility could be reached by reforming other policy regimes as well. In other words, this increased the credibility of monetary reforms.

However, it has proven difficult to quantify their ex-ante credibility as has been suggested in the theoretical part of the study. Whereas empirical estimations search for common influence of institutions for the whole sample, the case studies show that the relative importance of single institutions varies across countries. This makes the measurement of the credibility of a reform ex-ante even more difficult. Therefore, we will not make use of this proxy in the following Chapter 8 on policy options.

c) Strong commitment and no monetisation as necessary conditions for credibility and success

All the case studies show that monetary commitment defined comprehensively as a monetary regime (Chapter 2) is a prerequisite for the success of monetary reforms. On the one hand, those reforms that succeeded and were credible created a monetary regime that left the lowest discretionary power to the government. On the other hand, those monetary reforms without a strong commitment to stability, i.e. reforms that left too much discretionary power to the government were bound to fail. Besides commitment, the willingness of governments to do without seigniorage was essential for the success of monetary reforms. All those attempts where the reliance on seigniorage remained high inevitably failed.[30]

The cases validate another point made in the theoretical part of this study. The comprehensive interpretation of commitment included the exchange rate regime. A monetary policy that follows a nominal anchor *ceteris paribus* means higher commitment than a regime with flexible exchange rates. However, as other criteria can also differ between two monetary regimes the exchange rate policy necessarily cannot be an exclusively decisive element and distinctive feature for success or failure of the stabilisation efforts (see also Banerjee et al. 1995, p. 14). Estonia and Lithuania, for example, both introduced a currency board system. Still, the overall success of the reform was at least slightly different.

Thus, empirical evidence concerning the degree of commitment and the political need to rely on seigniorage to cover public expenditure is strong regardless of the applied analytical method. In general, stronger commitment is correlated to lower annual inflation rates on average after the monetary reform. Also, governments that relied upon the money press to finance their expenditure failed to stabilise their currencies.

d) Institutions have more relevance than shown by econometric methods

Six institutional factors have been identified as being relevant for the success of monetary reforms in the theoretical part of this study. The econometric analysis has turned out to provide relatively weak empirical evidence. The case studies clarify that it is poor data that accounts for the poor econometric

---

[30] The case studies do not allow to check the relevance of *PostBW*, the dummy for the disciplining effect of the Bretton Woods era since only one reform took place within this era. The fact that this reform, the German monetary reform of 1948, was a full success, however, cannot be taken as proof of this.

results. To start with, a lack of political stability can be responsible for the failure of even reasonably well-conciliated monetary reform. Fiscal stability is of importance particularly after a hyperinflation. In some positive instances, budget surpluses supported the monetary reform. On the other hand, governments could run considerable budget deficits without endangering the stabilisation efforts. As long as these could be financed on the capital markets, the monetary regime was credible. The flexibility of the labour market regime is seminal from a political economy point of view. If trade unionisation is very high, monetary policy with a high probability faces the pressure of accommodating high wage increases. This is a serious constraint to an austere monetary policy. The positive role of public opposition to inflation for a successful monetary reform can be seen across the complete sample. Openness to trade can provide a disciplinary element and improve the functioning of relative prices as signals of scarcity. Thus, it can be important when choosing the monetary regime. A currency board is only adequate in open economies. The two Baltic currency boards also emphasised the importance of the choice of the reserve currency.

To summarise, institutions matter; they help considerably with supporting strong monetary commitment in combination with a government that stops monetisation of budget deficits. If monetary and fiscal policies are unlikely to stop the inflationary process, institutions are unable to prevent inflation. An appropriate institutional setting is a necessary, but not sufficient condition for a credible monetary commitment. It must be combined with another condition, the determination of the government to stabilise. Only both together are credible.

e) The role of external help

External help can be of crucial importance. It can consist of economic knowledge like in Germany 1948 where the Allies imposed the alternative on Germany which was superior to the suggestions made by German economists. In addition, the help exerted pressure on the government to pursue reforms against the pretended interests of large groups in society. Thus, external factors could play the role of scapegoats.

Notwithstanding, the case studies also reveal that external influences can become a mixed blessing. Other cases illustrate that plans to introduce rule-bound policies which minimise or at least reduce discretionary powers are not always welcome to international organisations. Some authors argue that this is due to the nature of these institutions; their interest in interventionist possibilities is said to be great (Vaubel 1991b; Frey 1991). Mundell (1969) argues that the academic interest of employees in IOs is rather low. Other than known solutions are said to be unwelcome.[31] Whether or not these positions are well funded, there may be a third explanation which is a completely different argument and which is not rested in political economy. It may easily happen that the consulted IO and the country in question cannot agree on the proper remedy for the problems at hand. This may also be an explanation for the different opinions of the IMF and the respective governments in Poland and in Argentina. In numerous instances, however, the IOs or external consultants argue in favour of more rather than less commitment and comprehensiveness. Often the reform fails when the IOs cannot impose their ideas on the country. This can be seen in Argentina 1985 where the government not only did not follow the advice of a foreign expert mission, but also tried to claim that it actually followed this advice, i.e. to make use of a potential scapegoat.

But even if the external advice is both the appropriate remedy and accepted by the government, its success depends on the willingness of the reform country to make a commitment and – most important – to adhere to it. In other words, without domestic commitment, a monetary reform is bound to fail. To conclude, external help can do considerable good for the reform process if, and only if, the domestic government is willing and able to make a credible commitment and stick to it.

31 Reading the publications of the IMF's and World Bank's staff these days does not justify the view that they are not interested in the latest methods and theories. Still, one obtains the impression that the methodical perspective is rather narrow and concentrated on traditional macroeconomics. The broader perspective, taken in this study, cannot be found.

8. Economic Policy Options

The final objective of this study is to use the theoretical and empirical findings of the positive analysis to draw monetary policy conclusions. We try to apply the results to countries who at present are suffering from severe inflation. Considering the institutional setting in the respective country, in this chapter we discuss monetary policy options. Special reference is given to the political economy nature of inflation.

The chapter is divided into six sections. The following section deals with the feasibility of monetary reforms and the role economists and foreign agencies can play. In the second section, the monetary policy implications from the results are derived. These implications will influence the policy options for a number of countries that might consider reforming their monetary policy. Candidates for monetary reform are identified on the basis of considering their inflation rates and reflecting their policy objectives in section III. In section IV, a policy simulation for five countries is carried out. The results are used to check whether these countries should opt for actual policy recommendations given in the literature. Section V discusses options for three countries with severe monetary problems, namely Russia, Ecuador and Venezuela. In the final section, we discuss options for two countries that have improved their monetary policy a great deal during the 1990s (Chapter 7), namely Argentina and Poland.

I. THE TYRANNY OF STATUS QUO AND FEASIBILITY OF REFORM

a) Political reasons for inflation also impede remedy

An important question as regards economic policy reform is the question of its political feasibility. Inferior economic performance leads to both a theoretical and an empirical debate about a better policy regime. Once such an improved regime is identified, policymakers try to implement the new set of rules. In general however, the identification of a better policy system is only a necessary condition for the turnaround in economic policy. The sufficient condition is the successful search for ways to implement the new economic policy regime. There are obstacles in the form of organised pressure groups and constituencies who prefer the certainty of the status quo to the uncertainty of the post-reform situation. The policy reformer's task is to convince these groups.

It has been argued throughout this study that long periods of inflation are neither caused by permanently erroneous monetary policy[1] nor by evil monetary policymakers. Rather, it has been shown that the reasons for monetary crises can be found out in a political economy analysis (Chapter 2). Either a lack of instruments in other policy areas or organised interests prevent a monetary policy that aims at stability. Both reasons are closely related as the empirical analysis documents: if, for instance, the government is not able to overcome vested interests on the labour market, it will have a very limited set of policy instruments to combat high unemployment. It will also be very difficult for it to make flexible labour market laws or to liberalise the wage-setting process. In such a situation, naturally, monetary policy will become very attractive as an instrument of reducing unemployment, especially before general elections. Similarly, the inability to raise taxes fosters the reliance on seigniorage.

Thus, a government willing to reform its monetary regime in order to stabilise the economy and to make monetary policy credible will have to overcome exactly those vested interests that have forced the inappropriate monetary policy upon it. Is this possible? At first glance, enforcing a monetary reform that benefits virtually the whole society looks easy. It even looks easier than to pursue a reform of other policy areas like trade policy since the negative long-run effects of inflation are so obvious (Chapter 2, section I). Overall political consensus about the need for reform seems to be within reach. However, a distinction between the short run and the long run reveals that reform is always difficult to implement. Whereas in the long run, all members of society have better prospects with low inflation, in the short run, there well may be a trade-off. Some groups gain at the expense of others, e.g. the borrowers are happy with inflation, in particular if indexation as a protection from the costs of inflation is not permitted. With indexation being permitted, inflation might be a way of compensating for other loopholes in the economic order, e.g. labour market rigidities. In this case, a reform is

1 However, it cannot be ruled out that the beliefe in the Phillips trade-off has caused part of the observed inflation rates throughout the pos-war period. See also subsection 2.II.b.

even more difficult to implement. Thus, there is a trade-off between winners and losers of a monetary reform to be overcome in real political life.

The remainder of this section deals with this issue. The endeavour is not as pointless as one may think at first glance. One argument is rooted in the political process itself. The relative costs and benefits of a political regime distributed to certain groups within society are not fixed. Rather, there is a dynamic development of the pay offs. The longer the period of severe inflation lasts, the more the gains from inflation vanish and the more the losses become unbearable. Consequently, the number of winners also shrinks and the crowd of losers increases. Their relative positions change.[2] It then becomes politically attractive for the government to take into consideration the losers' perspective. With the demand side of the political market switching, a monetary reform will become increasingly feasible. In other words, social states where some permanently gain at the expense of others cannot survive very long (Buchanan 1995).

However, it may be very expensive to wait for a switch on the demand side of the political market as a signal for political suppliers to react and change the monetary policy. In addition, a monetary reform is a sudden change of monetary policy. It is not predictable if and when it will become a relevant alternative for the government to introduce a new monetary regime only through changes on the demand side. It is plausible – and can be observed – that the permanent worsening of the economic situation does not necessarily cause reform. If, however, the society as a whole learns pathologically, i.e. a reform can only be enforced after a severe crisis, this is a costly experiment.[3] Thus, one cannot merely wait for it.

Economic policy reform can be politically enhanced by a comprehensive reform package which may be necessary in a situation of a severe economic crisis. If not only monetary policy is to be changed, but also other policy areas such as fiscal policy, regulations or trade policy, the short-term distributional effects are completely unclear ex ante (Rodrik 1996, pp. 28f). In such a setting, every group and all individuals may feel comfortable with a comprehensive reform. This argument is analytically different from the 'crisis-triggers-reform' argument. Obviously, the economic reform in New Zealand in the 1980s was very much based on this logic, albeit it was also driven by crisis (Bollard 1994, pp. 96–99).

---

2 For a basic analysis see Becker (1983, 1985).

3 See also Williamson (1994, pp. 11f). However, it has to be clarified that the 'crisis-triggers-reform' hypothesis can become a tautology if applied in reversed direction. A statement such as: the fact that a reform does not take place shows that the crisis is not severe enough yet makes the hypothesis worthless (Rodrik 1996, p. 27).

b) The role of economic advisers in monetary policy

Some economists argue that the analyst who gives economic advice to politicians should take into account the problems of implementations mentioned above.[4] The claim behind this demand is to accept the status quo as a relevant alternative. This would increase the analyst's consciousness for political feasibility. Following this line of reasoning, the policy adviser ideally selects all those policy options which she/he believes can be easily implemented politically. A main criterion for the suitability of policy options is the degree of consensus on these options which is possible in the short term within the society. There are several objections against such a procedure.

Normally, economic researchers and analysts work on three tracks. First, a positive analysis is carried out. Theoretical deliberations are made with the final goal of a better understanding of the economic, or in this instance monetary situation. Causes and consequences of bad monetary performance and success or failure of subsequent monetary reforms are analysed. Second, these considerations are tested empirically. Third, policy implications are derived and policy options for countries that are facing severe inflation are discussed.[5] Following the strategy of concentrating on reform options which are politically feasible at once would probably narrow the analyst's view. Even if driven by the best of intentions to be as comprehensive as possible in the analysis, there may be a preselection bias. In this case, the analysis is not comprehensive enough and some monetary reform proposals are excluded from the very beginning. In a static setting this means that not all existing knowledge is exploited. In addition, in a dynamic view, the efforts to search for new and innovative solutions of monetary problems in the future might be reduced under the constraint of feasibility.

Moreover, by trying to restrict one's advice to politically appealing policy options, an economist can easily fail to fulfil the main tasks for which she/he is paid, partly by the public. These tasks are positive theoretical analysis and empirical assessment combined with policy advice. It is not intended that economists make decisions on which alternatives have or have not to be considered (v. Hayek 1990, p. 19).[6] Economists claiming to filter relevant alternatives certainly pretend having knowledge about political feasibility.

---

4 See e.g. Franz (2000, pp. 65–68) who particularly refers to the presentation style but also recommends to advisers to consider the governments' special situation.

5 For an analysis of the possible division of labour between economists on the three tracks see Freytag (1998c).

6 With this limitation, von Hayek does not connect the denial of a normative focus for economists. Instead, he is strongly sympathetic with normative, even appealing work. In his 1990 paper, he argues in favour of the 'denationalisation of money' which is politically very difficult to implement. Nonetheless, he is aware that economists offer alternatives to the society which compete with other options, either presented by other economists or scholars from different social sciences.

This holds in a static perspective, but becomes even more relevant in a dynamic view. Alternatives that are politically impossible to realise today may well be feasible in the future.[7] This, however, is beyond the knowledge of any economist. In addition, the way and speed new ideas are considered in politics is unclear (von Weizsäcker 2000, pp. 51f). Thus, the richness of (competing) policy regime options can be of crucial importance for the possibilities of the society to opt for the best monetary (but also other policy) regime.

As for monetary policy, there is evidence supporting this dynamic view. During the 1990s, the objective of price stability has been increasingly accepted as the main, if not the only objective of monetary policy. Until the 1980s, there was a widespread belief in politics that monetary policy could be used for other policy objectives as well (Chapter 2). Consequently, a number of central banks remained under the direct control of the government in order to support general economic policy. Not least thanks to the great number of contributions on the ineffectivity of monetary policy for other objectives, price stability has become the focus of monetary policy in an increasing number of countries. Although the chances to switch the focus of monetary policy in the short run were low, these – theoretically profound and empirically rich – contributions did not primarily consider the political feasibility of stability. Finally, they added to policy changes.

Nevertheless, that neither means that economists have no influence on political feasibility nor that they should not focus on it. Instead, the better economists fulfil their original tasks, the more relevance their proposal can claim and the easier a policymaker can overcome political pressure or the unwillingness of her/his constituency. Put differently, a thorough theoretical analysis supported by detailed empirical evidence derived from statistical analysis and case studies is an auxiliary for the political feasibility of appropriate reform proposals. Knowledge enhances feasibility: the better and more detailed the knowledge about success and failure of monetary reforms in the past, the better the chances to implement a good reform. This procedure can be supported technically by means of econometrics. The results of the empirical analysis can be made productive in policy simulation (section IV). All available information (including planned values) is translated into institutional factors, a desirable degree of stability (expressed as rate of inflation π^*) is added and the equation is solved for the degree of legal commitment, using the regressors obtained in the estimations (Chapter 6, section III). The degree then has to be translated into a monetary regime.

---

7 As Keynes put it: 'I am sure that the power of vested interests is vastly exaggerated compared with the gradual encroachment of ideas' (Keynes 1936, p. 383).

Arguments which are both theoretically convincing and empirically valid do not only influence the political decision making directly. They also exert pressure on those who are against a reform; they reverse the burden of proof. This has been proven in many instances of economic policymaking. More often than publicly acknowledged, a thorough economic analysis gradually has changed the relative position of interests within the society. The procedure normally is as follows: first, those groups who benefited from the status quo ante oppose the proposal very strongly and it is claimed that the proposal is infeasible, usually by politicians representing these groups. By the time the proposal is read and perceived by many other groups and individuals. It is publicly discussed and thus contributes to a switch on the demand side of the political market (see above). If external pressures also contribute to a higher political feasibility (see below), the proposal slowly infiltrates the political process.[8]

Of course, this does not exclude the necessity that economists take the potential for consensus into consideration when offering reform proposals. Again, the better the proposal is backed economically, the more sense it makes and the higher the general approval it gets. In addition, one can assume that in the long run when all arguments have been acknowledged by the public, only those reform proposals that are economically most meaningful will finally find consensus.[9] To summarise, economists should not exclusively concentrate on immediately politically feasible reform alternatives, but rather search for the economically best alternative. Thus, looking at the monetary economic problem at hand from a political point of view, an improved understanding of the relation between monetary commitment and the institutional setting is crucial for the chances of potentially successful monetary reforms being implemented.

c) External help as an enforcement mechanism

A government planning a monetary reform can make use of international assistance. It trades discretionary power for support with the stabilisation

---

8 One can find many instances for such a pattern of reform. In Germany 1991, the Deregulierungskommission scrutinised the necessity of the level of regulation in eight sectors in Germany and offered a detailed proposal, not simply for deregulation, rather for re-regulation for each of these sectors (Deregulierungskommission 1991). The first public reactions were extremely opposing, in some cases hostile. However, the report contributed to a fruitful public debate which at the end the of 1990s has not ended. In particular, it exerted pressure on highly regulated sectors that previously had a strong, nearly impregnable position. Within less than one decade, some of the sectors (e.g. energy, insurance) have become deregulated and have opened up to competition. Although one cannot calculate the magnitude of the impact of the report, the author is convinced that it at least increased the speed of reform in some instances.

9 This is emphasised by Pies (1999). He does not, however, explicitly distinguish the short and the long run.

programme. Thus, in the first place, external help touches a very important aspect, namely the issue of sovereignty. International economic policy assistance is sometimes assessed critically because national governments have to give up degrees of freedom in decisionmaking. Governments do not like to share their powers with foreign institutions, be it on a bilateral or on a multilateral level. However, as we have argued throughout this study, governments only have a limited sovereignty, regardless of whether they call for international economic help or not. Governments do not operate in isolation from the society's groups in a kind of laboratorium. Their power is restricted factually by rent-seeking activities. Following this reasoning, international help is a blessing rather than a curse for governments. Their sovereignty increases because they can escape the grip of their interest groups. Viewed from this perspective, external help can be extremely beneficial.

Yet, the empirical chapters have shown mixed evidence. Almost all reform countries relied on external help. Either they asked for foreign advice or they accepted contingent support by the IMF or World Bank. It turned out that external help did not prove to be decisive for the success or the failure of a monetary reform. One can identify two dimensions of external support in the context of enforcement: first, it is mainly foreign expertise and policy advice. In this case, it can be treated analytically like internal economic advice. Its role has been discussed in the foregoing subsection (see above). The second dimension regards the function of international organisation as a scapegoat. The help of international organisations, either through financial assistance made contingent upon certain reforms or by directly implementing a reform, can be made responsible for effects of a monetary reform that negatively influence previously privileged groups. Thus, the government can try to raise the chances to implement a proposal for monetary reform that has been identified as the best available. In the following, we concentrate on this dimension.[10]

As shown in the case studies, external assistance did not prove to contribute to success generally. The question then is under which circumstances this strategy is able to support the political feasibility of a monetary reform. In other words, when does the scapegoat function of IOs work? The answer is simple and straightforward: if and only if the government is determined to implement the reform package. Without internal commitment, external support is pointless! The reason behind this pessimistic view is that there is no enforcement mechanism for international treaties, not even for bilateral ones. Thus, if the IMF runs a stabilisation programme in

10 We do not discuss the issue of foreign exchange regime which is part of the search for the best reform and will be dealt with in the next section.

one of its member countries and the country does not stick to the conditions agreed on ex ante, there is no way to force the country to obey the treaty. There is even no adequate way to enforce repayment.

Nevertheless, there is a good argument not to discard external help with a monetary reform. If the government is determined to stabilise and if it overcomes the vested interests benefiting from the status quo in the short run, it could go ahead without external help. However, as mentioned earlier, there is no stable equilibrium on the political market. Those interest groups losing by the reform may try to force the government to deviate from the once made commitment. In such a setting, an external strengthening of the reform, e.g. by accepting contingent help with the reform as the 'concession' traded for help, improves the chances of success and feasibility of the reform. The time span during which the domestic political climate is advantageous for reform may well be rather small; political support by foreign institutions can be crucial. Thus, external help cannot be a sufficient condition for successful implementation of a monetary reform.

On a domestic constitutional level, this systematic relationship between a domestic commitment and an international fixing can be legalised. This can be done by giving citizens the right to sue the government if it does not follow international agreements it has concluded. Each citizen can check whether the government deviates from such an agreement or not and can take it to court. In case the government indeed deviates, it has to be convicted and sentenced to adhere to the agreement (Freytag 2001b). This suggestion is along the lines of Jan Tumlir's suggestion of giving direct effect to multilateral agreements in trade policy (Tumlir 1983). The incentive structure of this proposal is simple: it would certainly strengthen the commitment to stability and would be a strong disincentive to favour certain interest groups at the expense of others through inflation. It would not, on the other hand, deprive the government of the necessary flexibility to react to shocks. Thus, like in commercial policy, the international course is a device to protect the public from its own government in that the government is forced to pursue policies that are in the interest of the economy as a whole.[11]

The logic of why there may be a majority within a country to implement Tumlir's proposal is the following: citizens today agree on an economic order whose future distributive outcome is uncertain but which is regarded as being fair. Ex ante, everyone can support this order (Brennan and Buchanan 1983). Once there are distribution effects, there will be rent-seeking activities to alter this outcome. This constitutional rule will generate difficulties for such activities. It has to be emphasised that there is no need for international co-

11 Needless to say that under such a legal setting these policies are in the interest of the government as well. Political and economic rationality converge.

operation to introduce the rule domestically. Every country can implement the constitutional right of compliance to international treaties on its own. In addition, the suggestion is independent of the contemporary state of monetary policy. It would even be advantageous to implement this in times of good overall economic performance to avoid increasing resistance also against the actual monetary policy.

d) Conclusion: monetary reform can be implemented

As a general economic policy lesson it can be summarised that in a crisis a new and better monetary policy regime has good chances of being implemented successfully provided the government is determined to stabilise. Even a determined government is constrained by political economy considerations as shown in the theoretical model (Chapter 4, section IV). The government's will to stabilise can be enhanced if the goal of price stability is fixed on the constitutional level. In this case, there is a consensus in the society. Nevertheless, the determination to improve on the monetary regime is only a necessary condition for the reform's success.

In a reform process, resistance by affected interest groups has to be overcome. Besides the government's determination the work of economic advisers as well as international organisations is helpful. The advisers should take political feasibility of policy options into consideration only via the quality of theoretical and empirical research. The better their work, the more difficulties interest groups have when advocating their case. Similarly, international assistance is no guarantee for the successful implementation of an adequate monetary policy. Without a political will to implement a stabilisation programme, it will not work. In a constitutional decision allowing citizens to sue their government if it does not adhere to international agreement made by itself, the role of external help can be enhanced.

II. MONETARY POLICY LESSONS

a) No simple and uniform way out of a monetary crisis

The focus of the foregoing section has not been primarily on the topical aspects of monetary reform. It has been discussed how to enforce a monetary reform and the contribution economists can make to enforcement. We now discuss in particular monetary policy lessons derived from the study. What should a monetary reformer consider? First of all, there is no simple and uniform solution for monetary problems. Although this is pretty much a trivial insight, it is important to notice for often monetary policy recommendations are very similar for whole groups of countries, regardless of their institutional setting and of the deeper causes of their monetary problems. The study has strongly supported the view that unrefined discussion such as 'orthodox versus heterodox', 'central bank versus currency board' or 'fixed versus flexible exchange rates' are not adequate and do not contribute significantly to a sustainable solution of the problem.

In the course of the study, some new policy implications have been made explicit. Credibility of a monetary reform can be raised by considering the institutional setting in the country. Thereby, credibility can theoretically be judged ex ante, i.e. before the reform takes place. Thus, the study allows for differentiated answers to the question of the appropriate monetary policy. Despite the fact that the causes of the monetary problem are very similar in almost all cases of chronic inflation or hyperinflation, the adequate reform steps may well differ to a very large extent. In addition, the healthy influence of monetary commitment and the negative impact of the money press as the main instrument to finance public expenditure on the fate of a reform have been confirmed.

The less the search for the correct monetary policy regime is driven by ideological or even quasi-religious impetus, the more the new regime will be credible. Those economists who argue in favour of a certain policy regime, e.g. free banking or a currency board regardless of the causes of the crisis and the institutional factors, seem to be driven by such an impetus. Rather, the economic policymaker and reformer has to analyse the situation in the individual country carefully before selecting one monetary regime. Nevertheless, some aspects of monetary reform can be regarded as being basic. These aspects will be the subject of this section.

b) Enhancing credibility

Credibility is crucial for the success of monetary policy, in particular a monetary reform. One major implementation problem for policymakers and reformers in the past has been caused by the fact that credibility only could be judged ex post, using interest differentials, government bond prices and the like. In this study, we have developed an ex-ante proxy for credibility (Chapter 4, section V) which proved to be weakly significant in the econometric analysis. Credibility can be enhanced if the degree of legal commitment is adjusted to the factual outcome of five institutional factors, namely political stability, fiscal stability, labour market flexibility, openness of the country and public opposition to inflation. If a nominal anchor is part of the legal commitment the choice of the reserve currency is also important.

To generate high credibility, monetary commitment should be high when political stability is high, when the public budget can be balanced, when labour markets are flexible enough to react to a disinflation programme, especially through flexible wages, when the country faces competition from outside and when public opposition to inflation is reasonably high. However, these conditions are not necessarily given. Hence, the degree of commitment is dependent on institutional details. In other words, the monetary reformer has to assess the institutional features and choose the appropriate degree of commitment. The degree of commitment has to be 'translated' into a monetary regime. *Figure 4.1* on page 85, can be used as a guideline. The best procedure in this context is to exclude certain strategies successively. This can be best demonstrated using two institutional factors as examples. First, a strictly rule-oriented monetary policy that is exclusively dedicated to price stability does not consider changes in employment. Thus, to reach full employment, high labour market flexibility is required. If, however, the labour market is rigid and the rigidity cannot be eliminated for political reasons, monetary policy is regularly forced to make allowances for it. In this case, for instance flexible exchange rates or a crawling peg might be superior to an unchangeable fixing of the exchange rate. Second, a low degree of openness may seem counterproductive to a currency board or to dollarisation since in a more or less closed economy it is difficult to earn the foreign exchange necessary to run the monetary regime smoothly. Another – probably less binding – alternative is preferable.

However, there is one qualification of this general policy lesson. One cannot expect credibility to be enhanced through a very low degree of commitment in cases when the institutional factors also have low values, i.e. when political stability is low or when the labour markets are inflexible. A very schematic interpretation of the model in Chapter 4 would lead to this conclusion. We already have made this point when discussing the model. Another example will clarify the problem. If the government is unable to balance its budget and will certainly remain so, a monetary regime that does not prohibit monetesing budgets will not raise credibility.

In such cases, the government has not only the task of introducing a new monetary policy regime but of reforming other economic policy areas as well. In the first place, a comprehensive policy reform includes both monetary and fiscal policy; it should be extended to encompass the liberalisation of foreign trade. The Argentine convertibility law is an instructive case in point. Besides the introduction of the currency board, the government started a privatisation programme to balance the public budget sustainably and opened the Argentine market unilaterally to foreign trade. It may also be possible to use a strong monetary commitment to trigger reforms in other policy areas. Of course, this argument can also hold when reversed. Reform experiences in economic history strengthen the argument: in many countries during the 1980s, economic policy reforms were comprehensive rather than gradual (Williamson 1994). Enforcement will be easier if many policy areas are involved.

Moreover, it has turned out in the study that some institutional factors are more restricting than others for the fate of monetary reforms. Political stability seems to be crucial. Whereas for instance labour market inflexibilities can be considered quite easily by choosing a flexible monetary regime, allowing for little inflation (as compared to the status quo ante), it may become extremely difficult to successfully introduce a new monetary regime during a period of political instability, no matter how urgent the need. Political stability indeed is the most important prerequisite for success as has been shown by the case studies (as opposed to the econometric studies). This example additionally makes it clear that it is sometimes necessary to make an overall economic or even political reform.

At any rate, a considerable minimum degree of legal monetary commitment is inevitable to make a stabilisation programme work. Monetary reforms that do not consider this basic necessity cannot contribute to stabilisation and, therefore, are bound to fail. The credibility of monetary reforms can be enhanced when the elements of economic order are in accord with each other. For this purpose, an overall economic reform sometimes is necessary; in other cases it may be enough to pursue a monetary reform.

c) Strict separation of monetary and fiscal policy necessary for success

Most severe cases of inflation in history that have been analysed in this study were rooted in the inability or unwillingness of the state to cover its expenditures by taxes or by ordinary financing on capital markets. As both the case studies as well as the estimates have made clear, one distinctive reason for success or failure of reforms is the ability or inability to end this public behaviour and to strictly separate fiscal and monetary policy. Fiscal policy has to be pursued without the money press. Besides the necessity of monetary commitment the need to finance public expenditure without falling back to seigniorage is essential.

Although in the econometric analysis fiscal stability proved to contribute significantly to low inflation, economic policy should not confuse the necessity to stop monetisation with the need to balance the public budget at any rate. As many cases have shown, a moderate public debt can be in accordance with stabilisation. Its impact on the price level crucially depends on how the debt is financed. Ideally, public debt should be denominated in international currency such as the US dollar or the Euro. It should be placed on the international capital market and pay a competitive interest. This would give the correct incentive for the government to be as thrifty as possible as well as to use the imported capital for highly profitable investments.[12]

d) Conditions for a successful monetary reform

To summarise this chapter hitherto, the conditions for a successful reform are briefly listed.[13] It has to be reiterated that without a strong political determination to stop inflation and to stabilise, monetary reforms remain incredible. The following steps are not necessarily to be made in this order.

1. The reasons for the monetary situation have to be carefully examined. Economic advice by domestic and foreign consultants can be very helpful.
2. The public perception and interest group behaviour needs to be taken into account. External help (e.g. by IOs) may overcome special interest opposition to reform easily (Tumlir's proposal).
3. A 'reform off the peg' only has limited chances of becoming a success.
4. Instead, the new monetary regime should be in accord with the institutional setting. Econometric results can be used by simulating monetary policy (Chapter 6, section V).
5. If necessary, other parts of the economic order should be subject to reform as well.
6. Monetisation of public debt has to be excluded from the very beginning both by abolishing it by central bank law and by creating the presuppositions for a balanced budget.

One determinant for the success of a monetary reform identified in the econometric chapter was a dummy which stood for the international monetary discipline imposed by the Bretton Woods system and the absence of international price shocks (*PostBW*).[14] It is self-evident that a domestic policymaker has no opportunity creating this kind of disciplinary atmosphere. However, compared to the 1980s international monetary discipline has increasingly grown. A monetary reformer can claim this evidence as a case in favour of stabilisation. In addition, there are world-wide attempts to discuss and implement a so-called 'new international financial architecture'. Although the contributions to the discussion are very controversial, they all

---

12 Profitability in this context means social returns on investment.

13 In a similar manner, but much more general, Williamson and Haggard (1994) have summarised a catalogue of presuppositions for successful reforms from a number of country reports collected in Williamson (1994). This catalogue is called the Washington Consensus.

14 Technically, the dummy has taken the value 1 for the time span after 1973 and was a positively significant determinant of post-reform inflation.

seem to go in the direction of enhancing international discipline and stability.[15]

III. CANDIDATES FOR MONETARY REFORMS

a) A brief overview: inflation is not dead

In early 1999, the public debate changed its focus very pronounciated. Instead of an intensified discussion of inflation, fears of deflation and another great depression became popular. However, these fears vanished very quickly during 1999 and in early 2000. In this period, prices for raw materials increased and interest rates were raised by central banks all over the world. Rather than deflation, inflation became a topic again. There is no reason to fear that there is another phase of sharp inflation in the world economy to come, but one still can find a number of countries where either inflation has not been successfully combated in the last years or where inflation is on the upspring again. Hence, there are some countries which suffer from high annual inflation and which apparently are in need for reform.

Table 8.1 gives an overview of those countries which, in the personal judgement of the author or according to other sources, are candidates for a monetary reform since early 2000. The third column shows the reason why the country is assessed to be in need of a monetary reform. However, there is no simple correlation suggesting that high inflation always demands monetary reform and low inflation does not. It should be clarified that not all countries suffering from high inflation necessarily demand a monetary reform. There may be cyclical or external reasons for temporarily high inflation.[16] Monetary reform also sometimes seems to be justified for countries with low inflation rates and which obviously do not call for reform. In some cases, the reform is warranted by undeniably unsustainable macroeconomic policies, e.g. fiscal policy. In other instances, the country in question may be very ambitious concerning the future monetary policy. The

---

15 See e.g. Eichengreen (1994) and the numerous contributions to this debate in IMF publications. There has also been a huge and controversial discussion in politics.

16 A case in point is the situation in Indonesia at the end of 1997. The annual inflation rate was increasing and the rupiah depreciated heavily against the US dollar. Although it was widely acknowledged that the causes for this situation were located in microeconomic distortions and insufficient banking regulations (e.g. Radelet 1998), a currency board was suggested to solve the problem (Schuler 1998) which was not a monetary one. The government was enthusiastic about this idea and took efforts to implement it. Only international disapproval caused the government to finally stop the plan (World Bank 1999).

actual monetary policy regime may not be well-enough suited to guarantee that these ambitions will be met in the future. Before we begin with policy simulations to discuss reform proposals made for some of the countries listed in *Table 8.1*, we briefly discuss the relation of monetary problems and the institutional setting in sub-Saharan Africa.

Table 8.1 Potential Candidates for Monetary Reform

Country	Av. annual inflation rate 1991–98 in per cent[1]	Reason for judgement
1. Africa		
Angola	588.1	Persistent inflation
Congo, Dem. Rep. of	1,192.4	Volatile inflation
Ghana	25.3	Persistent inflation
Nigeria	34.6	Persistent inflation
São Tomé and Príncipe	42.3	Persistent inflation
Sierra Leone	37.0[2]	Persistent inflation
2. Asia		
Indonesia	13.7	Financial crisis
3. Middle East and Europe		
Turkey	80.5	Persistent inflation
4. Western Hemisphere		
Argentina	19.3	Suspected unsustainability
Ecuador	35.8	Severe economic crisis
Venezuela	49.9	Persistent inflation
5. Central and Eastern Europe		
Poland	32.0	Application to access the European Union
Romania	119.3[3]	Persistent inflation
Russian Federation	202.7	Severe economic crisis

Notes: [1]: calculated as in equation (A.12b);[2]: 1990–97; [3]: October 1990 as basis.

Source: IMFa, own calculations.

b) Sub-Saharan Africa: policy simulations pointless

Compared to other continents, in particular Latin America, African inflationary experience is moderate. There are countries which have had an almost stable currency for decades (Burkina Faso, Republic of Congo, The Gambia). Partly, these countries have assured stability by means of a monetary union that pegs its currency to the French franc. The French Franc Zone (CFA) consists of 14 countries organised in two monetary unions with their own central bank each (Monga 1997, p. 103). Average annual inflation rates in these countries in the 1990s did not exceed 10 per cent. Nevertheless, among the potential candidates for monetary reform, there are a number of sub-Saharan African countries (*Table 7.3*). Inflation in Africa has very rarely been hyperinflation, but rather chronic inflation. In a nutshell, inflation in Africa has not been among the highest in the world, but also has not been negligible. Despite this assessment, inflation normally is not mentioned when the chief problems in Africa are discussed. In a recent symposium about 'Slow growth in Africa' in the *JEP*, the institutional setting in sub-Saharan Africa was extensively discussed. The papers in this symposium identify a number of economic problems responsible for its backwardness. Although inflation is not dealt with explicitly, the papers clearly identify the institutional constraints for a potential monetary reform.

Collier and Gunning (1999) employ a scheme with four factors which they call domestic destiny (climate, low life expectancy, poor soil quality, low population density, high natural resource endowment per capita), domestic policy (corruption, preferential treatment of urban population at the expense of rural population, low quality of public services, too big a public sector), external destiny (landlocked population, narrow range of exportable commodities, dependence on foreign aid) and external policy (import substitution, non-tariff barriers, multiple exchange rates). In their view, the main reason for the poor (often even negative) economic growth is domestic policy. This view is supported by the fact that Africa has become more diverse in the 1990s (ibid., p. 19). If the African development was exclusively driven by external factors or by destiny, substantial differences would not be noticeable. In addition, Ndulu and O'Connell (1999), emphasise the role of governance in Africa as a main obstacle for economic growth. Political instability and intranational distributional conflicts impede economic development.

There are other determinants of underdevelopment. First, the dependence of many African countries on a limited number of, in some instances only one, primary commodities as the only export products sets them at risk if the prices for these commodities are volatile or declining relatively over time.

This has regularly been the case (Deaton 1999).[17] Second, investment in human capital is insufficient and misallocated (Schultz 1999): the social returns on primary and secondary education are much higher than those of investment in post-secondary education. Nevertheless, the emphasis in many countries is put on post-secondary education of urban middle-class children who do not necessarily consider the whole country's interests adequately when exploiting their investment in human capital (Ndulu and O'Connell 1999). In addition, deficiencies in public health are costly in terms of development (Schultz 1999).

This evidence has two implications. First, the institutional shortcomings in these countries seem to be overwhelming[18]. It is questionable whether a monetary reform in e.g. Angola or the Democratic Republic of Congo would make sense if not accompanied by an overall reform. Second, the chaotic situation, in general, makes it very difficult to assess the institutional setting meaningfully and to derive policy conclusions. Two institutional factors can easily be calculated, namely openness and fiscal stability. The other factors cannot be seriously computed. Rather one has to guess. Hence, it can be taken for granted that political stability as measured in this study, in general, is rather low, probably close to zero. It is questionable whether labour market regulations exist; their flexibility cannot be assessed. One may suspect that it is high because of the lacking framework. Public opposition to inflation cannot be measured. Often, there is no perceptible public opinion, let alone freedom of the press. Therefore, we refrain from discussing policy options in the African countries with the help of instruments applied in this study. We do not include the African countries with monetary problems in the policy simulations.

Nevertheless, one can think of one exception by taking recourse to the past. Three of the countries listed in *Table 7.3* are former members of the West African Currency Board, namely Ghana, Nigeria and Sierra Leone. The fourth participant was the Gambia. From 1913 to 1971, the board was run successfully. It not only managed to keep the West African Pound stable but also maintained an adequate money supply. This was particularly difficult because of the payment habits of the local population which led to a very volatile demand for money (Clauson 1944, p. 8; Freytag 1999). Only after the countries gained independence from the UK, they abandoned the currency board one after the other and established central banks. The monetary performance of the board, however, was much better than of any new central bank.

---

17 The reasons for this dependence are irrelevant in this context.

18 See also Leipold (1997).

It can be assumed that the West African Currency Board was compatible with the institutional setting of those days. On the constitutional level, the institutions were British. Economic relations with the mother country were also close. In particular, it was relatively easy to obtain access to international capital flows in order to increase and decrease, respectively, the monetary base since British banks had branches in West Africa.

Currently, the institutional setting is different and probably not that favourable for a currency board. Nevertheless, it may be an alternative to today's central banks in the three countries to re-establish the West African Currency Board. To illustrate the possible merits of this idea, we take the Nigerian case. In mid-1999, a civilian government replaced the army. It immediately started to combat corruption and to privatise many of the state enterprises with the help of the IMF. Given that it is thoroughly determined to pursue economic reforms and given that the political situation is not very stable, there is a case for either a new West African Currency Board or another monetary regime set up by the IMF as an agent of the Nigerian government. The government's efforts to further reform the economic order may be strengthened by such an arrangement with an external agency responsible for monetary policy.

However, these deliberations are not strictly derived from the analysis of this study. To summarise this subsection, the political and economic situation in sub-Saharan Africa is very much an obstacle for economic reform, in particular monetary reform. With the tools developed in this study, it is almost impossible to discuss adequate policy options. In the following three sections, we come to policy conclusions for countries that can be analysed with the instruments of the study.

IV. POLICY SIMULATIONS FOR FIVE CANDIDATES

In the late 1990s, several countries were suffering from monetary problems (*Table 7.3*). These problems have led to a number of policy proposals. We want to use the instruments developed in this study to test whether some of the recommendations are viable. The proceeding is along the lines of the empirical part (Chapters 6 and 7). We start by calculating an 'optimal' degree of commitment C_{uw}* using equations (6.8) and (6.9) of Chapter 6. As an outcome of Chapter 6, the results of the econometric analysis very much depend on the specification of the variables and the quality of the data. Moreover, a certain degree of commitment cannot be assigned exactly to a monetary regime (apart from very low values of *C*). This makes it necessary to discuss each case in more detail following the policy simulation.

In particular, five countries are in the focus of the following three sections. Ecuador, Venezuela and Russia had monetary problems in early 2000. In Ecuador, two potential monetary regimes were publicly discussed: a currency board system and dollarisation. For Venezuela, a currency board system was put forward by domestic and foreign economists. The reform options suggested for Russia range from a currency board to a crawling peg. The latter was suggested after the 1999 crisis.

The situation in these countries differs much from the situation in the two countries analysed in section VI. Argentina and Poland both managed to stabilise their economies during the 1990s. Hence, recommendations to reform their monetary regime were directed at safeguarding the successes. As a reply to the contagion effects of the Brazilian crisis in 1999, it was proposed that Argentina should abandon its currency board and introduce dollarisation. The second case was Poland. Although it reformed its monetary regime in 1995, another regime change was suggested. Instead of the central bank system with an external crawling peg introduced in 1995, a currency board with the Euro as a reserve currency was regarded as being adequate. It was argued that this would enable Poland to access the European Monetary Union shortly after it becomes an EU member.

As for policy simulations, we exclusively take recourse to the estimations of specification 2 of the econometric analysis (Chapter 6, subsection III.b). In particular, estimations 13, 14 and 17 of *Table 10* are used. However, to make policy simulations work, we have to adjust equations (6.8) and (6.9) for two variables that only affect the level of C_{uw}*: these are *SEIGN* and *PostBW*. We assume that the government while pursuing a monetary reform is willing to completely refrain from seigniorage as a source for revenues. Therefore, the projected value of *SEIGN* is 0. We also neglect *PostBW* since it would generate the value 1 in every simulation regardless of the country in question. Both variables do not affect the structure of the degree of commitment among the five countries. The same is true for the intercept (β_0). Besides, it has no economic meaning and can be neglected as well. Thus, a policy simulation based on estimations 13, 14 and 17 uses equations (8.1a), (8.2a) and (8.3a), respectively:

$$C_{uw}^{*} = \frac{\beta_2}{\beta_1} PS2* + \frac{\beta_3}{\beta_1} FS1* + \frac{\beta_4}{\beta_1} OP4 + \frac{\beta_5}{\beta_1} POI* - \frac{\ln ACPI*}{\beta_1} \quad (8.1a),$$

$$C^*_{uw} = \frac{\beta_2}{\beta_1} PS2* + \frac{\beta_3}{\beta_1} FS1* - \frac{\ln ACPI*}{\beta_1} \qquad (8.2a),$$

$$C^*_{uw} = \frac{\beta_2}{\beta_1} EF2000 - \frac{\ln ACPI*}{\beta_1} \qquad (8.3a).$$

Inserting the parameter values of estimations 13, 14 and 17 yields:

$$C^*_{uw} = 0.237 \times PS2* + 0.839 \times FS1* + 1.4E-05 \times OP4 + 0.165 \times POI* - \frac{\ln ACPI*}{4.189} \qquad (8.1b),$$

$$C^*_{uw} = 0.269 \times PS2* + 0.944 \times FS1* - \frac{\ln ACPI*}{4.515} \qquad (8.2b),$$

$$C^*_{uw} = 1.435 \times EF2000 - \frac{\ln ACPI*}{3.088} \qquad (8.3b).$$

The further proceeding is as follows: first, the projection for the institutional factors on the right-hand side is made. The calculation is based on the sources used in Chapter 6 (see also Appendix 2). In addition, they reflect policy objectives. Different observers may deviate as regards their judgement on the feasibility of the projections. However, we try to be as realistic as possible, i.e. the projections do not differ too much from the latest figures. This is not only necessary to be impartial but also reflects the fact that the majority of the institutional factors cannot be influenced in the short run. The variable *OP*4 is not calculated as a projection since it covers the three years prior to the reform. Second, an objective for the average inflation rate for the five years after the monetary reform is set. We presume that the potential reform countries are rather ambitious. The planned inflation rate is between 2 and 5 per cent. In the case of Argentina, this is higher than the actual inflation rate in 1998 and 1999. There may be situations, even caused by external shocks, in which a higher inflation rate is inevitable. Third, C_{uw}* is calculated. The results are reported in *Table 8.2*.

The optimal degree of commitment for a potential reform country is the higher, the lower the envisaged inflation rate is, the closer to 1 the projected values of the institutional factors are and the higher the degree of economic freedom is. Two implications of the simulations are remarkable. First, an optimal degree of commitment for countries with severe monetary problems is less ambitious than for those countries which already have been successful in stabilisation. This is in line with the theoretical considerations. Second, regardless of the estimation on which the simulation is based this structure of the optimal degree of commitment among the two groups of countries is valid. Although the structure is similar for the simulation based on *EF*2000, it yields more extreme values than the other two. Hence, when using these results to assess the policy recommendations for these countries we mainly refer to equations (8.1b) and (8.2b). This is be done in the following sections.

Table 8.2: Policy Simulations

	ACPI*	PS2*	FS1*	OP4[1]	POI2*	EF 2000	C_{uw}* (8.1)	C_{uw}* (8.2)	C_{uw}* (8.3)
Ecuador	4	0.8	0.5	770	0.7	0.668	0.421	0.380	0.510
Venezuela	4	0.9	0.6	1,500	0.7	0.340	0.522	0.501	0.132
Russia	5	0.7	0.6	1,050	0.7	0.538	0.415	0.398	0.251
Argentina[2]	2	0.9	0.6	1,350	0.8	0.807	0.702	0.645	0.933
Poland	2	1.0	0.65	5,975	0.9	0.564	0.849	0.729	0.585

Notes: [1]: 1995–1997; [2]: This simulation has been run prior to the 2001 crisis (see subsection VI.a).

Source: See Appendix 4.

V. SEVERE CRISES CALL FOR REFORM: RUSSIA, ECUADOR AND VENEZUELA

a) Russia: external help may foster stability

Since the disintegration of the Soviet Union in 1991, Russia has had difficulties in managing the transition period well. This political situation has severe implications for the economic, in particular for the monetary policy. The economic order in Russia is still suffering from serious and outstanding shortcomings (Welfens 1998). More importantly, the state has not made earnest efforts to balance its budget. On the one hand, revenue is still insufficient, in particular tax revenue. Accumulated tax arrears in terms of GDP have doubled since 1995 and in 1998 accounted for almost 10 per cent of GDP (IMF 1999a, p. 139). On the other hand, the government has not managed to control its expenditures. The stock of foreign and domestic debt steadily grew in the 1990s. Each depreciation of the rouble increases the burden of debt denominated in foreign currency. In late 1998, Russia felt the need to partly declare a moratorium (Götz 1999, pp. 10f). Due to a tax reform and due to a higher growth rate, tax revenues have risen since 1998 (Fischer 2001). Still, Russia's situation in mid-2001 was extremely difficult, notwithstanding rather high growth rates in 1999 and 2000.

The fiscal problems have caused two reactions. First, the state has built up huge pension and wage arrears, both in public services and in state enterprises. In sum, enterprise arrears comprised approximately 45 per cent of GDP in 1998 (IMF 1999a, p. 139). This evidence clarifies the fact that the soft budget constraints of the socialist era have not been hardened yet. The firms do not have incentives to work more efficiently. There also is no bankruptcy law. Moreover, and probably more important, there is a growing tendency of breaching agreements if the state does not fulfil its financial duty as employer or customer. Public moral deficiencies lead to decreasing individual moral standards. Under such circumstances, it becomes increasingly difficult to establish a market-oriented economic order in the future. Second, the fiscal problems have led to another wave of monetisation which was prohibited by the central bank law of December 1994. Despite the ban, the central bank indirectly gave loans to the government by holding about 70 per cent of governmental bonds (commonly with the state-owned Sberbank) (Götz 1999, p. 11). The first economic plan, initiated directly after the crisis in 1998, contained the intention to legally rely on monetisation, but was dismissed by the IMF (ibid., pp. 8f).

In addition, there has been an increase in barter trade which in 1998 accounted for about half of all industrial sales (IMF 1999a, p. 141). Even taxes were paid in real goods instead of in money. The system of relative prices as a tool of enhancing information about scarcity obviously did not work.[19] After the real depreciation of the rouble in late 1998, barter trade decreased. However, this development did not document a behavioural shift of Russian enterprises, but reflected higher profitability of using cash instead of trading real assets, in particular for export-oriented industries (Gaddy and Ickes 2000). The causes of barter still exist. Consequently, the demand for money has been very low compared to the demand for money in industrialised countries. Real balances fell between 1991 and 2000.

External controls of Russian economic policy through international organisations did not work properly either. The IMF has been criticised for

19 Barter trade is not only costly, but also shifts resources from value-adding sectors to those destroying values. It also reduces the trust in markets and their ability to allocate resources due to scarcities.

focusing too extensively on macroeconomic data and for paying too little attention to the institutional setting in Russia (Welfens 1998, 1999). By making the help dependent on certain macroeconomic indicators, both the IMF and the Russian government neglected the microeconomic perspective: institutional factors did not play a major role in the decision of helping and – even more important – of how to help. Thus, external help proved to be an obstacle rather than a help to transition. In addition, between 1991 and 1998 the IMF gave contingent help of about 63 billion US dollars to Russia and added even more during 1999.

The monetary regime, in particular the central bank law of December 1994, provided a rather high legal degree of commitment (C_{uw} = 0.611). As an element of this commitment, the US-dollar exchange rate was fixed. Despite such a strong commitment, the stabilisation process in Russia after 1994 has not been sustainable. The annual inflation rate fell from more than 200 per cent in 1994 to 11 per cent in 1997. However, it rose again in 1998 and remained high throughout 1999 and 2000. With about 20 per cent it was above the target of 14 per cent for 2001 (Banco Central de Venezuela 2002). The exchange rate towards the US dollar had to be adjusted frequently. In 1998, Russia gave up the peg and introduced managed floating. This evidence has led to several reform proposals for the Russian monetary regime. The policy simulation carried out in the foregoing section revealed that an optimal degree of commitment ($C_{uw}* \approx 0.4$) is lower than the actually chosen degree.

A currency board for Russia was suggested before the 1994 monetary reform by Hanke, Jonung and Schuler (1993) and in September 1998 by a member of the Russian government. In principal, a minimum degree of commitment of C = 0.4 is required for a currency board to work. This condition is met by the policy simulation. However, a CBS obviously would not coincide with the institutional setting of the country. Political stability has to be assessed as being low, although the President has been in office for almost a decade. There was an unsuccessful coup *d'état* in the early 1990s, and there is a political reprisal, at least in the provinces. In addition, corruption is high which makes life rather insecure. Thus, the government's power is limited. The low level of fiscal stability has already been mentioned. Labour market flexibility cannot be regarded as being high, although the data for *LM*73 suggest the opposite (Appendix 3). It seems to be difficult to lay off workers and to reduce employment on the firm level regardless of the speed of the decline in production (IMF 1999a, pp. 30–32). In addition, the wage differentiation seems to be low (Gimpelson and Lippolt 1999). Openness of the country in terms of foreign trade by GDP in the 1990s was rather high. In 1998, nearly 50 per cent of GDP was exported and imported.

However, one has to consider that the GDP was continuously declined over this period (IMF 1999a, p. 38). Calculated as foreign trade per capita, openness is moderate. Finally, it cannot be assessed whether there is substantial public opposition to inflation in Russia. In a nutshell, a currency board may be too rigid to deal with the inflexibilities of the institutional setting in Russia. It might finally force the government to give up the board which would make further efforts to stabilise even more difficult.

As an alternative, it has been suggested to introduce a crawling peg because of the institutional setting in Russia (Welfens 1998, 1999). According to Welfens, the anchor should be a basket consisting of the US dollar and the Euro. A crawling peg is perfectly consistent with the results of the policy simulations. A lower degree of commitment would provide more flexibility for the Russian government as long as distortions in other policy areas are not removed. Technically, the exchange rate should be based on a market rate. It would be the economically best way to detect it by letting the rouble float against the reserve currencies for a limited period, e.g. 90 days. Thereafter, a base rate would be fixed with a band (e.g. ± 10 per cent). A monthly or quarterly crawl would be introduced next. Both the band and the crawl could be successively reduced when the stabilisation efforts have been fruitful.

To make a crawling peg work and to reduce the annual inflation rate sustainably, one has to assume a determined government which is strong enough to implement the first step of this 'reform chain'. Götz (1999, pp. 7f) has put forward a very interesting argument which makes this assumption not look as heroic as it seems: he has observed that political majorities in the government and in the Duma, the Russian parliament, in 1999 for the first time are very similar. Both are dominated by former communists and nationalists. Under such circumstance, the Duma will have difficulties in opposing political initiatives by this government for principal reasons. This happened regularly with former administrations. Following Götz, the paradox result of this anti-democratic coalition can be that it enhances parliamentarism and thereby political stability.

Applied to monetary policy, this coalition may come to the conclusion that inflation must be avoided and, therefore, should try to start a stabilisation programme. One reason for the change of mind might be that stable money can increase real tax revenue. The second reason can be international advice in favour of stabilisation combined with the prospects of further financial aid. However, good advice does not remove the main cause of unsustained Russian monetary policy, namely the threat of permanent monetisation of public budget deficits, either explicitly (and illegally) via borrowing from the central bank or implicitly through the central bank purchasing government bonds on the secondary market. In section IV, we have assumed that the projection for *SEIGN* is zero. This assumption can only be valid if the government protects itself strongly from printing money.

One alternative to escape this vicious circle is to delegate monetary policy to an international organisation, namely the IMF. Instead of a domestic agency, an external agency would be pursuing Russian monetary policy. Thus, the only difference with the actual monetary policy regime would be the nationality and the legal status of the monetary policymakers. The Russian government would conclude a contract with the IMF where the details of monetary policy are fixed. This contract would have a fixed term and could be prolonged if both parties desired. The actual Russian central bank law would have to be changed only slightly, especially the limitations to lending would have to be tightened. Two questions arise: (1) how can such an arrangement be made attractive for the Russian administration? (2) how should the monetary regime be ideally designed?

Ad 1): As such, the arrangement looks rather unattractive to the Russian government. It would be forced to give up national sovereignty in a period of political instability. Hence, to avoid this impression and – on the contrary – converse this proposal into a bargain for the Russian government, the contract should have additional elements. First, with the new monetary regime as an asset, Russia could be made a full and equal member of the G8, having all rights and duties a member normally has. Although Russia has been made a full member of G8 – created in Birmingham 1998 – there still exists G7 both at the summit and the ministerial level. The G7 regularly meets exclusively before the G8 summit officially starts (Hajnal 1999, pp. 26f). It can be assumed that Russia is still underrepresented in the G8 process. By a further integration into it, Russia would be able to obtain more international political weight. This appreciation is an internal political advantage. Second, the IMF could combine its engagement as the monetary agency with financial aid. For instance, the Fund could step in for the central bank by taking Russian governmental bonds into its portfolio and replacing them by foreign exchange. This would be a simple operation on the asset side of the central bank's balance sheet. Hence, the Russian government could advocate the contract in public as a concession to get the financial aid which would be a net transfer rather than a credit. Third, Russian citizens could be involved in the monetary regime. For instance, one or two Russian monetary policymakers could become members of the governing board of the monetary agency. It could be an element of the contract that the Russians gradually take over the monetary policy.

Ad 2): The second question is concerned about the details of monetary policy conducted by the IMF. As mentioned above, the central bank law would not necessarily have to be changed very much. To introduce a new currency would be unnecessary. Lending to the Russian government would have to be strictly prohibited. Price stability should be made the only objective of monetary policy, for given the IMF's inclination to flexibility, the Fund does not seem to be completely immunised against the logic of the Phillips curve, although its irrelevance has often been shown. However, price stability should not be defined as strictly as, e.g., within EMU. It could be defined as being reached with an annual inflation rate of 5 per cent rather than with lower ones. The crawling peg may help with meeting this objective. Political influence on monetary decisionmaking by the Russian government would have to be strictly rejected.[20] Thus, the IMF would run an independent central bank on behalf of the Russian government. From a theoretical monetary perspective, there is no difference between an independant central bank and a domestic central bank.

As a consequence of this arrangement, the Russian government by its own determination and by the help of external institutions could be induced to reform even more than the Russian monetary regime. The relatively austere monetary policy of the IMF would at least prevent monetisation of fiscal budget deficits. Thus, in the first place the government in collaboration with the Duma would be forced to find ways to finance its expenditures. As for the reputation of the IMF, by this arrangement it would rise as well because the Fund would match responsibility and competence.

b) Dollarisation in Ecuador

In Ecuador, consumer price inflation was more than 20 per cent per annum from 1983 through 1999. Accordingly, the sucre permanently depreciated against the US dollar within a flexible exchange rate system. This development has caused the Ecuadorian government to publicly announce its intention to officially dollarise the economy in early 2000. It received the approval of the IMF immediately. The dollarisation was planned as follows: from April 1 to September 30, 2000, both the US dollar and the sucre should be legal tender. Their ratio should be 25,000 sucre per 1 US dollar. After that, the US dollar was to become the only legal tender in Ecuador. Following the policy simulation for Ecuador, both a CBS and dollarisation is in the range of the optimal degree of commitment ($C_{uw}^* \approx 0.4$). In addition, the degree of economic freedom in Ecuador is rather high which leads to a higher optimal degree of commitment following equation (8.3b).

However, the institutional setting in Ecuador cannot be regarded as being in line with a very strong commitment. First, dollarisation makes the country

---

20 That does not exclude an escape clause for the government. In this case, however, the whole monetary regime is abandoned.

vulnerable to external shocks as it is dependent on oil exports (Rülle and Knees 2000). Moreover, the political situation at the end of 1999 was rather unstable. The latest (civilian) government took over after a coup *d'état* by the army. Fiscal stability is low rather than high. Thus, dollarisation can be seen as the signal to stop monetisation of public budget deficits and to increase fiscal discipline. As for public opposition to inflation, it may be high since indexation is only permitted for social security expenditures. Ecuador was hit by a flooding in 1998 which can be seen as an external shock (Appendix 2, subsection III.d). This certainly contributed to the poor economic situation at the beginning of 2000. As long as there is not a similar shock in the near future, one can expect a higher fiscal discipline which makes a case for a strong commitment.

While Ecuador opts for dollarisation, it will make sense to use the IMF as external protector. Although the government seems to have broad support in parliament, the IMF can support the reform by making further help contingent on the government's willingness to adhere to such a monetary regime. Indeed, the IMF and other IOs (World Bank, Inter-American Development Bank and the Corporación Andina de Fomento) reacted promptly to the new monetary regime by announcing they would financially support Ecuador's ambitious reform plans contingent on further reform steps to be taken by the Ecuadorian government (IMF 2000).

c) A currency board for Venezuela?

Another country that has experienced chronic inflation for the last 20 years is Venezuela. Annual inflation rates were between 6.3 and 99.9 per cent and rather volatile. In the 1990s, on average, inflation was about 50 per cent per year. However, a hyperinflation could be avoided in the past. Nevertheless, in the late 1990s the country was hit by a severe economic crisis that not only affected price stability. The public budget slipped into a deficit again, after two years of fiscal surplus (1996 and 1997). The deficit has been financed only to a low extent with the help of monetary policy; seigniorage as defined in Appendix 2 (*SEIGN*) has not exceeded the value of 0.071 in the period of 1995 through 1998. Official employment figures indicate a rise in unemployment to about 12 per cent of the workforce in the late 1990s (IMF 1999b). As compared to 1993, real GDP per capita in 1998 fell by 4 per cent. In 1999 the situation did not improve. The recession has contributed to a rather 'good' monetary performance: the 1999 inflation rate is estimated to be below 25 per cent (Duscha 1999).

The reasons for this poor economic performance are purely domestic. Economic policy in any area in Venezuela has not been focused on rules, but rather on discretion. A long established problem of Venezuela is its high share of public enterprises, the most important being the petroleum sector. This has at least two disadvantageous consequences: first, the low efficiency of state-owned firms contributes to a meagre return on investments. Second, the state strongly depends on petroleum turnovers and, thus, on the oil prices. Due to this dependence on oil, Venezuela has suffered from the Dutch disease (Moll 1994), i.e. other industries did not have much chance to develop. This was even increased by the government controlling the allocation of foreign exchange (World Bank 1996). In addition, the government has introduced price controls, in particular for prices of public services and fuel which are kept very low. Indexation is widely prohibited.

In terms of the institutional setting, Venezuela is in a mixed state. Openness is high and has increased throughout the 1990s. The sum of exports and imports accounts for about 60 per cent of GDP. Fiscal stability is very fragile and highly dependent on oil sales (see above). There is no exact knowledge about public opposition to inflation. Nevertheless, given that price controls exist and that annual inflation rates have not been skyrocketing and despite the abolition of indexation, they can be regarded as being moderate. Wages are set centrally. The labour market regime is not likely to contribute to the flexibility of the labour force and to a rise in employment in due course. As regards political stability, there is no clear evidence. The new government, inaugurated in late 1998, tried to weaken the opposition through decrees which is generally assessed as being undemocratic. Notwithstanding, the government seems to have broad support in the public. The main question from a reformer's point of view is whether or not this support would last in case a comprehensive reform package is intended.

Monetary policy is pursued by the Banco Central de Venezuela. The Venezuelan central bank law forces the central bank to follow several objectives, among others to support the government's general economic policy. Direct loans to the government as well as local authorities are prohibited. The central bank is not responsible for the regulation of the banking sector which is given to a specialised agency. This agency has been successful after the 1994/95 banking crisis (IMF 1998, pp. 18–26).[21] In the last two decades, the exchange rate system was changed several times. At the end of 1999, Venezuela had a crawling peg system with a unified exchange rate fixing the Bolivar to the US dollar. There are no convertibility restrictions. Thus, the formal degree of monetary commitment is on a medium level. Nevertheless, the overall economic order is not likely to increase stability in the next few years.

This evidence has led to suggestions that should completely reform its economic order. The core of the reform package is the introduction of a

21 However, the regulation has to be improved.

currency board (Cordeiro 1998). Following him, the bolivar should be pegged to the US dollar. The question is whether such a strong commitment is adequate. The policy simulation for Venezuela yielded an optimal degree of legal commitment which makes a currency board viable ($C_{uw}* \approx 0.52$). For the simulation we assumed a rather high political stability and an ambitiously planned annual post-reform inflation rate. Given these assumptions are realistic, a CBS may well contribute to credibility and stability in Venezuela.

In case Venezuela follows the advice to introduce a currency board, some aspects can be important. As experiences with currency boards in other countries have shown, a high backing of the money base with foreign exchange (80 to 100 per cent) is crucial. In August 1999, Venezuela's reserves were too small to cover the money base: about two-thirds of the money base were covered by international reserves (Banco Central de Venezuela 1999), but it can be expected that privatisation revenues and petroleum sales will allow the threshold to be reached relatively fast.[22] To introduce a new currency seems to be unnecessary. As for the organisational structure, again there are some lessons to be drawn from foreign experiences. The board could have two departments, the issue and the banking departments. The issue department would be responsible for the exchange of US dollar into bolivars and vice versa and the investment of foreign reserve. The banking department would administer excess foreign exchange as well as old assets like governmental bonds. To the extent of the excess foreign reserves, the banking department could act as a central bank. The establishment of the CBS could consist of the following steps (Hanke and Schuler 1994, pp. 59–62):

1. Prior to the regime switch, the introduction of a currency board with the US dollar as reserve currency is announced.
2. For a short – previously fixed – time (≤ 90 days) the bolivar floats against the US dollar. Thereby, the 'correct' exchange rate is determined.
3. After that, the exchange rate to the US dollar is fixed taking the market rate.
4. The central bank is dissolved and the board is introduced. It immediately starts its operations.

The political feasibility of the economic reform seems to be reasonably high. Because of the severe economic crisis and the sluggishness of the economy in the last two decades, there are many supporters of reforms. In

[22] In addition to a monetary reform, a privatisation law and a unilateral liberalisation of foreign trade should be considered. Both were successfully pursued in Argentina in 1991 (Chapter 7).

addition, the actual inflation is costly and there is public support for a currency board. Under the – inevitable – assumption that the government is determined to pursue and implement a reform, a currency board has good chances of being implemented.

VI. ANOTHER MONETARY REFORM FOR ARGENTINA AND POLAND?

a) Argentina: is the CBS sustainable?[23]

Although Argentina has been subject to contagion effects during the crises in Mexico 1994/95 and Brazil 1999/2000, the success of its currency board system cannot be denied. Nevertheless, during 1999 a decision was made to give up the currency board and to dollarise the Argentine economy. The first step was made by the government in January 1999 announcing plans to introduce the US dollar as the single legal tender. It already became a legal tender besides the peso with the establishment of the currency board system in April 1991 (Chapter 7).

This proposal has been supported by Hanke and Schuler (1999) who not only inspect all arguments pro and contra dollarisation in their paper, but also provide a manual for the regime switch and a very simple dollarisation law. It is worth scrutinising their arguments for they are appealing. The main arguments in favour of dollarisation are the following (ibid., pp. 406–408): first, Argentines are already sceptical about the peso and to a large extent hold the US dollar. To take the consumers' sovereignty seriously would inevitably lead to dollarisation. Second, the transition costs of an official dollarisation would be extremely low as the de-facto dollarisation of the Argentine economy is high. Third, interest rates will decrease when all transactions are made in the US dollar. Fourth, following a government memorandum, dollarisation promises an additional two percentage points to the trend rate of economic growth. Fifth, property rights will be directly enforced, if Argentines do not only hold the right to demand US dollars when they wish, but hold US-dollars directly. Finally, the authors claim that historical evidence is on their side: in developing countries, central banks

---

23 The main line of argument of this subsection eas developed before 2001. As the problem of the crisis has not been inflation, we do not discuss the current situation but a suggestion related to monetary policy.

were less successful with guaranteeing stability than more rule-based systems, among them currency boards (ibid., p. 411; Schuler 1996).

In addition, they dismiss all counter-arguments (Hanke and Schuler 1999, pp. 408–412): first, some observers argue that dollarisation diminishes monetary flexibility even below the level reached by the board. Hanke and Schuler simply declare flexibility as undesirable. In the Argentine case, the government's sovereignty has already been given up by implementing the currency board system. Second, as for the function of the central bank as lender of last resort, they argue that it can be executed by the government or another state agency. Third, and similarly, the exchange rate's function as shock absorber and instrument of economic policy would be abandoned if the economy was dollarised. Following Hanke and Schuler, other policy variables can easily step in. Fourth, some people fear that the US dollar may become unstable which cannot be regarded as being a serious argument.

The arguments in favour of dollarisation surely make sense economically. However, they hold almost equally currency boards as well. Only the fact that interest rates on peso-based loans are higher than on US-dollar-based loans would be a case in favour of dollarisation. However, the Argentine government will have to pay higher interests on international capital markets, as long as the risks in Argentina are perceived higher than in other countries, regardless of the currency the debt is denominated in. The US-dollar-denominated governmental bonds (BONEX) have always borne a higher interest than US bonds. The two percentage points higher trend rate of growth cannot be proven. Against it stands the loss in seigniorage from issuing pesos. Consumers' sovereignty which, following Hanke and Schuler, is a major advantage of dollarisation, is already taken seriously. The Argentine citizens can hold as high a share of their money in US dollars as they wish, and they can make almost all payments in US dollar. If they really wished, they could hold even more US dollars. This argument against the CBS in favour of dollarisation is weak, too.

So, it has to be examined whether the currency board is about to break down which would make an even stronger external commitment necessary. There are no signs for such a development. Rather, it can be suspected that the announcement of the Argentine government to dollarise was made to quieten the international public and to repeat its will to commit to strict monetary policy rules. Due to the fiscal and political crisis in the country, in 2001 the policy in Argentina changed again. The currency board arrangement was slightly changed, giving the government the option to add the Euro as a reserve currency. The crisis even led many people to speculate about an untimely end of the currency board and the introduction of a less strict commitment (e.g. Hausmann 2001).

As it indeed seems inappropriate to give up a currency board in a weak position (Chapter 4, subsection II.c), we would not recommend the pursuit of a monetary reform a few years after the establishment of a well-functioning currency board in either direction. In addition, the optimal degree of commitment obtained through the policy simulation ($C_{uw}* \approx 0.7$) is quite close to the actual degree of commitment($C_{uw} = 0.798$). Given the fact that the Argentine currency board has worked extremely well (annual inflation rate in 1998 and 1999 near zero) and given the Argentine experience with repeated monetary reforms, there seems to be no need for another reform attempt.[24] Rather, it seems necessary to sort out fiscal problems immediately[25] and in a few years time opt for a more flexible monetary regime.

b) Poland and its way to the European Monetary Union

Argentina and Poland can be well compared. Both countries have only recently introduced a new monetary regime; both reforms have been successful (although in the Polish case less convincing by) and both are subject to debates about the future monetary policy. The arguments in the Argentine case are all well known and the situation has not changed recently. Thus, no case for another reform can be made. This is different in Poland: since the monetary reform in 1995, it has been necessary to tighten the monetary and fiscal regime. Moreover, new arguments for monetary policy have been put forward. The main reason for Poland to rethink its monetary regime is its determination to join the European Union (EU) and finally the European Monetary Union (EMU). To meet this ambitious objective, efforts to reform the economic order are necessary. But even without this objective, changes '...are indispensable in their own right if the momentum of the catch-up process is to be maintained' (OECD 1998, p. 11). Therefore, it has been suggested that Poland introduces a currency board with the Euro as reserve currency (Freytag 2001a). This – politically certainly controversial – suggestion will be discussed in what follows.

To begin with, one has to clarify whether or not Poland is well suited for a currency board. The policy simulation has revealed that a currency board is certainly within the range of the possible monetary regimes for Poland. Under the assumption that Poland strives for stability (2 per cent average annual inflation rate in the following five years), the optimal degree of commitment is rather high ($C_{uw}* \approx 0.8$). Thus, a currency board as a strong commitment is suitable.

---

24 Obviously, advocating dollarisation mirrors belief rather than analysis: 'Because Argentina does not have an orthodox currency board and has been unwilling to make the system orthodox,..., dollarization is desirable' (Hanke and Schuler 1999, p. 407).

25 The main problem seems to be the unsettled relationship between the central government and the 23 provinces of the country. The latter obviously do not care about fiscal stability.

This assessment can be confirmed by a closer look at the institutional setting. Political stability in Poland can be regarded as being high. Poland has become a democracy of Western style and will be one of the first Eastern and Central European countries to join the EU. Fiscal stability is improving. However, the causes of past problems have not been completely erased. During the 1990s, public spending regularly exceeded public revenues. This would be a minor problem if the public budget deficits were transitory in nature, e.g. caused by a recession. However, public deficits were caused by structural problems: first, still too many enterprises are state-driven and produce high losses. This is partly due to an inappropriate privatisation law.[26] Second, the tax system is working inefficiently. A third factor contributing to ongoing fiscal problems in the present and future is the organisation of the old-age protection system. It seems unable to deal with the demographic development in Poland where the share of retired persons who have earned a claim on the system probably will rise sharply. Given these circumstances, the government has been permanently tempted to plea for inflation to solve its budget problem. Since the early 1990s, the NBP has increasingly lent money to the central government and public enterprises (Ugolini 1996, p. 17). Although there is progress as regards fiscal policy, it seems too early to '...conclude that Poland runs sustainable fiscal policy and can be regarded as a successful reformer' (Budina and van Wjinbergen 1997, p. 57). There are still many potential threats to fiscal sustainability. In mid-2001, fiscal policy in Poland turned out to be unsustainable. It is expected that in the year 2002 the budget deficit will amount to almost 10 per cent of GDP. In addition, although the government seems to be determined to refrain from seigniorage as a means to finance its expenditures, political pressure arose to ease monetary policy (Ludwig, 2001).

As for labour market flexibility, it can be regarded as still being rather low (Chapter 7, section III). The wage-setting process in Poland seems to be rather corporatist in nature and may systematically lead to wages higher than economically feasible (OECD 1998, pp. 87–89). The degree of openness is high (*Table 8.1*). It can also be taken for granted that there is a remarkable public opposition to inflation. Indexation is not permitted, prices have been mainly freed in the 1990s and the public experienced rather high inflation during this decade.

Even under the realistic assumption that the government is firmly determined to keep the price level stable, the actual monetary regime (central bank with a crawling peg) does not completely rule out the danger of persistent inflation of about 10 per cent or even higher, depending on external

---

26 See OECD (1998, chapter III). For an overview see also Donges and Wieners (1994) and Bornstein (1997).

influences. Apart from the fact that inflation at this level is costly, Poland wants to join the EU soon, and there is no guarantee that Poland may never become subject to contagion of financial or monetary crises elsewhere (IMF a, May 1998, pp. 83–88). Hence, the foregoing analysis has made clear that there may be a case for establishing a currency board in Poland.

The introduction of the currency board may be part of an overall reform that is credible. Given that the pressure to allow for monetary expansion incompatible with stability arises from fiscal problems, a high degree of commitment can be introduced simultaneously with a fiscal reform. The latter seems inevitable, as otherwise Poland would have difficulties to be among the first to join the European Union, let alone the EMU (Ludwig 2001). It can be assumed that such an effort will be credible. Poland is a case for an overall reform as discussed in Chapter 4, section IV of this study.

Table 8.3: Foreign Trade of Poland: EU, Central and Eastern Europe and the Rest of the World 1992–1999[1]

	1992	1993	1994	1995	1996	1997	1998	1999
Imports from EU	53.1	57.3	57.5	64.7	63.9	63.8	65.6	64.9
Imports from CEE	16.3	13.4	14.1	15.4	15.6	14.9	13.1	14.2
Imports from ROW	30.6	29.3	28.4	19.1	20.5	21.3	21.3	20.9
Exports to EU	57.9	63.3	62.7	70.0	66.3	64.2	68.3	70.5
Exports to CEE	15.4	13.2	14.5	17.2	20.5	24.3	20.5	17.0
Exports to ROW	26.7	23.5	22.8	12.8	13.2	11.5	11.2	12.5

Notes: [1]: as per cent of overall trade.
Source: OECD 1998, p. 154,;Polish Official Statistics (2001).

Given that the Euro will remain a sound currency, it is adequate to become the reserve currency for the currency board, as the following considerations show. By choosing the Euro, Poland could, first, import stability and, second, protect itself as much as possible from real external shocks in the reserve country (EMU). Many other currencies will be pegged to the Euro, at least all those currencies pegged to the D-Mark in early 2000. These are to a great extent currencies of countries whose firms compete with the firms in Poland. A nominal appreciation of the Euro, therefore, would not worsen price and non-price competitiveness of the Polish firms relative to their competitors in third countries. Moreover, the production structure in EMU differs from the production structure of the Polish economy. Hence, productivity shocks in EMU members would not negatively affect many firms there (Statistisches Bundesamt 1996, pp. 79–114). In addition, Polands foreign trade with potential EMU members (that is EU members) has been steadily intensifying since the end of cold war (*Table 16*). Poland also trades a great deal with Central European countries and has stabilised its trade share with these countries. This provides another reason why the effects of a potential nominal appreciation of the Euro will be small.

Finally, some remarks on the political feasibility of a currency board for Poland. By introducing a currency board, the government gives away all discretionary power in monetary policy. This gives reason for the argument that the introduction of a currency board is equal to a loss in sovereignty. This argument implicitly assumes that discretionary power of governments automatically means sovereignty. However, the Polish government does not voluntarily run budget deficits which then contribute to inflation. Rather, it should eagerly try to quickly bring down inflation. Moreover, rule-oriented monetary policy provides the opportunity for the government to gain a reputation and for the monetary policy to become credible. In addition, a stronger monetary commitment can help with implementing sustainable fiscal policy and even a more flexible labour market which currently is rather rigid. Thus, instead of bringing a loss in sovereignty, the CBS in fact raises the sovereignty of the government in relation to vested interests in the country.

Further help to improve the economic order in general can be expected externally as the following considerations show. A currency board normally is not meant to be a permanent institution. If, and only if, monetary policy has reached credibility and has successfully stabilised will it be appropriate to establish a central bank again. Since it is planned that Poland will go for membership in the EMU, it should be part of the reform that the currency board will be abandoned as soon as Poland will have met the Maastricht criteria. It will become a member of the EMU immediately afterwards. Such an arrangement[27] provides another advantage: if it is difficult to pursue a monetary and fiscal policy which is compatible with stability for political economy reasons, it will be similarly difficult to introduce a currency board on the same political economy grounds. Thus, a way to implement the monetary reform is by making the monetary regime switch (the CBS) part of the accession negotiation with the EU. In this scenario, the EU would insist on a credible monetary regime such as the currency board for a transition period before Poland eventually becomes a EMU member. From the point of view of the Polish government, the dirty work is done by the EU. Internal reform is backed by external pressure.

---

[27] For a detailed analysis of the potential reform process itself see Freytag (2001b).

9. Summary and Conclusion

I. SUMMARY IN BRIEF

Success and failure of monetary reforms in history have been analysed in numerous contributions. Despite this rich and fascinating literature, progress as regards the probability of a reform being successful can hardly be perceived. Especially during recent crises in Latin America and Eastern Europe, the gathered expertise did not reach unambiguous conclusions and policy proposals. Rather, many proposals contradicted each other, partly using inconsistent methods. The study presented here has obtained considerable stimulus by the perception of various shortcomings in the literature on monetary commitment and the appropriate monetary regime to be introduced by a reform. One problem is that many contributions to the literature on commitment versus discretion do not employ a comprehensive definition of commitment. Either it is not fully elaborated what is meant by commitment, or commitment is set equal to central bank independence. The conclusions derived from these studies for economic policy are often highly questionable. We focused on this problem in Chapter 2.

A second, somewhat related shortcoming of the macroeconomic literature, is the almost entire neglect of institutions or problems with the economic order. Given the complexity of the models applied in the macroeconomic literature, the lack of institutions in the analysis is understandable. As long as this strand of literature is used as input for subsequent policy-oriented research, one can interpret this as a trade of clarity against complexity. Thus, this procedure makes perfect sense. However, if the outcome is used to derive immediate policy conclusions and to propose reforms, the quality of the recommendation has to be doubted. We make use of this literature as input for our analysis of the relation of commitment and institutions as a prerequisite for successful reforms in Chapters 3 and 4.

A third problem is that discussions within economics science about changes in the monetary regime are often carried out with considerable personal involvement and less so with a clear analytical mind. To give an example, monetary stabilisation programmes are often characterised as being 'orthodox' or 'heterodox'. These attributes are better used when dealing with questions of faith than with economic analyses. Unfortunately, especially those regimes characterised by a high degree of legal commitment and by a high success in history are advocated with much – almost religious – emphasis. The fact that proposals are backed by personal emphasis rather than by analytical clarity is likely to give discredit to good policy regimes and worsens the position of those policymakers in government and in the civil service who are in favour of rule-bound policy. We try to make a case for a rule-bound monetary policy by a careful theoretical analysis (Chapters 2 through 4) which is tested empirically in Chapters 5 through 7. Both econometrics and case studies are employed. Thereby, the basis for a discussion of credible policy options (Chapter 8) can be laid. Before drawing some general conclusions from the study, we first summarise the results in seven short statements.

1) Monetary reforms are only successful in creating credibility and stability, if the government makes a commitment to a rule-bound monetary policy.

We have found a strong theoretical argument for this thesis which has been backed by empirical scrutiny. It has turned out in both the econometric analysis and the case studies that monetary reforms inevitably failed when there was no or a very low commitment by the government. The variable for the legal degree of commitment, *C*, is significantly negative correlated with the post-reform inflation rate throughout all the estimations. The case studies forcefully added to this outcome.

2) In addition, legal monetary commitment needs to be backed by a strong determination of the government to stabilise. Otherwise, even strong commitment is not sufficient for a success.

It is very difficult for a government to establish a credible rule-bound monetary policy if it does not give the impression that it is strongly willing to execute the reform and that it will under no circumstances deviate from the new regime. This demands a minimum of political stability (variable *PS*), as the case of Paraguay (high *C* but low *PS*) shows.

3) Similarly important is the requirement that governments strictly separate monetary and fiscal policy.

If the government in the post-reform period is unable to finance its expenditure through tax and tariff revenues or via borrowing on ordinary capital markets or if the government is unwilling to cut expenditures, the reform is bound to fail. In all cases analysed in Chapter 7 and throughout the complete sample of the 29 monetary reforms in Chapter 6, it is a distinctive feature for the success of reforms whether the government abstains from the money press or not. This is a well-known conclusion drawn in the literature on monetary commitment and reform confirmed in this study by the application of an alternative method.

4) There is no *per se* superior monetary regime to be introduced by a monetary reform.

In history, some policy regimes have been more successful than others, particularly in developing countries. Among the most successful types of monetary policy, the currency board system has an impressive track record. Nevertheless, this does not mean that every developing country should introduce a currency board without a careful and detailed analysis of the economic order and its relation to monetary policy; in other words, the institutional setting. To the contrary, a currency board system demands for a number of institutional prerequisites which are not met by every country in question.

5) Institutions are important constraints for a monetary policy reform. The commitment has to be made in accordance with the institutional setting.

Apart from political stability, there are other relevant institutional factors that have to be taken into account when pursuing a monetary reform. Fiscal stability, labour market flexibility, openness and public opposition to inflation restrain the reformer's choice. Those countries relying on a nominal anchor have to consider the properties of a potential reserve currency. Alternatively, a variable for economic freedom has proved to cover the institutional setting satisfactorily. In addition, we have developed an ex-ante proxy for credibility that is based on the relationship between monetary commitment and the institutional setting in a country. It allows us to assess the chances of a monetary reform being successful in advance. Although theoretically appealing, the ex-ante measure has not proven to be econometrically robust. It has to be further improved to definitely be of use for policy options. Especially, the data set applied in the empirical analysis has to be further advanced. Similarly, tested individually in the econometric chapter, the institutional factors have only shown a mixed performance. However, jointly and in addition to both monetary commitment and a proxy for seigniorage, they can very well explain the post-reform inflation rate. The case studies confirm the importance of institutions as constraints.

6) External help can improve the probability of a successful monetary reform. However, it is not a substitute for both commitment and determination of the government to stabilise.

External help is a common feature of a great number of reforms regardless of their fate. External advisers can be used to dignify a reform attempt; the assistance of international organisations (IOs) is an appropriate scapegoat for internal reforms. IOs do the dirty work of governments. However, unless the government is not full-heartedly resolute in its efforts to stabilise, the reliance on external assistance is of no use. This result is mainly drawn from the case studies.

External help can be made politically worthy by fixing it in the domestic constitution. This can be done by giving the citizens the right to sue the government in case it does not adhere to international agreements and contracts it has signed. If the charge proves to be justified, the government has to be sentenced by the domestic constitutional court to comply with the agreement. The internal sovereignty of the government as the citizens' agent and in relation to organised interests is enhanced by this proposal.

7) Credible policy advice neither simplifies the matter nor does it claim the *per se* superiority or inferiority of certain policy regimes. Instead, it has to consider institutional details very carefully.

To consider these restrictions as an adviser surely enhances the quality of policy advice. The advice then is based on thorough analysis and, thus, exerts pressure on those groups in the society opposing the monetary reform. The policy adviser is not forced to consider the feasibility of proposals derived from careful theoretical reasoning and backed by empirical assessment. Rather, the better the advice is supported by painstaking enquiry, the higher its political feasibility will be.

II. FURTHER RESEARCH

The objective of the study has been to contribute to the knowledge about why monetary reforms in history have had so different a destiny. The study is meant to broaden the perspective by confirming some known upshots as well as by generating new knowledge. It is trivial to mention that every research output is only valid until a more strongly founded alternative is uncovered. This generally holds. Notwithstanding, there is undoubtedly also the case for further research based on the results of this study. In this sense, future analysis can focus on two major fields.

First, the analysis of monetary reforms can be deepened along the lines of this study. Although the results are rather promising and confirm well-known insights as well as exploring new territory, there is potential for further improvement on the outcome. This can be done in two ways. First, the number of cases can be increased. We have investigated 12 monetary reforms out of a sample of at least 70 reforms that have taken place in the 20th century. Additional cases may confirm the results of this study; they may also reveal that there are other country-specific features of monetary policy and reform.

Second, and more importantly, the data used in the econometric chapter of this study is far from perfect. In particular, the international comparison of labour market flexibility has to be improved. But also other institutional factors probably can be modelled in a better way. It is furthermore desirable to increase the knowledge on legal monetary commitment. In fact, it seems that the access to central bank laws and statutes has been made considerably easier via the Internet than was the case some years ago. The same may hold for other data used in the econometric analysis. There is much to be done, both conceptionally and concerning the database. Given the new technical opportunities, optimism seems to be justified.

Whereas the first direction of further analysis is dealing exactly with our economic problem, a second field of further research we have identified in the course of this study is dedicated to a different question. It makes sense to apply the theoretical concept used here to monetary policy of industrialised countries that do not change their monetary regime. It can be asked whether the monetary performance in those countries depends on the relationship between monetary commitment and the institutional setting. In particular, the empirical research on this topic hitherto has focused on central bank independence (CBI) as the variable for monetary commitment and has neglected institutions as constraints. Consequently, the results of these studies are rather disappointing. They do not confirm a correlation between CBI and low inflation unambiguously. A more comprehensive approach may be fruitful.

For this purpose, the theoretical model presented here has to be slightly altered. The threats to stability identified in the political economy framework are others than in case of regime switches after a period of severe inflation. Instead of the need for seigniorage, the inflexibility of labour markets and the government's inability to combat unemployment may exert pressure on governments to opt for permissive monetary policy. The theoretical model has to be adjusted to meet this argument. However, the method is similar. Costs of commitment have to be modelled correspondingly.

The econometric approach can be extended to a time series analysis. For each industrialised country there is a huge database available. The degree of monetary commitment as well as the institutional setting is subject to permanent change. Given the number of countries that can be investigated and the long time for which data exists, in a panel analysis, it may be possible to operate with a far bigger sample than we do in the enquiry of monetary reforms. In addition, the data of the institutional setting may be of higher quality for industrialised countries only. The international comparability certainly is higher. Moreover, it is also possible to assess each country in a time series analysis which can be an alternative, if the institutional factors are not easily comparable over several countries.

III. CONCLUSIONS

Monetary policy is one of the most important, if not the most important, economic policy fields. It affects the daily life and well-being of the whole economy with no exceptions. History is full of examples of poor monetary policy. The causes for this poor performance have been revealed by economists many times and long ago. Governments were unable to pursue adequate policies in other fields of economic order without falling back on monetary policy. Consequently, economic history is also history of monetary reforms. They always have been and probably always will be subject to both controversial political debates and mindful economic investigation.

This study is a contribution to the latter and has aimed at a better understanding of why some monetary reforms failed and others succeeded. It has confirmed the general acknowledgement that monetary commitment rather than discretion is a device to stabilise expectations and to create credibility of monetary policy. Monetary reforms without commitment to rules are most likely bound to fail. Besides this, it has been confirmed again that reforms of other policy fields are sometimes inevitable, fiscal policy being of utmost significance. In addition, the study has tried to add in other determinants of success or failure of reforms, namely institutions. The explanatory power of our model is higher than that of many models in the relevant literature. This is a very promising outcome, notably given that the issue at hand has an enormous political relevance.

Consequently, the final and outstanding objective of this endeavour is to provide policy options that enable governments of countries with monetary problems to choose the monetary regime with the highest probability of success. We have argued that this is given when the economic order or, to put it differently, the institutional setting is considered. Both theory and evidence have supported this argument. We have also elaborated policy options for five countries based on our findings.

Since economic policymaking is such a difficult field, in particular implementing an economic reform, all policy recommendations have been substantially backed by thorough analysis. We hope that the instruments developed here provide both good economic foundation and political feasibility. We are aware of the fact that reform is a long and strenuous process; however, we are convinced that better economic understanding is the best economists can contribute to ease this process. It is up to the politicians to put this increasing knowledge into practice.

Appendix 1: Sample of Countries

In Appendix 1, the countries used for the cross-sectional analysis reported in *Table 1*, Chapter 2, section II, p 19, are listed.

Table A.1a Sample of 51 Countries

Africa			
Burundi	Ethiopia	Ghana	Kenya
Mauritius	Nigeria	Sierra Leone	South Africa
Swaziland	Tanzania	Uganda	
Asia			
Bhutan	China	Fiji	India
Korea	Malaysia	Nepal	Pakistan
The Philippines	Sri Lanka	Thailand	
Europe and Middle East			
Bahrain	Cyprus	Iran	Israel
Jordan	Oman	Turkey	United Arab Emirates
Latin America and Caribbean			
Argentina	Belize	Bolivia	Chile
Costa Rica	Dominican Republic	Ecuador	El Salvador
Guatemala	Guyana	Haiti	Honduras
Mexico	Nicaragua	Peru	Uruguay
Venezuela			
Middle and Eastern Europe			
Czech Republic	Poland	Romania	Russian Federation

Table A.1b Sample of 28 Countries with Annual Inflation Rates of at Least 10 Per Cent

Africa			
Burundi	Ethiopia	Ghana	Nigeria
Sierra Leone	Swaziland	Tanzania	
Asia			
China	India	Pakistan	
Middle East and Europe			
Iran	Israel	Turkey	
Latin America and Caribbean			
Bolivia	Costa Rica	Ecuador	El Salvador
Guatemala	Haiti	Honduras	Mexico
Nicaragua	Peru	Uruguay	Venezuela
Middle and Eastern Europe			
Poland	Romania	Russian Federation	

Table A.1c Sample of 25 Transition Countries

Albania	Belarus	Bulgaria	Croatia
Czech Republic	Estonia	Hungary	Latvia
Lithuania	Macedonia	Moldova	Poland
Romania	Slovak Republic	Slovenia	Ukraine
Russian Federation	Armenia	Azerbaijan	Georgia
Kyrgyz Republic	Mongolia	Tajikistan	Turkmenistan
Uzbekistan			

Appendix 2: Detailed Explanations and Alternative Specifications of the Variables

MEASURING COMMITMENT

To measure the degree of commitment, an index of commitment has been introduced in Chapter 2. The index is constructed along the lines of an index of central bank independence (Cukierman 1992). It is the (unweighted and weighted) average of the following ten criteria which characterise the monetary regime.

- Various *objectives* of monetary policy can be thought of, e.g. price stability, employment, external equilibrium etc. If price stability is the only objective, the commitment is the highest.
- The higher the *constitutional level* on which the monetary regime is laid down, the higher the commitment.
- The lower the *discretionary power* left to the government, the higher the degree of commitment.
- *External obligations*, like an external anchor or contingent help by the IMF or other IOs, also raise commitment.
- The *appointment and dismissal procedures* of monetary policymakers have influence on the degree of commitment.
- Limitations on *lending* to the government is crucial for the degree of commitment. If lending is allowed, commitment is low.
- *Convertibility* restrictions also diminish the degree of commitment since they indicate that the government is not willing to accept international competition for mobile resources.
- *Competitive elements* in the monetary regime, e.g. the legally admitted circulation of a foreign currency, indicate a high degree of commitment.
- *Regulatory issues* exert influence of the degree of commitment. However, if monetary authorities have regulatory power, the effect of the degree of commitment is ambiguous.
- The same holds for the *accountability* of the monetary authorities. They should be accountable but not subject to directives. The boundaries between the two are not perfectly clear.

Table A.2 shows the codings of these criteria in detail.

Table A.2 Codings of the Index of Commitment

Criterion	Com-pon ent	Explanation	Numerical codings
Objectives of monetary policy	*obj*	1. Price stability only goal	1.00
		2. Other objectives mentioned	0.50
		3. No goals for monetary policy	0.00
Level on which monetary regime is established	*const*	1. Constitution	1.00
		2. Central bank law	0.66
		3. Decree	0.33
		4. Not fixed at all	0.00
Discretionar y power left to the government	*gov*	1. No power left to the government	1.00
		2. Exchange rate consulted between government and monetary authority	0.66
		3. Exchange rate regime completely left to government	0.33
		4. Government may override monetary authority as regards monetary policy	0.00
External pledge of the government	*extern*	1. Exchange rate fixed to a hard currency and money base fully backed with foreign reserves	1.00
		2. Exchange rate fixed	0.75
		3. Crawling peg	0.50
		4. Conditional help accepted	0.25
		5. No external pledge	0.00
Conditions of appointment and dismissal of monetary CEO	*Ceo*	1. CEO must be a reputed expert	1.00
		2. No expertise demanded	0.00
	Diss	1. Appointment with fixed term and dismissal only after bad performance	1.00
		2. No rules for dismissal	0.50
		3. Dismissal unconditioned or linked to resignation of governments and single politicians	0.00

Criterion	Com-pon ent	Explanation	Numerical codings
Limitations on lending to the government	*Lim*	1. Monetary authority is prohibited to give credit to the public	1.00
		2. Monetary authority is allowed to purchase public bonds in hard currency on the secondary market	0.66
		3. Monetary authority is allowed to purchase public bonds in any currency on the secondary market and to give the statr limited credit	0.33
		4. No limitations on lending	0.00
Convertibility restrictions	*conv*	1. Full convertibility	1.00
		2. Partial convertibility	0.75
		3. Convertibility for current account transactions only	0.50
		4. Convertibility for capital account transactions only	0.25
		5. No convertibility	0.00
	mult	1. One exchange rate	1.00
		2. Multiple exchange rate	0.00
Competitive elements in the monetary regime	*comp*	1. A hard currency can be used for all transactions	1.00
		2. A hard currency can be used for some transactions	0.66
		3. A hard currency may be held	0.33
		4. No holdings or transactions in hard currencies allowed	0.00
Financial market regulation	*reg*	1. Financial market regulation is assigned to a separated bureau	1.00
		2. Financial market regulation is assigned to monetary authority	0.50
		3. No financial market regulation	0.00
Accountability of the monetary authority	*acc*	1. Obligation to inform the public on a regular basis	1.00
		2. Obligation to inform the parliament in public hearings	0.66
		3. Obligation to inform the government without publicity	0.33
		4. No accountability	0.00

The reason why C will be calculated both as a weighted average (C_{w1} through C_{w2}) and as an unweighted average (C_{uw}) of all determining factors is rather simple. There are arguments for and against both methods. Normally, not all factors are of the same importance. By giving them different weights, these variations in importance can be taken into account properly. However, the perception of the importance of certain factors differs among individuals. The results then lose their intersubjective contestability. The weighting even may be abused to immunise the research from critique. As a consequence, the weighting has to be substantiated carefully. On the other hand, not to weight the factors would circumvent this problem. It can be assumed that several researchers would reach an agreement on the factors themselves rather than on the weight given to them. The disadvantage of this method is that differences in importance will be neglected which eventually may lead to biased results when estimating the influence of commitment on monetary performance.

Table A.3 Weights Given to the Components

Criterion	Component	Unweighted (C_{uw})	Weighted (C_{w1})	Weighted (C_{w2})	Weighted (C_{w3})
1. Objectives	*Obj*	0.10	0.15	0.15	0.20
2. Constitutional level	*Const*	0.10	0.05	0.05	0.05
3. Discretionary power	*Gov*	0.10	0.15	0.15	0.15
4. External obligations	*Extern*	0.10	0.15	0.15	0.20
5. Appointment/ dismissal procedures	*Ceo*	0.05	0.05	0.025	0
	Diss	0.05	0.05	0.025	0
6. Limitations on lending	*Lim*	0.10	0.10	0.20	0.20
7. Convertibility restrictions	*Conv*	0.05	0.10	0.10	0.10
	Mult	0.05	0.05	0.05	0.05
8. Competitive elements	*Comp*	0.10	0.05	0.05	0.05
9. Regulatory issues	*Reg*	0.10	0.05	0.025	0.00
10. Accountability	*Acc*	0.10	0.05	0.025	0.00
Sum		1.00	1.00	1.000	1.00

The unweighted index of commitment C_{uw} attributes the same weight to each of the ten criteria. The weighted index mainly attribute more weight to the objectives of monetary policy, governmental influence, external obligations, convertibility and limitations on lending. Less (partly no) weight is given to appointment and dismissal procedures, competitive elements, regulatory issues and accountability. *Table A.3* shows how the different components are weighted.

Different Specifications of the Institutional Factors

In this section, the institutional factors identified in Chapter 3 are specified and made internationally and intertemporally comparable. Again, the heterogeneity of the monetary reforms in the sample demands great care and, nonetheless, causes the data to have some weaknesses. The institutions that affect the success of a monetary reform are political stability, fiscal stability, labour market flexibility, openness of the country and public opposition to inflation. In addition a variable describing the reserve currency is introduced for those reforms which make use of a nominal anchor. Alternatively, a comprehensive variable for economic freedom is computed that includes the whole institutional setting.

Political stability

Political stability in this context means that a political system is stable rather than long-term survival of a government. Following this view, Italy, for instance, has a high political stability, although there has been a frequent change of government since World War II. We also connected political stability with political freedom. The specification has to take this into account. We do this by composing the variables *PS*1 and *PS*2 of three elements: unsuccessful irregular executive transfers (*coup d'état*, *UIET*), successful irregular executive transfers (*SIET*) and political reprisals in the year of monetary reform (*REPRIS*). The latter is a dummy, its outcome being 1 or 0, depending on whether or not political reprisal exists. *UIET* and *SIET* are the numbers of coups in the 25 years prior to the monetary reform. The time span of 25 years has been chosen since it approximately represents a generation and will be remembered well by the public. This specification is more precise and produces more variety in the sample than merely distinguishing democratic and undemocratic political systems. The exact specification is as follows:

$$PS1 = 0{,}5(1 - 0{,}4UIET - 0{,}6SIET)^2 + 0{,}5REPRIS \qquad \text{(A.1a)},$$

$$PS2 = 0{,}5(1 - 0{,}4UIET - 0{,}6SIET) + 0{,}5REPRIS \qquad \text{(A.1b)}.$$

$0 \leq PS1, PS2 \leq 1$ holds for both indicators. The difference between $PS1$ and $PS2$ is simply that the quadratic term in $PS1$ lays emphasis on countries with either very many or very few coups. Otherwise, both specifications are rather similar.

Fiscal stability

An indicator of fiscal stability should meet two conditions. Ideally, it should not be exclusively based on historical performance, and it should also be possible to calculate it at the moment of the monetary reform. Obviously, at the moment of the reform data of the future is not available; not even data of the recent past. Nevertheless, the condition is important from a methodological perspective. If a monetary and a fiscal reform are made simultaneously and if the fiscal reform is successful, the credibility of the monetary reform is *ceteris paribus* high, at least higher than without the fiscal reform. An indicator of fiscal stability should cover this fact. It would not cover this fact, if it did not include future fiscal policy. As long as one analyses reforms of the past, fiscal policy after t, the moment of the monetary reform[1] can be included in the calculation of the indicator.[2]

These requirements exclude the stock of public debt, tax arrears and the annual budget deficit in the year of the reform. All these indicators are purely backward-oriented. We choose a mix of past and future data. The indicator is built on the fiscal balance (FB = revenues minus expenditure) of the state which is divided by the GDP and has several specifications:

$$FS1 = \frac{1/8 \sum_{s=t-2}^{t+5} FB_s / GDP_s + 1}{2}, \text{ where } s \text{ denotes time} \quad \text{(A.2a)},$$

$$FS2 = \frac{1/8 \sum_{s=t-2}^{t+5} FB_s / GDP_s + 0.209}{1.068} \quad \text{(A.2b)},$$

$$FS3 = 1/8 \sum_{s=t-2}^{t+5} FB_s / GDP_s \quad \text{(A.2c)}.$$

1 As opposed to the theoretical model of section 4.V, $t+1$ is a precisely defined period, namely the first year after the reform. The period $t+1$ in the model, is called $t+1$ to $t+5$ (the first five years after the reform) in the econometric asessment (Chapter 6).

2 If the credibility of a planned monetary reform is to be assessed, a prognosis of future fiscal policy has to be included in the indicator.

All three specifications use the average fiscal balance per GDP in *t*-2 through *t*+5. *FS*1 uses a hundred per cent fiscal deficit and a 100 per cent surplus as a benchmark whereas *FS*2 uses a benchmark closer to reality: the average deficit of Israel between 1978 and 1985 (20.9 per cent of GDP) as the highest deficit and the surplus of Hong Kong between 1981 and 1988 (85.9 per cent). Both indicators are restricted between 0 and 1, making them comparable to *C*. *FS*3 is just the average of fiscal balances per GDP without restriction which does not allow us to calculate the ex-ante proxy for credibility of a reform with the help of *FS*3. In an estimation of variant 2 of the model, it nevertheless may be useful. Naturally, these indicators are highly correlated to each other.

Labour market flexibility

Labour market flexibility ideally reflects the ability of the labour force to adjust to structural change. It depends on various factors, the most important being the regulation of the labour market. The regulation in the countries in the sample is very patchy. To compare the *labour market regime* over such a time horizon and so many countries as in our sample is complicated as well. Thus, instead of analysing labour market regimes, we look at the actual flexibility of the labour force which may be affected by several factors, among them the labour market regime, but also technological change and the state of development a country is in. Our indicator of labour market flexibility (*LM*), therefore, is rather simple. It is the gross shift in per cent of the work force between the three sectors – Agriculture, Industry and Services – between 1950 and 1977 which is divided by 66 (the maximum gross shift in 121 countries, Taylor and Jodice 1983a, pp. 257–259). *LM* is restricted between 0 and 1.

$$LM = GrossShifts / 66 \qquad \text{(A.3a).}$$

The outcome of this variable and the econometric results (Chapter 6, section III) are rather unsatisfactory. The specification has at least three weaknesses: first, it cannot be distinguished whether the shifts are due to real flexibility or politically initiated moves, in particular in centrally planned economies.[3] In these countries the government was able to and did give orders to thousands of people to move from rural areas to newly erected industrial areas. Second, it cannot be ruled out that shifts in the work force are affected by and dependent on other institutional factors. Third, the period covered by *LM* is different from the time of the monetary reform.

---

[3] The outcome for the former Soviet Union is among the highest in the sample of 121 countries (Taylor and Jodice 1983a, pp. 257–259).

These shortcomings can be conquered. First, the causes for intersectoral labour mobility might be of minor relevance. Even if mobility is politically motivated, its existence shows the actual mobility. This can be seen as a sign that the workforce might be able to react to structural change. This reduces the pressure on monetary policy to take employment into account. Furthermore, the correlation between *LM* and other institutional factors is not very high (*Tables 7* and *8*). Third, although the time span covered by *LM* and the actual period before the reforms does not coincide, it is fair to assume that the labour force mobility in a country normally is not subject to sudden changes. Therefore, it can be regarded as a reasonable approximation. In addition, there are other arguments in favour of *LM*: it allows us to compare all countries in the sample and it is directly observable whereas other indicators which try to reflect the labour market regime have to be composed. As long as no better alternative is available we work with a variable based on *LM*.

One property of *LM* is that its outcome for advanced countries is lower than less developed countries. Industrialised countries had already experienced a great deal of structural change from agriculture to industry and to services in 1977 when the period covered by *LM* ended. Structural change proceeded more rapidly in developed countries than in developing countries until the 1960s. Thereafter it slows down. We have chosen the year 1973 as a benchmark year. A way to improve the empirical content of *LM* is to adjust it for this difference in structural change. *LM73* is defined as follows:

$$LM73 = GrossShifts / 66 * \frac{GDP\ per\ Capita_{1973}}{GDP\ per\ Capita\ US_{1973}} \qquad \text{(A.3b).}$$

Openness of the country

The potential (politically and technologically possible) level of openness has changed throughout this century. In the years before World War I, capital flows and trade were relatively unrestricted. Global integration was very intense (Freytag and Sally 2000). This changed dramatically after the war. Protectionism grew and trade flows decreased. After World War II, trade among the industrialised countries was instituted rapidly by the multilateral trading system. As opposed to trade flows, capital flows were restricted until the end of the Bretton Woods System. Since then, not only capital markets have been integrated increasingly, but also developing countries increasingly took part in the international division of labour. These different stages of internationalisation make it very difficult to compare the monetary reforms of this century with respect to their openness.

In this study, capital transactions are covered by a dummy variable (*PostBW*) that will be introduced in the next section. Thus, we restrict the indicator for openness, *OP*, to trade. This raises the comparability of the monetary reforms in the sample. Because the intensity of foreign trade of a country in general is rather stable and changes only slowly, we only observe three years, *t*-2 through *t*. We have five different specifications. For *OP*, we define a country as completely open when the fraction $(EX + IM)_s / GDP_s$ is 0.5. To norm *OP* between 0 and 1, we have to multiply the average fraction with 2 and set every value above 1 equal to 1. This indicator generates rather peculiar results, for instance that Russia has been a completely open economy in the early 1990s.

$$OP = 1/3 \sum_{s=t-2}^{t} \frac{(EX + IM)_s}{GDP_s} * 2 \qquad \text{(A.4a)},$$

with $$OP = 1, \text{ if } \quad 1/3 \sum_{s=t-2}^{t} \frac{(EX + IM)_s}{GDP_s} * 2 > 1 .$$

Therefore, we have to alter the indicator. *OP*2 is based on foreign trade per capita. To norm the indicator to $0 \le OP2 \le 1$, we take the German (1990) trade per capita (10,324.76 US $) as the benchmark, that is Germany is completely open and $OP2_{Germany}$ equals 1.

$$OP2 = 1/3 \frac{\sum_{s=t-2}^{t} (EX + IM)_s \, per\, Capita}{10{,}324.76} \qquad \text{(A.4b)}.$$

The result derived here seems more reliable. Russia in the early 1990s has the outcome 0.07 which can be assumed as being at least close to reality. However, it seems plausible that the extreme case in the sample cannot be regarded as the only truly open country. Thus, when constructing *OP*3, we define a country with 2,000.00 US $ trade per capita per year as completely open and again set every value above 1 equal to 1.

$$OP3 = 1/3 \frac{\sum_{s=t-2}^{t} (EX + IM)_s \, per\, Capita}{2{,}000} \qquad \text{(A.4c)}.$$

with $$OP3 = 1, \text{ if } 1/3 \frac{\sum_{s=t-2}^{t} (EX + IM)_s \, per\,Capita}{2{,}000} > 1.$$

The remaining two indicators have the same content as *OP*1 and *OP*2. They are not restricted between 0 and 1. *OP*4 is equivalent to *OP*2, and *OP*5 to *OP*.

$$OP4 = 1/3 \sum_{s=t-2}^{t} (EX + IM)_s \, per\,Capita \qquad \text{(A.4d)},$$

$$OP5 = 1/3 \sum_{s=t-2}^{t} \frac{(EX + IM)_s}{GDP_s} \qquad \text{(A.4e)}.$$

Public opposition to inflation

Public opposition to inflation is another delicate issue. It has to be operationalised so that one is able to compare it over the sample. Posen (1993) introduces the concept of 'financial opposition to inflation' (*FOI*). He argues that effective opposition against the inflationary bias is given if the financial sector is strong and able to express its interests. He employs four proxies for an anti-inflationary, well-organised financial sector (ibid., pp. 47–51). We do not have to explain this in detail here for the concept of Posen is too narrow to incorporate every aspect of public opposition against inflation.[4] Nevertheless the idea of focusing on interest groups rather than on organisation is quite appealing.

Another variable for the culture of stability could, therefore, be an index of corporatism. Grüner (1998, pp. 24–28) argues that the more different interest groups stand in contrast to each other, the less the chances are for economic stability in general and monetary stability in particular. In other words, a corporatist structure in a society gives evidence about its culture of stability. It is, however, very difficult to calculate an appropriate index and to determine the direction of causality. To give an example: Germany and Italy are both regarded as corporatist countries. Culture of stability in Germany has been regarded as being high since the 1950s, whereas in e.g. Italy it was seen as being low through 1990 and only after 1990 seems to have gradually

4 Nevertheless, Posen (1993) claims that he both explains low inflation and a high degree of CBI with high *FOI*. Unfortunately, the results are not very convincing (e.g. ibid., figures 2 and 3, pp. 51f). Other relevant variables seem to be omitted.

increased. Thus, it is not clear whether a corporatist structure indicates high or low culture of stability in a country.

Hence, we choose a composition of past experience and actual regulations as a proxy for public opposition to inflation. The former inflation record is especially relevant for a country after a hyperinflation. People are very sensitive as regards stability: since they have knowledge about the cost of inflation on average they strongly oppose another hyperinflation. Again, the time horizon is 25 years before the reforms, roughly a generation. One part of the indicator is the number of years with an inflation rate of at least 100 per cent per annum (*H*), divided by 25. The other elements are dummies for repressed inflation (*REPIN*), that is prices are at least partly fixed, [5] and indexation of wages, taxes, government bonds etc. (*INDEX*). It is a dummy, taking the values 0 or 1. Public opposition to inflation (*POI*) is modelled in two specifications:

$$POI = (\frac{H}{25} + REPIN + (1 - INDEX))/3 \qquad \text{(A.5).}$$

Both the experience of hyperinflation and repressed inflation lead to higher public opposition to inflation. People know that prices would be higher and fear it. In addition, price indexation decreases the peoples' opposition to inflation as they believe that they are protected against it. Hence, *POI* increases with *H* and the value 1 for *REPIN* and 0 for *INDEX*.

Properties of the reserve country

To measure how appropriate the reserve currency is, we calculate the institutional factor *properties of reserve currency* (*RC*). It is composed of two elements: first, the number of foreign countries fixing the exchange rate towards the same reserve currency is calculated by taking those five countries apart from the reserve country with which its trade is most intense: if all five are pegged to the reserve currency, RC_{er} is 1, with four currencies being pegged, RC_{er} is 0.8 and so on. The measure of the trade share Rc_t is simply the quotient of bilateral trade between the reform country and the reserve country and the reform country's total international trade. Production structure RC_{ps} could be calculated by using a bilateral Grubel–Lloyd index (intra-industry trade) of the bilateral trade. Since the data is not available for most countries in the sample, we neglect the production structure. *RC* is calculated as follows:

5 This definition explicitly includes the fixing of prices of food, utilities etc. for an urban population which is usual in many Latin American countries.

$$RC = (RC_{er} + RC_t)/2 \qquad \text{(A.6).}$$

Economic freedom

In what follows we introduce a comprehensive index as an alternative to the application of a combination of five institutional factors, the index of economic freedom by Gwartney and Lawson (1997). Their index consists of 17 components, separated into four groups (*G*). These groups are (Gwartney and Lawson 1997, p. 4):

1. Money and inflation (protection of money as a store of value and medium of exchange); 4 components, weight: 15.7 per cent.
2. Government operations and regulations (freedom to decide what is produced and consumed; 6 components, weight 34.6 per cent.
3. Takings and discriminatory taxation (freedom to keep what you earn); 3 components, weight: 27.2 per cent.
4. Restraints on international exchange (freedom of exchange with foreigners); 4 components, weight 22.5.

Every component can have an outcome between 0 and 10. Gwartney and Lawson calculated the weighted average in five years (1975, 1980, 1985, 1990, 1995). We use the index a little differently. Because the first group (money and inflation) is what we want to explain, we eliminate it from the index, but use the results that Gwartney and Lawson reached in their study. Our sample consists of 21 reforms. In case there is no result for the year of the reform, we take the result available soonest after the reform as we assume that the change in the overall economic system coincides with the monetary reform. For instance, in case of Argentina's reform in 1991, we apply the Gwartney–Lawson index (*GL*) of 1995. Our index *EF* is calculated as follows:

$$EF = \frac{(G2*0.346 + G3*0.272 + G4*0.225)_{GL}}{0.843*10} \qquad \text{(A.7).}$$

Thus, we restrict the outcome to a value between 0 and 1, and we have eliminated the influence of monetary issues on the index of economic freedom.

Similarly, *EF*2000 is calculated as the weighted average of five groups (except for monetary policy and alternative currencies) of the 2000 index of economic freedom by Gwartney, Lawson and Samida (2000, p. 7) (*GLS*) which is composed of 23 components in seven groups:

1. Size of government, 2 components, 11 per cent.
2. Structure of the economy and the use of markets, 4 components, 14.2 per cent.
3. Monetary policy and price stability, 3 components, 9.2 per cent (omitted).
4. Freedom to use alternative currencies, 2 components, 14.6 per cent (omitted).
5. Legal structure and property rights, 3 components, 16.6 per cent.
6. International exchange: trade, 5 components, 17.1 per cent.
7. Freedom to exchange in capital and financial markets, 4 components, 17.2 per cent.

$$EF2000 = \frac{(G1*0.11 + G2*0.142 + G5*0.166 + G6*0.171 + G7*0.172)_{GLS}}{0.762*10}$$

OTHER EXOGENOUS VARIABLES

Seigniorage and the demand for money

As argued in Chapter 6, section I, we compose a variable that includes the demand for money and the attitude towards seigniorage. The variable *SEIGN* is constructed as the change in (basic) money divided by the sum of the change in basic money and the total revenue of the government (Cukiermann 1992, pp. 48f). Since this indicator must be forward-looking it is calculated as the unweighted average of the five years following the monetary reform (*SEIGN*). Otherwise, it would contain elements of the pre-reform era with seigniorage as the government's main motive to inflate. As a consequence, for an ex-ante assessment of a monetary reform one has to use a projection instead of actual values.

$$Seign = 1/5 * \sum_{s=t+1}^{t+5} \frac{M_s - M_{s-1}}{R_s + M_s - M_{s-1}} \qquad \text{(A.8).}$$

This variable does not fully stand the critique formulated in Klein and Neumann (1990).[6] It is by no means clear that the change in money can be completely transferred to the government. Rather, it can be expected that it is not the case. However, Klein and Neumann analyse industrialised countries

6 See also Honohan (1996) and Baltensperger and Jordan (1997) as well as Chapter 6, section I.

where the magnitude of seigniorage as compared to public revenues is small[7]. In most of the countries in our sample, this is different. For instance in Argentina, *SEIGN* was up to 50 per cent of total revenues before 1991. A few years later, it dropped down to 1 per cent. This indicator obviously contains enough information to be empirically relevant. In addition, *SEIGN* can be calculated for the entire sample.

The influence of capital flows

Finally, we use a dummy variable for the influence of high capital mobility on post-reform inflation. Very simply, this variable has the outcome 0 when the reform takes place before 1973 and 1 when it takes place after the end of Bretton Woods. It is called *PostBW*.

$$PostBW = 0 \text{, if } t \leq 1973 \text{, and } PostBW = 1 \text{, if } t > 1973 \qquad \text{(A.10).}$$

As mentioned earlier in this chapter, theoretically it remains an open question whether increasing capital mobility after Bretton Woods is a disciplining factor or not. Both answers are plausible.

Growth differentials: exogenous or endogenous?

Under regular circumstances, developing countries grow faster than industrialised countries. The reason is that productivity growth is higher in developing countries which itself is due to a lower stock of capital there. The marginal return is higher than in capital-abundant countries. This faster growth regularly leads to higher inflation in developing countries via a real appreciation. However, often productivity growth is slower in developing countries despite a lower capital stock. Corruption, a lacking financial sector and many more factors contribute to sluggishness. Moreover, high inflation also seems to be an obstacle for growth. Thus, the causality is not clear. Nevertheless, we construct a variable showing the growth difference of the country towards the USA, the richest economy.

$$BAL = 1/7 * \sum_{s=t-1}^{t+5} (gGDP_s - gGDP_{s,USA}) \qquad \text{(A.9).}$$

The variable *BAL* does not need to be normed between 0 and 1. We will test both hypotheses, i.e. positive growth differences increasing inflation; and high inflation causing negative growth differences.

---

[7] In two later papers, Neumann (1992) and (1996) analyse Japan (in comparison with Germany) and the USA.

External shocks
Sometimes, the success of the monetary reform may be impeded by external shocks, such as a war, an earthquake, a flood etc. In this case, credibility of a monetary reform may be of minor importance: although credibility is high, post-reform inflation is also high. To explain such a phenomenon, we use a dummy (*SHOCK*) which has the outcome 1, if a shock occurred in the first three years of the reform, and the outcome 0 otherwise.

$$SHOCK = 1 \qquad \text{(A.11)},$$

if it occurs between *t* and *t+3*. For this study, we do not use SHOCK as almost every country in the sample was subject to an external shock, but with a greater sample it may well be a good dummy.

THE DEPENDENT VARIABLE: INFLATION

According to Chapter 6, subsection II.a, inflation is measured as CPI and has to be calculated as an average over some time after the reform, supposedly five years. We distinguish two general concepts of taking the time dimension into account. First, the annual inflation rates are weighted differently. An average inflation that pays regard to the disinflation process is calculated. Later periods are given higher weights. Second, we calculate an average inflation rate of the five years after the reform.

$$WCPI = \frac{\pi_t + 2*\pi_{t+1} + 3*\pi_{t+2} + 4*\pi_{t+3} + 5*\pi_{t+4} + 10*\pi_{t+5}}{25} \qquad \text{(A.12a)},$$

$$ACPI = ((P_{t+5} / P_t)^{0.2} - 1)*100 \qquad \text{(A.12b)}.$$

THE DATA AND ITS SOURCES

General comments
Most variables used in the econometric chapter of this study as well as in the case studies are composed ones. They are either composed of data available in statistics like the *IMF Yearbook, International Financial Statistics or the United Nations Yearbook of International Trade Statistics*. This data is accessible to everyone. The resulting variables are easily comprehensible for

readers. Any disagreement will be restricted to the construction and specification of the variable, but will not be about its value. Or the variables consist of components with discrete codings like in the case of *C*. The value of *C* to a certain degree is left to the disposition of the investigator. Here, disagreement can occur not only on the correct construction and specification, but also about the outcome of the variable. There are other variables composed comparably.

The character of the data is not homogeneous. In many cases, we can draw upon official international statistics. Although they differ in quality depending on the condition of the national statistical sources, this data can be regarded as being solid. In other cases, in particular Greece, Hong Kong, Korea and Paraguay, we can make use of official information that was given upon request. This data are considered as being similarly reliable. There are other instances, where the source of the data are papers and books published by other scholars without always obtaining detailed information about the origin of the data. For other data, we have had to read old newspapers and magazines to extract the necessary information. Therefore, it is necessary to describe in detail the sources of the data.

Sources in particular

To begin with, the index of commitment *C* is made of ten components. An important source for these components is the central bank law of the respective country, particularly for details about internal relations between the central bank and the government. Many central bank laws today are available on the Internet. A complete collection of central bank homepages is given by the Institute for Economic Policy (http://www.uni-koeln.de/wiso-fak/iwp/). A list of central bank laws and directives can be found also; Mark Bernkopf (http://patriot.net/~bernkopf/) as well as at the New York University (www.law.nyu.edu/centralbankscenter/). To complete the list, we draw upon the library of the Deutsche Bundesbank in Frankfurt/Main. Central bank laws are also reprinted in Aufricht (1962). Some central bank laws and further information (Israel, Slovenia, Hong Kong, Ukraine) have been sent to the author upon request. A valuable source, especially for external monetary relations of countries as well as for monetary history, is *Picks Currency Yearbook* and its successor, the *World Currency Yearbook*, edited by Philip Cowitt. They were published between 1955 and 1989. External features can also been found in IMF (d). Besides these collections, many papers and books are valuable. Among them, we particularly make use of Bähr (1994), Bennett (1993, 1994), Buch (1993), Cukierman (1992, pp. 371–411), (Fischer 1986), Fischer, Hiemenz and Trapp (1985), Greenwood (1983), Mastroberardino (1994, pp. 161–171; 187–197) and Schuler (1996).

For the computation of institutional factors, a number of sources are used. Before we describe the sources by variables, one remark has to be made about the German monetary reform in 1948, the oldest reform in the sample. For various independent variables, different issues of Statistisches Bundesamt (a, varous issues) and SVR (1966) are consulted. In general, the subsequent sources are used.

The indicators of political stability *PS1* and *PS2* are based on the following sources. Indicators of *coups d'états* (*SEIT* and *UIET)* are taken from Taylor and Jodice (1983b, pp. 89–94). They report of irregular transfers until 1977. For the period from 1978 through 1994 we consult back issues of *The Economist* to collect information about *coups d'états*. The same holds for the component *REPRIS*: on the basis of reading old issues, we decided whether to assign a 1 or a 0. The variables for fiscal stability (*FS*1, *FS*2, *FS*3) are mainly based on IMF (a), IMF (b) and IMF (c). Only the data for Hong Kong and Korea are based on national statistics which have been sent to the author. Labour market flexibility is calculated considering Taylor and Jodice (1983a, pp. 257–259). For the calculation of *LM*73 we additionally use IMF data. All indicators of openness (*OP* through *OP*5) are based on the *United Nations Yearbook of International Trade Statistics*. Additionally, IMF (a), IMF (b) and (c) are used. For the calculation of the indicators of Public opposition to inflation *POI* we make use of IMF (c) data for the component *H. REPIN* is based on back issues of *The Economist*, and for *INDEX* we refer to Fischer (1983) as well as to Bruno and Piterman (1990) and to Corbo and Solimano (1991). Properties of reserve currencies *RC* are computed with data from the *United Nations Yearbook of International Trade Statistics* and *Statistisches Bundesamt* (1994a and 1994b). Finally, the index of economic freedom *EF and EF2000* is a modified version of the index composed by Gwartney Lawson (1997) and by Gwartney, Lawson and Samida (2000), respectively. We only change the weights they have introduced, but use their results.

The calculation of the other independent variables, in particular the influence of seigniorage *SEIGN* and growth differentials *BAL*, is purely based on IMF (a through c) data. The same holds for the dependent variable consumer price inflation (A*CPI*, W*CPI*).

Appendix 3: Calculated Degree of Commitment

Table A.4 The Index of Commitment for the Sample of 29[1]

Country	Year	C_{uw}	C_{w1}	C_{w2}	C_{w3}
Argentina	1991	0.798	0.882	0.873	0.898
Argentina	1985	0.462	0.479	0.462	0.474
Bolivia	1987	0.540	0.545	0.466	0.450
Bolivia	1963	0.540	0.545	0.466	0.450
Brazil	1994	0.495	0.520	0.482	0.507
Brazil	1989	0.238	0.225	0.188	0.175
Brazil	1986	0.346	0.354	0.317	0.342
Chile	1975	0.474	0.412	0.350	0.350
Estonia	1992	0.787	0.825	0.837	0.825
Germany (East)	1990	0.665	0.624	0.649	0.599
Germany	1948	0.707	0.687	0.712	0.699
Greece	1954	0.424	0.341	0.312	0.299
Hong Kong	1983	0.674	0.750	0.804	0.833
Israel	1985	0.503	0.495	0.478	0.490
Israel	1980	0.495	0.441	0.411	0.374
Korea	1962	0.441	0.396	0.308	0.283
Latvia	1992	0.632	0.658	0.628	0.616
Lithuania	1994	0.715	0.783	0.829	0.850
Mexico	1987	0.378	0.345	0.291	0.275
Mexico	1993	0.628	0.687	0.641	0.624
Nicaragua	1990/91	0.662	0.704	0.649	0.624
Nicaragua	1988	0.441	0.412	0.358	0.333
Peru	1991	0.578	0.637	0.624	0.641
Peru	1985	0.445	0.454	0.383	0.375
Russia	1994	0.611	0.653	0.632	0.641
Slovenia	1991	0.511	0.516	0.507	0.491
Ukraine	1992	0.187	0.266	0.266	0.291
Uruguay	1993	0.457	0.479	0.425	0.433
Uruguay	1975	0.440	0.445	0.391	0.400

[1] For sources see Appendix 2, section V.

Appendix 4: The Institutional Factors Calculated

Table A.5 Institutional Factors for the Sample of 29[1]

Country	Year	WCPI	ACPI	PS1	PS2	FS1
Argentina	1991	29.467	8.304	0.748	0.852	0.496
Argentina	1985	1,644.219	577.611	0.190	0.308	0.487
Bolivia	1987	15.546	16.325	0.807	0.892	0.466
Bolivia	1963	6.672	7.290	0.314	0.396	0.482
Brazil	1994	255.037	113.820	0.500	0.500	0.491
Brazil	1989	3,490.500	736.850	0.476	0.488	0.462
Brazil	1986	10,677.184	1,310.680	0.476	0.488	0.501
Chile	1975	81.759	78.620	0.431	0.464	0.496
Estonia	1992	69.365	37.629	0.961	0.980	0.507
Germany (East)	1990	3.001	3.534	0.976	0.988	0.494
Germany	1948	1.083	1.000	1.000	1.000	0.504
Greece	1954	3.106	3.070	1.000	1.000	0.495
Hong Kong	1983	6.323	5.804	1.000	1.000	0.929
Israel	1985	31.951	23.791	1.000	1.000	0.427
Israel	1980	248.804	196.547	1.000	1.000	0.395
Korea	1962	19.444	18.905	0.916	0.956	0.478
Latvia	1992	33.651	35.234	0.961	0.980	0.495
Lithuania	1994	19.079	27.932	0.961	0.980	0.495
Mexico	1987	31.774	35.783	1.000	1.000	0.469
Mexico	1993	21.150	22.100	1.000	1.000	0.499
Nicaragua	1990/91	130.046	14.494	0.431	0.464	0.454
Nicaragua	1988	5,395.121	1,009.235	0.431	0.464	0.433
Peru	1991	38.731	31.650	0.887	0.940	0.473
Peru	1985	3,836.255	823.342	0.866	0.928	0.465
Russia	1994	69.506	59.247	0.446	0.472	0.478
Slovenia	1991	15.216	18.196	0.976	0.988	0.500
Ukraine	1992	592.113	215.226	0.476	0.488	0.455
Uruguay	1993	23.637	28.536	0.909	0.952	0.496
Uruguay	1975	60.111	56.535	0.916	0.956	0.493

1 For sources see Appendix 2, section V.

Table A.5 (continued)

Country	Year	FS2	FS3	OP1	OP2	OP3
Argentina	1991	0.189	-0.007	0.134	0.050	0.259
Argentina	1985	0.171	-0.026	0.122	0.040	0.208
Bolivia	1987	0.132	-0.067	0.251	0.021	0.110
Bolivia	1963	0.162	-0.036	0.345	0.004	0.020
Brazil	1994	0.179	-0.018	0.145	0.038	0.198
Brazil	1989	0.124	-0.076	0.138	0.036	0.188
Brazil	1986	0.198	0.002	0.177	0.029	0.150
Chile	1975	0.188	-0.008	0.294	0.032	0.167
Estonia	1992	0.209	0.014	1.174	0.194	1.000
Germany (East)	1990	0.185	-0.012	0.496	1.000	1.000
Germany	1948	0.204	0.009	0.215	0.014	0.073
Greece	1954	0.187	-0.009	0.199	0.006	0.028
Hong Kong	1983	1.000	0.859	1.501	0.791	1.000
Israel	1985	0.059	-0.146	0.601	0.357	1.000
Israel	1980	0.000	-0.209	0.762	0.338	1.000
Korea	1962	0.154	-0.045	0.142	0.002	0.008
Latvia	1992	0.186	-0.010	0.715	0.089	0.458
Lithuania	1994	0.187	-0.009	1.233	0.131	0.677
Mexico	1987	0.137	-0.063	0.222	0.040	0.208
Mexico	1993	0.193	-0.003	0.205	0.080	0.411
Nicaragua	1990/91	0.110	-0.092	0.529	0.024	0.125
Nicaragua	1988	0.070	-0.134	0.379	0.030	0.154
Peru	1991	0.145	-0.054	0.178	0.031	0.158
Peru	1985	0.129	-0.071	0.281	0.027	0.138
Russia	1994	0.154	-0.044	0.422	0.074	0.379
Slovenia	1991	0.195	0.000	0.961	0.719	1.000
Ukraine	1992	0.150	n.a.	0.631	0.028	0.146
Uruguay	1993	0.188	-0.008	0.309	0.114	0.589
Uruguay	1975	0.182	-0.015	0.231	0.028	0.144

Table A.5 (continued)

Country	Year	OP4	POI	LM73	LM	RC
Argentina	1991	517.581	0.533	0.162	0.394	0.178
Argentina	1985	415.192	0.147	0.162	0.394	0.172
Bolivia	1987	220.106	0.067	0.038	0.303	0.303
Bolivia	1963	39.590	0.387	0.038	0.303	0.692
Brazil	1994	395.268	0.173	0.068	0.303	0.207
Brazil	1989	376.121	0.120	0.068	0.303	*
Brazil	1986	299.631	0.067	0.068	0.303	0.216
Chile	1975	334.167	0.360	0.097	0.364	0.372
Estonia	1992	2,007.822	0.680	0.220	0.682	0.244
Germany (East)	1990	10,324.759	0.667	0.099	0.242	*
Germany	1948	145.707	0.680	0.178	0.242	0.553
Greece	1954	56.911	0.667	0.172	0.470	*
Hong Kong	1983	8,165.536	0.333	0.065	0.167	0.097
Israel	1985	3,685.976	0.067	0.083	0.182	0.110
Israel	1980	3,489.482	0.000	0.090	0.182	0.095
Korea	1962	16.343	0.333	0.103	0.712	0.205
Latvia	1992	915.513	0.680	0.220	0.682	*
Lithuania	1994	1,354.955	0.707	0.220	0.682	0.006
Mexico	1987	416.738	0.347	0.201	0.636	0.458
Mexico	1993	822.681	0.373	0.201	0.636	0.460
Nicaragua	1990/91	249.359	0.413	0.095	0.606	0.220
Nicaragua	1988	308.714	0.373	0.095	0.606	0.169
Peru	1991	315.767	0.413	0.078	0.379	*
Peru	1985	276.065	0.360	0.078	0.379	0.221
Russia	1994	758.956	0.373	0.220	0.682	0.024
Slovenia	1991	7,420.333	0.720	0.168	0.652	*
Ukraine	1992	291.117	0.667	0.220	0.682	0.011
Uruguay	1993	1,178.473	0.373	0.203	0.258	0.334
Uruguay	1975	287.571	0.347	0.077	0.258	0.346

Table A.5 (continued)

Country	Year	EF	EF2000	BAL	PostBW	SEIGN
Argentina	1991	0.699	0.793	2.99	1.000	0.113
Argentina	1985	0.325	0.384	-3.97	1.000	0.506
Bolivia	1987	0.503	0.633	0.50	1.000	0.101
Bolivia	1963	n.a.	n.a.	0.97	0.000	0.151
Brazil	1994	0.437	0.620	0.54	1.000	0.059
Brazil	1989	0.343	0.500	1.00	1.000	0.175
Brazil	1986	0.308	0.417	1.17	1.000	0.296
Chile	1975	0.364	0.394	1.42	1.000	0.113
Estonia	1992	0.597	0.664	-3.35	1.000	0.134
Germany (East)	1990	0.583	0.783	0.26	1.000	0.044
Germany	1948	n.a	n.a.	3.32	0.000	0.068
Greece	1954	n.a.	n.a.	4.12	0.000	0.086
Hong Kong	1983	0.955	0.920	4.21	1.000	0.184
Israel	1985	0.219	0.449	0.56	1.000	0.037
Israel	1980	0.201	0.373	3.83	1.000	0.044
Korea	1962	n.a.	n.a.	2.69	0.000	0.143
Latvia	1992	n.a.	0.608	-3.89	1.000	0.063
Lithuania	1994	0.583	0.623	-4.29	1.000	0.084
Mexico	1987	0.452	0.631	0.03	1.000	0.139
Mexico	1993	0.635	0.733	-0.17	1.000	0.066
Nicaragua	1990/91	0.213	0.590	-0.15	1.000	0.055
Nicaragua	1988	0.213	0.299	-4.19	1.000	0.214
Peru	1991	0.466	0.761	1.98	1.000	0.099
Peru	1985	0.424	0.303	.2.90	1.000	0.517
Russia	1994	0.342	0.508	-8.77	1.000	0.197
Slovenia	1991	n.a.	0.613	1.40	1.000	0.037
Ukraine	1992	0.288	0.237	-15.16	1.000	0.125
Uruguay	1993	n.a.	0.740	1.47	1.000	0.033
Uruguay	1975	n.a.	0.667	2.40	1.000	0.244

Notes: *: no reserve currency.

References

Ábel, István, John P. Bonin and Pierre L. Siklos (1994), 'Crippled Monetary Policy in Transforming Economies: Why Central Bank Independence Does not Restore Control?', in: Pierre L. Siklos (ed.) *Varieties of Monetary Reforms: Lessons and Experiences on the Road to Monetary Union*, Kluwer, Boston, Dordrecht, London, pp. 367–382.

Agénor, Pierre-Richard and Mark P. Taylor (1992), 'Testing for Credibility Effects', *IMF Staff Papers*, Vol. 39, pp. 545–571.

Ahrensdorf, Joachim (1959/60), 'Central Bank Policies and Inflation: A Case Study of Four Less Developed Economies, 1949–57', *IMF Staff Papers*, Vol. 7, pp. 274-301.

Akhand, Hafiz A. (1998), 'Central Bank Independence and Growth: A Sensitivity Analysis', *Canadian Journal of Economics*, Vol. 31, pp. 303–317.

Akhtar, M.A. (1995), 'Monetary Goals and Central Bank Independence', *BNL Quarterly Review*, No. 195, pp. 423–439.

Alesina, Alberto (1988), *Macroeconomics and Politics*, NBER Macroeconomics Annual, The MIT Press, Cambridge/Mass.

Alesina, Alberto and Guido Tabellini (1988), 'Credibility and Politics', *European Economic Review*, Vol. 32, pp. 542–550.

Anyadike-Danes, M.K. (1995), 'Comment on "Measuring the Independence of Central Banks and Its Effect on Policy Outcomes" by Cukierman, Webb and Neyapti', *The World Bank Economic Review*, Vol. 9, pp. 335–340.

Aufricht, Hans (1962), *Central Bank Legislation*, International Monetary Fund, Washington D.C.

Backhouse, Roger E. (1998), *UncriticalRrealism*, Department of Economics, University of Birmingham, mimeo.

Backus, David and John Driffill (1985), 'Rational Expectations and Policy Credibility Following a Change in Regime', *Review of Economic Studies*, Vol. 52, pp. 211–221.

Bade, Robin and Michael Parkin (1988), *Central Bank Laws and Monetary Policy*, University of Western Ontario, October 1988, mimeo.

Bähr, Christa (1994), *Ansätze zu einer Theorie der Währungsreform: Währungsreformen nach offenen und zurückgestauten Inflationen*, Institut für Wirtschaftspolitik, Köln.

Bailey, Martin J. (1956), 'The Welfare Cost of Inflationary Finance', *The Journal of Political Economy*, Vol. 64, pp. 93–110.

Balassa, Bela (1964), 'The Purchasing-power Parity Doctrine: A Reappraisal', *The Journal of Political Economy*, Vol. 72, pp. 584–596.

Baliño, Tomás J.T., Charles Enoch et al. (1997), *Currency Board Arrangements: Issues and Experiences*, IMF Occasional Paper 151, Washington D.C.

Baltensperger, Ernst and Thomas J. Jordan (1997), 'Principles of Seigniorage', *Schweizerische Zeitschrift für Volkswirtschaft und Statistik*, Vol. 133, pp. 133–151.

Banaian, King, Richard C.K. Burdekin and Thomas D. Willett (1998), 'Reconsidering the Principal Components of Central Bank Independence: The More the Merrier?' *Public Choice*, Vol. 97, pp. 1–12.

Banco Central de Venezuela (1999), *Boletín Mensual*, August 1999, http://www.bcv.org.ve.

Banco Central de Venezuela (2002), *Boletín Mensual*, January 2002, http://www.bcv.org.ve.

Banerjee, Biswajit, Vincent Koen, Thomas Krueger, Mark S. Lutz, Michael Marrese and Tapio O. Saavalainen (1995), *Road Maps of the Transition: The Baltics, the Czech Republic, Hungary, and Russia*, IMF Occasional Paper 127, Washington D.C.

Bank of Lithuania (1996), *Annual Report*, Riga.

Barro, Robert J. (1983), 'Inflationary Finance under Discretion and Rules', *Canadian Journal of Economics*, Vol. 16, pp. 1–16.

Barro, Robert J. (1995), 'Inflation and Economic Growth', Bank of England, *Quarterly Bulletin*, Vol. 35, pp. 166–175.

Barro, Robert J. and David B. Gordon (1983), 'Rules, Discretion and Reputation in a Model of Monetary Policy', *Journal of Monetary Economics*, Vol. 12, pp. 101–121.

Baxter, Marianne (1985), 'The Role of Expectations in Stabilization Policy', *Journal of Monetary Economics*, Vol. 15, pp. 343–362.

Becker, Gary S. (1983), 'A Theory of Competition Among Pressure Groups for Political Influence', *Quarterly Journal of Economics*, Vol. 98, pp. 371–400.

Becker, Gary S. (1985), 'Public Policies, Pressure Groups and Dead Weight Costs', *Journal of Public Economics*, Vol. 28, pp. 329–347.

Belke, Ansgar (1996), *Politische Konjunkturzyklen in Theorie und Empirie: Eine kritische Analyse der Zeitreihendynamik in Partisan-Ansätzen*, Mohr (Siebeck), Tübingen.

Bennett, Adam G.G. (1993), 'The Operation of the Estonian Currency Board', *IMF Staff Papers*, Vol. 40, pp. 451–470.

Bennett, Adam G.G. (1994), 'Currency Boards: Issues and Experiences', *IMF Paper on Policy Analysis and Assessment*, PPAA/94/18, p. 25, Washington D.C.

Bergsten, C. Fred and John Williamson (1994), 'Introduction', in: John Williamson (ed.) *The Political Economy of Policy Reform*, Institute for International Economics, Washington D.C., pp. 3–7.

Bernholz, Peter (1990), 'Notwendige und hinreichende Bedingungen zur Beendigung der Hyperinflationen', in: J.-M. Graf von der Schulenburg and Hans-Werner Sinn (eds.) *Theorie und Wirtschaft*, Festschrift zum fünfundsiebzigsten Geburtstag von Hans Möller, Mohr (Siebeck) Tübingen, pp. 62–88.

Bernholz, Peter (1995), 'Necessary and Sufficient Conditions to End Hyperinflations', in: Pierre L. Siklos (ed.) *Great Inflations of the 20th Century*, Edwar Elgar, Aldershot and Brookfield, pp. 257–287.

Bernholz, Peter and Hans Gersbach (1992), 'The Present Monetary Theory of Advanced Inflation: A Failure?', *Journal of Instituional and Theoretical Economics*, Vol. 148, pp. 705–719.

Bernholz, Peter and Hans Jürgen Jaksch (1989), 'An Implausible Theory of Inflation, *Weltwirtschaftliches Archiv*, Vol. 125, pp. 359–370.

Bernkopf, Mark (2001), Mark Bernkopf's Central Bank Resource Center, http://patriot.net/~bernkopf/.

Birnbaum, Eugene A. (1957), 'The Cost of a Foreign Exchange Standard or of the Use of a Foreign Currency as the Circulating Medium', *IMF Staff Papers*, Vol. 5, pp. 477–491.

Blackburn, Keith and Michael Christensen (1989), 'Monetary Policy and Policy Credibility: Theories and Evidence', *Journal of Economic Literature*, Vol. 27, pp. 1–45.

Blinder, Alan S. (1996), 'Central Banking in a Democracy', Federal Reserve Bank of Richmond, *Economic Quarterly*, Vol. 82/4, pp. 1–14.

Blinder, Alan S. (1997), 'Distinguished Lecture on Economics in Government: What Central Bankers Could Learn from Academics – and Vice Versa', *The Journal of Economic Perspectives*, Vol. 11, No. 2, pp. 3–19.

Bofinger, Peter (1991), *Festkurssysteme und geldpolitische Koordination*, Nomos, Baden-Baden.

Bofinger, Peter, Julian Reischle and Andrea Schächter (1996), *Geldpolitik: Ziele, Institutionen, Strategien und Instrumente*, Verlag Franz Vahlen, München.

Böhm-Bawerk, E. (1914), 'Unsere passive Handelsbilanz', *Neue Freie Presse* of 6/8 and 9 January 1914, in: Franz X. Weiss (ed.) *Gesammelte*

Schriften von Eugen von Böhm-Bawerk, Wien, Reprint Sauer & Auvermann, Frankfurt a.M. 1968, 1, pp. 499–515.

Bollard, Alan (1994), 'New Zealand', in: John Williamson (ed.) *The Political Economic of Policy Reform*, Institute for International Economics, Washington D.C., pp. 72–110.

Bomhoff, Eduard J. (1992), 'Monetary Reform in Eastern Europe', *European Economic Review*, Vol. 36, pp. 454–458.

Bonin, John P. et al. (1998), *Banking in Transition Economies*, Edward Elgar, Cheltenham and Northampton.

Bornstein, Morris (1997), 'Non-standard Methods in the Privatization Strategies of the Czech Republic, Hungary and Poland', *Economics of Transition*, Vol. 5, pp. 323–338.

Brennan, Geoffrey H. and James M. Buchanan (1981), *Monopoly in Money and Inflation: The Case for a Constitution to Discipline Government*, Institute for Economic Affairs, Hobart Paper 88, London 1981.

Brennan, Geoffrey H. and James M. Buchanan (1983) *The Reason of Rules: Constitutional Political Economy*, Cambridge University Press, Cambridge.

Broaddus, J. Alfred Jr. (1995), 'Reflections on Monetary Policy', Federal Reserve Bank of Richmond, *Economic Quarterly*, Vol. 81/2, pp. 1–11.

Brunner, Karl and Allan H. Meltzer (1993), *Money and the Economy: Issues in Monetary Analysis*, Cambridge University Press, Cambridge.

Bruno, Michael (1993), *Crisis, Stabilization and Economic Reform: Therapy by Consensus*, Clarendon Press, Oxford.

Bruno, Michael and Sylvia Piterman (1990), 'Israel's Stabilzation: A Two-Year Review', in: Michael Bruno et al. (eds.) *Inflation Stabilization*, The MIT Press, Cambridge/Mass. and London, pp.3–47.

Buch, Claudia M. (1993), 'Das erste Jahr der Krone – Estlands Erfahrungen mit der Währungsreform', *Die Weltwirtschaft*, pp. 441–465.

Buchanan, James M. (1983), 'Monetary Research, Monetary Rules, and Monetary Regimes', *Cato Journal*, Vol. 3, pp. 143–146.

Buchanan, James M. (1995), 'Individual Rights, Emergent Social States and Behavioral Feasibility', *Rationality and Society*, Vol. 7, pp. 141–150.

Buchheim, Christoph (1990), *Die Wiedereingliederung Westdeutschlands in die Weltwirtschaft*, Institut für Zeitgeschichte, München.

Buchheim, Christoph (1998), 'Die Errichtung der Bank deutscher Länder und die Währungsreform in Westdeutschland', Deutsche Bundesbank (ed.) *Fünfzig Jahre Deutsche Mark*, C.H. Beck, München, pp. 91–138.

Budina, Nina and Sweder van Wjinbergen (1997), 'Fiscal Policies in Eastern Europe', *Oxford Review of Economic Policy*, No. 2, pp. 47–64.

Buiter, Willem H. (1999), *Alice in Euroland*, CEPR Policy Paper No. 1, London.

Cagan, Phillip (1956), 'The Monetary Dynamics of Hyperinflation', in: Milton Friedman (ed.) *Studies in the Quantity Theory of Money*, The University of Chicago Press, Chicago, London and Toronto, pp. 25–117.

Calvo, Guillermo (1978), 'On the Time Consistency of Optimal Policy in a Monetary Economy', *Econometrica*, Vol. 46, pp. 1411–1428.

Campillo, Marta and Jeffrey A. Miron (1997), 'Why does Inflation Differ across Countries?', in: Christina D. Romer and David H. Romer (eds.) *Reducing Inflation, Motivation and Strategy*, National Bureau of Economic Research, Studies in Business Cycles, Vol. 30, pp. 335–357.

Canavese, J. Alfredo and Guido Di Tella (1990), 'Inflation Stabilization or Hyperinflation Advoidance? The Case of the Austral Plan in Argentina, 1985–87, in: Michael Bruno et al. (eds.), *Inflation Stabilization*, The MIT Press Cambridge, Massachusetts, London, pp. 153–190.

Cardoso, Eliana (1991), 'From Inertia to Megainflaton: Brazil in the 1980s', in: Michael Bruno et al. (eds.) *Lessons of Economic Stabilization and Its Aftermath*, The MIT Press, Cambridge, Mass. and London, pp. 143–189.

Cargill, Thomas F. (1995), 'The Statistical Association between Central Bank Independence and Inflation', *BNL Quarterly Review*, No. 193, pp. 159–172.

Cavallo, Domingo F. (1993), 'The Convertibility Plan', in: Nissan Liviatan (ed.) *Proceedings of a Conference on Currency Substitution and Currency Boards*, World Bank Discussion Papers No. 207, Washington D.C., pp. 37–40.

Cavallo, Domingo F. and Joaquin A. Cottani (1997), 'Argentina's Convertibility Plan and the IMF', *American Economic Review, Papers and Proceedings*, Vol. 87, pp. 17–22.

Chortareas, Georgios E. and Stephen M. Miller (2000), *Optimal Central Bankers Contracts and Common Agency*, Paper Presented at the 2000 Annual Meeting of the Public Choice Society, March 12-14, Charleston, SC.

Clauson, G.L.M. (1944), 'The British Colonial Currency System', *The Economic Journal*, Vol. 54, pp. 1–25.

Collier, Paul and Jan-Willem Gunning (1999), 'Why Has Africa Grown Slowly?', *The Journal of Economic Perspectives*, Vol. 13, No. 3, pp. 3–22.

Colombatto, Enrico and Jonathan Macey (1996), 'Exchange-rate Management in Eastern Europe: A Public Choice Perspective', *International Review of Law and Economics*, Vol. 16, pp. 195–209.

Corbo, Vittorio (2000), 'Stabilisation Policies in Latin America: The Decade of Reckoning', in: Federico Foders and Manfred Feldsieper (eds.) *The Transformation of Latin America: Economic Developments in the Early 1990s*, Edward Elgar, Cheltenham and Northampton, pp. 11–33.

Corbo, Vittorio and Andrés Solimano (1991), 'Chile's Experience with Stabilization Revisited', in: Michael Bruno et al. (eds.) *Lessons of Economic Stabilization and Its Aftermath*, The MIT Press, Cambridge, Mass. and London, pp. 57–101.

Cordeiro, Jose Luis (1998), *La Segunda Muerte de Bolivar*, CEDICE, Cararcas.

Cowitt, Philip. P. (ed.) '*World Currency Yearbook*', current issues, International Currency Analysis Inc., New York.

Cukierman, Alex S. (1990), 'The End of High Israeli Inflation: An Experiment in Heterodox Stabilization', in: Michael Bruno et al. (eds.) *Inflation Stabilization*, The MIT Press, Cambridge, Mass. and London, pp. 3–47.

Cukierman, Alex S. (1992), *Central Bank Strategy, Credibility and Independenc: Theory and Evidence*, The MIT Press, Cambridge, Mass. and London.

Cukierman, Alex S. (1995), 'Rapid Inflation: Deliberate Policy or Miscalculation?', in: Pierre L. Siklos (ed.) *Great Inflations of the 20th Century*, Edward Elgar, Aldershot and Brookfield, pp. 125–182.

Cukierman, Alex S., Pantelis Kalaitzidakis, Lawrence H. Summers and Steven B. Webb (1993), 'Central Bank Independence, Growth, Investment and Real Rates', *Carnegie-Rochester Conference Series on Public Policy*, Vol. 39, North-Holland, Amsterdam, pp. 95–140.

Cukierman, Alex S. and Mariano Tommasi (1998), 'When Does it Take a Nixon to Go to China?', *The American Economic Review*, Vol. 88, pp. 180–197.

Cukierman, Alex S., Steven B. Webb and Bilin Neyapti (1992), 'Measuring the Independence of Central Banks and Its Effect on Policy Outcomes', *The World Bank Economic Review*, Vol. 6, pp. 353–398.

Cukierman, Alex S. and Steven B. Webb (1995), 'Political Influence on the Central Bank: International Evidence', *The World Bank Economic Review*, Vol. 9, pp. 397–423.

Da Empoli, Stefano (2000), *Central Banker's Behavior with Revolving Doors: A New Appraisal of the Optimal Contract Approach*, Paper presented at the 2000 Annual Meeting of the Public Choice Society, March 12–14, Charleston, SC.

Deaton, Angus (1999), 'Commodity Prices and Growth in Africa', *The Journal of Economic Perspectives*, Vol. 13, No. 3, pp. 23–40.

De Beaufort Wijnholds, Onno J. and Lex Hoogduin (1994), 'Central Bank Autonomy: Policy Issues', *Financial and Monetary Policy Studies*, Vol. 27, pp. 75–107.

Debelle, Guy and Stanley Fischer (1995), 'How Independent Should a Central Bank Be?', in: Jeffrey C. Fuhrer (ed.) *Goals, Guidelines, and Constraints, Facing Monetary Policymakers*, The Federal Reserve Bank of Boston, Boston, pp. 195–221.

DEG – Deutsche Investitions- und Entwicklungsgesellschaft (1996), *Wandel in Mitteleuropa III, Länderberichte : Estland, Lettland, Litauen*, DEG, Köln.

De Gregorio, José (1992), 'The Effects of Inflation on Economic Growth: Lessons from Latin America', *European Economic Review*, Vol. 36, pp. 417–425.

Delivanis, Dimitrios and William C. Cleveland (1949), *Greek Monetary Developments 1939-1948*, Indiana University, Bloomington.

Deregulierungskommission (1991), *Marktöffnung und Wettbewerb*, Poeschel, Stuttgart.

Deutsche Bundesbank (ed.) (1998), *Fünzig Jahre Deutsche Mark, Notenbank und Währung in Deutschland seit 1948*, C.H. Beck, München.

Deutsche Bundesbank (2000), 'Transparenz in der Geldpolitik', *Monatsbericht der Deutschen Bundsbank*, March 2000, pp. 15–30.

Dluhosch, Barbara, Andreas Freytag and Malte Krüger (1996), *International Competitiveness and the Balance of Payments: Do Current Account Deficits and Surpluses Matter?*, Edward Elgar, Cheltenham and Brookfield.

Domes, Jürgen and Michael Wolffsohn (1979), 'Setting the Course for the Federal Republic of Germany: Major Policy Decisions in the Bi-Zonal Economic Council and Party Images, 1947-1949', *Zeitschrift für die gesamte Staatswissenschaft*, Vol. 135, pp. 332–351.

Donges, Juergen B. (1985), *Kann die argentinische Wirtschaft gesunden? Vorschläge zur Überwindung einer Krise*, Institut für Weltwirtschaft, Kiel.

Donges, Juergen B. and Jürgen Wieners (1994), 'Foreign Investment in the Transformation Process of Eastern Europe', *The International Trade Journal*, Vol. 8, pp. 163–191.

Dornbusch, Rüdiger (1992), 'Purchase Power Parity', in: John Eatwell, Murray Milgate and Peter Newman (eds.) *The New Palgrave Dictionary of Money and Finance*, Macmillan, London, Basingstoke, pp. 236-244.

Dornbusch, Rüdiger and Stanley Fischer (1986), 'Stopping Hyperinflations Past and Present', *Weltwirtschaftliches Archiv*, Vol. 122, pp. 1–47.

Dowd, Kevin (1994), 'Free Banking', in: Peter J. Boettke (ed.) *The Elgar Companion to Austrian Economics*, Edward Elgar, Hants, pp. 408–413.

Dreyer, Jacob S., Gottfried Haberler and Thomas D. Willett (1978), *Exchange Rate Flexibility*, American Enterprise Institute, Washington D.C.

Driffill, John (1988), 'Macroeconomic Policy Games with Incomplete Information – A Survey', *European Economic Review*, Vol. 32, pp. 533–541.

Duscha, Waldemar (1999), *Wirtschaftsdaten Venezuela*, in: Homepage of CAVENAL, http://www.cavenal.com/1wirch.htm (May 7, 1999).

Ecker, Lowell L. (1933), 'The Hungarian Thrift Crown', *The American Economic Review*, Vol. 23, pp. 471–474.

Eesti Pank (Bank of Estonia) (a), *Eesti Pank Bulletin*, various issues, Tallinn.

Eichengreen, Barry (1994), *International Monetary Arrangements for the 21st Century*, The Brookings Institution, Washington D.C.

Eichengreen, Barry and Paul Masson et al. (1998), *Exit Strategies: Policy Options for Countries Seeking Greater Exchange Rate Flexibility*, IMF Occasional Paper 168, Washington D.C.

Eijffinger, Sylvester C.W. and Jakob de Haan (1996), *The Political Economy of Central-bank Independence*, Special Papers in International Economics, No. 19, International Finance Section, Department of Economics, Princeton University, Princeton.

Eijffinger, Sylvester C.W. and Martijn van Keulen (1995), 'Central Bank Independence in Another Eleven Countries', *BNL Quarterly Review*, No. 192, pp. 39–83.

Eijffinger, Sylvester C.W. and Eric Schaling (1993), 'Central Bank Independence in Twelve Industrial Countries', *BNL Quarterly Review*, No. 184, pp. 49–89.

Eucken, Walter (1923), *Kritische Betrachtungen zum deutschen Geldproblem*, Verlag Gustav Fischer, Jena.

Eucken, Walter (1955), *Grundsätze der Wirtschaftspolitik*, Mohr (Siebeck), Tübingen and Polygraphischer Verlag, Zürich.

Fischer, Bernhard (1986), *Brasilien ohne Inflation? Eine kritische Würdigung des Cruzado-Planes*, Institut für Weltwirtschaft, Kiel.

Fischer, Bernhard, Ulrich Hiemenz and Peter Trapp (1985), *Argentina: The Economic Crisis in the 1980s*, Mohr (Siebeck), Tübingen.

Fischer, Stanley (1981), 'Towards an Understanding of the Costs of Inflation: II', in: Karl Brunner and Allan H. Meltzer (eds.) *The Costs and Consequences of Inflation*, Carnegie-Rochester Conference Series on Public Policy, Vol. 15, North-Holland, Amsterdam, pp. 5–41.

Fischer, Stanley (1983), 'Indexing and Inflation', *Journal of Monetary Economics*, Vol. 12, pp. 519–541.

Fischer, Stanley (1994), 'The Costs and Benefits of Disinflation', *Financial and Monetary Policy Studies*, Vol. 27, pp. 31–53.

Fischer, Stanley (1995), 'Central Bank Independence Revisited', *American Economic Review, Papers and Proceedings*, Vol. 85, pp. 201–206.

Fischer, Stanley (1997), 'Applied Economics in Action: IMF Programs', *American Economic Review, Papers and Proceedings*, Vol. 87, pp. 23–27.

Fischer, Stanley (1998), 'Die asiatische Krise hat die Rolle des IWF verändert', *Handelsblatt* of July 16, 1998, p. 11.

Fischer, Stanley (2001), *The Russian Economy: Prospects and Retrospect*, Speech delivered at the Higher School of Economics, Moscow, June 19, 2001, http://www.imf.org/external/np/speeches/2001/061901.htm.

Fisher, Irving (1924), *Der schwankende Geldwert*, Walter de Gruyter, Berlin, German edition of *Stabilizing of the Dollar*.

Forder, James (1998), 'Central Bank Independence – Conceptual Clarifications and Interim Assessment', *Oxford Economic Papers*, Vol. 50, pp. 307–334.

Franco, Gustavo H.B. (1990), 'Fiscal Reforms and Stabilisation: Four Hyperinflation Cases Examined, *The Economic Journal*, Vol. 100, pp. 176–187.

Franz, Wolfgang (2000), 'Wirtschaftspolitische Beratung: Reminiszenzen und Reflexionen', *Perspektiven der Wirtschaftspolitik*, Vol. 1, pp. 53–71.

Freris, A.F. (1986), *The Greek Economy in the Twentieth Century*, Croom Helm, London and Sydney.

Frey, Bruno S. (1991), 'The Public Choice View of International Political Economy, in: Roland Vaubel and Thomas D. Willett (eds.) *The Political Economy of International Organizations: A Public Choice Approach*, Westview Press, Boulder, San Francisco, Oxford, pp. 9–26.

Freytag, Andreas (1998a), 'Einige Anmerkungen zur Wahl der Reservewährung eines Currency Boards', *Zeitschrift für Wirtschaftspolitik*, Vol. 47, pp. 3–19.

Freytag, Andreas (1998b) 'Geldpolitische Regelbindung als Teil der wirtschaftlichen Gesamtordnung: Der argentinische Currency Board', *ORDO*, Vol. 49, pp. 379–399.

Freytag, Andreas (1998c), 'Überwindung des Reformstaus durch Verbesserung der Politikberatung?', in: Uwe Mummert and Michael Wohlgemuth (eds.) *Aufschwung Ost und Reformstau West*, Nomos, Baden-Baden, pp. 348–360.

Freytag, Andreas (1999), 'Der Westafrikanische Currency Board: Erfahrungen und Lehren daraus für die Währungspolitik', *Vierteljahresschrift für Sozial- und Wirtschaftsgeschichte*, Vol. 86, pp. 39–48.

Freytag, Andreas (2001a), 'Getting Fit for the EU: A Currency Board for Poland', in: Thomas Moser und Bernd Schips (eds.) *EMU, Financial Markets and the World Economy*, Kluwer, Dordrecht, pp. 231–251.

Freytag, Andreas (2001b), 'Internal Macro-policies and International Governance', in: John Kirton, Joseph Daniels and Andreas Freytag (eds.) *Guiding the Global Economy – The G8's Role at 25*, Ashgate, Aldershot et al., pp. 21–32.

Freytag, Andreas (2001c), 'Does Central Bank Independence Reflect Monetary Commitment Properly? – Methodical Considerations', *BNL Quarterly Review*, No. 217, pp. 181–208.

Freytag, Andreas and Razeen Sally (2000), 'Globalisation and Trade Policy Response: 1900 and 2000 Compared', *Jahrbuch für Neue Politische Ökonomie*, pp.191–222.

Friedman, Milton (1951), 'Commoditiy Reserve Currency', *Journal of Political Economy*, Vol. 59, pp. 203–232.

Friedman, Milton (1987), 'Quantity Theory of Money', in: John Eatwell, Murray Milgate and Peter Newman (eds.) *The New Palgrave Money*, Norton, New York and London, pp. 1–40.

Fry, Maxwell J., Charles A.E. Goodhart and Alvaro Almeida (1996), *Central Banking in Developing Countries*, Routledge, London and New York.

Furstenberg, George M. von and Michael K. Ulan (1998), *Learning from the World' s Best Central Bankers*, Kluwer, Boston, Dordrecht, London.

Gaddy, Clifford G. and Barry W. Ickes (2000), *The Virtual Economy and Economic Recovery in Russia*, The Brookings Institution and The Pennsylvania State University, The William Davidson Institute, mimeo.

Gärtner, Manfred (1997), 'Central Bank Independence and the Sacrifice Ratio: The Dark Side of the Force', *Schweizerische Zeitschrift für Volkswirtschaft und Statistik*, Vol. 133, pp. 513–558.

Gerchunoff, Pablo L. (1993), 'Argentina', in: Paul H. Boeker (ed.) *Latin America's Turnaround*, ICEG, San Francisco, pp. 18–22.

Ghosh, Atish and Steven Phillips (1998), 'Warning: Inflation May Be Harmful to Your Growth', *IMF Staff Papers*, Vol. 45, pp. 672–710.

Giersch, Herbert, Karl-Heinz Paqué and Holger Schmieding (1992), *The Fading Miracle*, Cambridge University Press, Cambridge.

Gimpelson, Vladimir and Douglas Lippolt (1999), 'Private Sector Employment in Russia: Scale Composition and Performance', *Economics in Transition*, Vol. 7, pp. 505–533.

Glaß, Stefan (1996), *Für ein direktes Preisniveauziel in der Geldpolitik*, Institut für Wirtschaftspolitik, Köln.

Gomulka, Stanislaw (1995), 'The IMF Supported Programs of Poland and Russia, 1990–1994: Principles, Errors, and Results', *Journal of Comparative Economics*, Vol. 20, pp. 316–346.

Gomulka, Stanislaw (1998), 'Managing Capital Flows in Poland, 1995–98', *Economics of Transition*, Vol. 64, pp. 389–396.

Götz, Roland (1999), 'Von der Abwertung des Rubels zum Macht-, Programm- und Politikwechsel in Rußland', *osteuropa*, Vol. 49, pp. 3–15.

Greene, Joshua E. and Peter Isard (1991), *Currency Convertibility and the Transformation of Centrally Planned Econonomies*, IMF Occasional Paper 81, Washington D.C.

Greene, William H. (1997), *Econometric Analysis*, Prentice Hall, London et al.

Greenwood, John (1983), 'The Stabilisation of the Hong Kong Dollar', *Asian Monetary Monitor*, Vol. 7, No. 6, pp. 9–37.

Greenwood, John (1988a), 'Response to Dr. Jao', *Asian Monetary Monitor*, No. 6, Vol. 12, pp. 7–12.

Greenwood, John (1988b), 'Hong Kong's Monetary System, *Asian Monetary Monitor*, Vol. 12, No. 1, pp. 1–13.

Greenwood, John (1995), 'Hong Kong: The Debate on the Optimum Monetary System', *Asian Monetary Monitor*, Vol. 19, No. 2, pp. 1–5.

Grilli, Vittorio, Donato Masciandaro and Guido Tabellini (1991), 'Political and Monetary Institutions and Public Financial Policies in the Industrial Countries', *Economic Policy*, No. 13, pp. 342–392.

Grimes, Arthur (1991), 'The Effects of Inflation on Growth: Some International Evidence', *Weltwirtschaftliches Archiv*, Vol. 127, pp. 632–644.

Grotius, Fritz (1949), 'Die Europäischen Geldreformen nach dem Zweiten Weltkrieg II', *Weltwirtschaftliches Archiv*, Vol. 63, pp. 276–325.

Grüner, Hans Peter (1998), 'Einige Anmerkungen zu den Determinanten wirtschaftlicher Stabilität', *Zeitschrift für Wirtschaftspolitik*, Vol. 47, pp. 20–41.

Gulde, Anne Marie (1999), *The Role of the Currency Board in Bulgaria's Stabilization*, IMF Policy Discussion Paper 99/3, Washington D.C.

Gwartney, James D. and Robert A. Lawson (1997), '*Economic Freedom of the World*', 1997 Annual Report, The Fraser Institute, Vancouver.

Gwartney, James D., Robert A. Lawson and Dexter Samida (2000), '*Economic Freedom of the World*', 2000 Annual Report, The Fraser Institute, Vancouver.

Hadziiossif, Christos (1987), 'Economic Stabilization and Political Unrest: Greese 1944-1947, in: Lars Bærentzen, John O. Iatrides and Ole L. Smith (eds.), Studies in the History of the Greek Civil War 1945–1949, Museum Tusculanum Press, Copenhagen.

Hajnal, Peter I. (1999), *The G7/G8 System, Evolution, Role and Documentation*, Ashgate, Aldershot, Brookfield, Singapore and Sydney.

Hanke, Steve H. (1996), *A Tale of Two Pesos: A Comparison of Currency Policies In Mexico and Argentina*, The Heritage Lectures 552, Washington D.C.

Hanke, Steve H., Lars Jonung and Kurt Schuler (1993), *Russian Currency and Finance: A Currency Board Approach to Reform*, Routledge, London and New York.

Hanke, Steve H. and Kurt Schuler (1994), *Currency Boards for Developing Countries*, International Center for Economic Growth, Sector Study No. 9, San Francisco.

Hanke, Steve H. and Kurt Schuler (1999), 'A Monetary Constitution for Argentina: Rules for Dollarization', *Cato Journal*, Vol. 19, pp. 405–419.

Hansen, Gerd (1993), *Quantitative Wirtschaftsforschung*, Verlag Franz Vahlen, München.

Hart, Albert G. (1948), *Money, Debt and Economic Activity*, Prentice Hall, New York.

Hausmann, Ricardo (2001), 'A way out for Argentina', *Financial Times*, October 29, 2001, www.news.ft.com.

Havrilesky, Thomas and James Granato (1993), 'Determinants of Inflationary Performance: Corporatist Structures vs. Central Bank Autonomy', *Public Choice*, Vol. 76, pp. 249–261.

Hayek, F.A. von (1990), *Denationalisation of Money – The Argument Refined*, Institute of Economic Affairs, Hobart Paper Special 70, London.

Hayo, Bernd (1998), 'Inflation Culture, Central Bank Independence and Price Stability', *European Journal of Political Economy*, Vol. 14, pp. 241–263.

Henderson, David (1999), *The Changing Fortune of Economic Liberalism. Yesterday, Today and Tomorrow*, The Institute of Public Affairs and New Zealand Business Roundtable, Melbourne and Wellington.

Hetzel, Robert L. (1990), 'The Political Economy of Monetary Policy', in: Thomas Mayer (ed.) *The Political Economy of American Monetary Policy*, Cambridge University Press, Cambridge, pp. 99–114.

Hetzel, Robert L. (1997), 'The Case for a Monetary Rule in a Constitutional Democracy', Federal Bank of Richmond, *Economic Quarterly*, Vol. 83/2, pp. 45–65.

Heymann, Daniel (1991), 'From Sharp Disinflation to Hyperinflation, Twice: The Argentine Experience, 1985–1989', in: Michael Bruno et al. (eds.)

Lessons of Economic Stabilization and Its Aftermath, The MIT Press, Cambridge, Mass. and London, pp. 103–141.

Hochreiter, Eduard and Georg Winckler (1994), 'Die Wechselkurspolitik der Österreichischen Nationalbank (OeNB). Beispiel einer erfolgreichen Wechselkursbindung', in: Dieter Duwendag (ed.) *Geld- und Währungspolitik in kleinen, offenen Volkswirtschaften: Österreich, Schweiz, Osteuropa*, Schriften des Vereins für Socialpolitik, Gesellschaft für Wirtschafts- und Sozialwissenschaften, Neue Folge, Vol. 230, Duncker und Humblot, Berlin, pp. 17–41.

Holtfrerich, Carl-Ludwig (1980), *Die deutsche Inflation 1914–1923, Ursachen und Folgen in internationaler Perspektive*, de Gruyter, Berlin and New York.

Honohan, Patrick (1996), 'Does It Matter How Seigniorage Is Measured?', *Applied Financial Economics*, Vol. 6, pp. 293–300.

Institute for Economic Policy (2001), *Central Bank Adresses*, http://www.uni-koeln.de/wiso-fak/iwp/.

International Monetary Fund (website): http://www.imf.org.

International Monetary Fund (a), *World Economic Outlook*, various issues, Washington D.C., quoted as IMFa.

International Monetary Fund (b), *International Financial Statistics*, various issues, Washington D.C., quoted as IMFb.

International Monetary Fund (c), *International Financial Statistics Yearbook*, various issues, Washington D.C., quoted as IMFc.

International Monetary Fund (d), *Exchange Arrangements and Exchange Restrictions, Annual Report*, various issues, Washington D.C., quoted as IMFd.

International Monetary Fund (e), *Economic Reviews*, Public Information Notices, various issues, Washington D.C., quoted as IMFe.

International Monetary Fund (1998), *Venezuela: Recent Economic Developments*, IMF Staff Country Report No. 98/117, Washington D.C.

International Monetary Fund (1999a), *Russian Federation: Recent Economic Developments*, IMF Staff Country Report No. 99/100, Washington D.C.

International Monetary Fund (1999b), *Venezuela: Statiscal Appendix*, IMF Staff Country Report No. 99/111, Washington D.C.

International Monetary Fund (2000), *IMF, World Bank, IDB and CAF Prepared to Support Ecuador*, News Brief No. 00/24, Washington D.C, http://www.imf.org/external/np/sec/nb/2000/NB0014.htm.

Issing, Otmar (1997), 'Geldwertstabilität als ordnungspolitisches Problem', *ORDO*, Vol. 48, pp. 167–178.

Issing Otmar (1999), *The Eurosystem: Transparent and Accountable*, CEPR Policy Paper No. 2, London.

James, Harold (1986), *The German Slump: Politics and Economics 1924–1936*, Clarendon Press, Oxford.

James, Harold (1996), *International Monetary Cooperation Since Bretton Woods*, International Monetary Fund and Oxford University Press, Washington D.C., New York and Oxford.

James, Harold (1998), 'Die Reichsbank 1876 bis 1945', in: Deutsche Bundesbank (ed.) *Fünfzig Jahre Deutsche Mark*, C.H. Beck, München, pp. 29–89.

Jankowski, Richard (2000), *An Error-corrections Model of Reaction Functions: The Case of Exchange-rate Intervention*, Paper Presented at the 2000 Annual Meeting of the Public Choice Society, March 12–14, Charleston, SC.

Jenkins, Michael A. (1996), 'Central Bank Independence and Inflation Performance: Panacea or Placebo?', *BNL Quarterly Review*, No. 197, pp. 241–270.

Johnson, Bryan T., Kim R. Holmes and Melanie Kirkpatrick (1999), *1999 Index of Ecomomic Freedom*, Heritage Foundation and *The Wall Street Journal*, Washington D.C. and New York.

Johnson, Harry G. (1972), 'The Monetary Approach to the Balance of Payments', in: Johnson Harry G. (ed.) *Further Essays in Monetary Economics*, London, pp. 229–249.

Johnson, Harry G. (1977), 'A Note on the Dishonest Government and the Inflation Tax', *Journal of Monetary Economics*, Vol. 3, pp. 375–377.

Jordan, Jerry L. (1995/6), 'Governments and Money', *Cato Journal*, Vol. 15, pp. 167–177.

Kallas, Siim and Mart Sörg (1993), 'Estonia's Currency Reform of 1992', *Bank of Finland Bulletin*, No. 3, pp. 3–7.

Kenen, Peter B. (1994), *Ways to Reform Exchange-rate Arrangements*, Reprints in International Finance, Princeton University Press, Princeton.

Kennedy, Peter (1992), *A Guide to Econometrics*, The MIT Press, Cambridge, Mass.

Keynes, John M. (1924), *Monetary Reform*, Harcourt, Brace & Co., New York.

Keynes, John M. (1936), *The General Theory of Employment, Interest and Money*, Macmillan, London et al.

Kiehling, Hartmut (2000) *Die Bevölkerung in der Hyperinflation 1922/23*, Regensburg, mimeo.

Kiguel, Miguel A. and Nissan Liviatan (1991), 'The Inflation-stabilization Cycles in Argentina and Brazil', in: Michael Bruno et al. (eds.) *Lessons of Economic Stabilization and Its Aftermath*, The MIT Press, Cambridge, Mass. and London, pp. 192–239.

Killick, Tony (1995), 'Can the IMF Help Low-income Countries? Experiences with its Structural Adjustment Facilities', *The World Economy*, Vol. 18, pp. 603–616.

Kirchgässner, Gebhard (1996), 'Geldpolitik und Zentralbankverhalten aus der Sicht der Neuen Politischen Ökonomie', in: Peter Bofinger and Karl-Heinz Ketterer (eds.) *Neuere Entwicklungen in der Geldtheorie und Geldpolitik*, Mohr (Siebeck), Tübingen, pp. 21–41.

Klein, Martin and Manfred J.M. Neumann (1990), 'Seigniorage: What is it and Who Gets it?', *Weltwirtschaftliches Archiv*, Vol. 126, pp. 205–221.

Klopstock, Fred H. (1946), 'Monetary Reform in Liberated Europe', *The American Economic Review*, Vol. 36, pp. 578–595.

Klump, Rainer (ed.) (1989), '40 Jahre Deutsche Mark', *Beiträge zur Wirtschafts- und Sozialgeschichte*, Bd. 39, Franz Steiner, Wiesbaden.

Klump, Rainer and Richard Reichel (1994), 'Institutional Uncertainty and Economic Development', *Jahrbücher für Nationalökonomie und Statistik*, Vol. 213/4, Stuttgart, pp. 441–455.

Krueger, Anne O. (1998), 'Whither the World Bank and the IMF', *Journal of Economic Literature*, Vol. 36, pp. 1983–2020.

Krugman, Paul R. and Maurice Obstfeld (1994), *International Economics: Theory and Policy*, 3rd edition, Harper Collins College Publishers, New York.

Kydland, Finn E. and Edward C. Prescott (1977), 'Rules Rather Than Discretion: The Inconsistency of Optimal Plans', *Journal of Political Economy*, Vol. 85, pp. 473–491.

Laidler, David and Michael Parkin (1975), 'The Theory of Inflation', *The Economic Journal*, Vol. 85, pp. 741–809.

Laso, Eduardo (1958), 'Financial Policies and Credit Control Techniques in Central America', *IMF Staff Papers*, Vol. 6, pp. 427–460.

Lawson, Tony (1997), *Economics and Reality*, Routledge, London and New York.

Leipold, Helmut (1997), 'Institutionelle Ursachen der wirtschaftlichen Unterentwicklung in Schwarzafrika', in: S. Paraskewopoulos (ed.) *Wirtschaftsordnung und wirtschaftliche Entwicklung*, Lucius & Lucius, Stuttgart, pp. 415–445.

Leipold, Helmut (1998), 'Die große Antinomie der Nationalökonomie: Versuch einer Standortbestimmung', *ORDO*, Vol. 49, pp. 15–42.

Leschke, Martin (1996), 'Die Funktion der Moral in der liberalen Gesellschaft – Die Perspektive der konstitutionellen Ökonomik' in: Ingo Pies and Martin Leschke (eds.) *James Buchanans konstitutionelle Ökonomik*, Mohr (Paul Siebeck), Tübingen, pp. 75-99.

Little, I.M.D, Richard N. Cooper, W. Max Corden and Sarath Rajapatirana (1993), *Boom, Crisis, and Adjustment: The Macoreconomic Experience of Developing Countries*, Oxford University Press, Oxford et al.

Lohmann, Susanne (1992), 'Optimal Commitment in Monetary Policy: Credibility versus Flexibility', *The American Economic Review*, Vol. 82, pp. 273–286.

Loungani, Prakash and Nathan Sheets (1997), 'Central Bank Independence, Inflation and Growth in Transition Economics', *Journal of Money, Credit and Banking*, Vol. 29, pp. 381–399.

Lucas, Robert E. Jr. (1996), 'Nobel Lecture: Monetary Neutrality', *Journal of Political Economy,* Vol. 104, pp. 661–682.

Ludwig, Michael (2001), 'Als Finazminister soll Marek Belka die Staatsfinanzen wieder in Ordnung bringen', *Frankfurter Allgemeine Zeitung* of October 1, 2001, p. 18.

Lutz, Friedrich A. (1949), 'The German Currency Reform and the Revival of the German Economy', *Economica*, Vol. 16, pp. 122–142.

Machinea, Jose Luis and Jose Maria Fanelli (1990), 'Stopping Hyperinflation: The Case of the Austral Plan in Argentina, 1985–87', in: Michael Bruno et al. (eds.), *Inflation Stabilization*, The MIT Press Cambridge, Mass. and London, pp. 111–151.

Makinen, Gail E. (1984), 'The Greek Stabilization of 1944-46', *The American Economic Review*, Vol. 74, pp. 1067–1074.

Marengo, Silvia and Augustin Vilar (2000), 'Central Bank Policies in Transition Economies: The Latin American Case', in: Federico Foders and Manfred Feldsieper (eds.) *The Transformation of Latin America. Economic Developments in the Early 1990s*, Edward Elgar, Cheltenham and Northampton, pp. 35–61.

Marsh, David (1992), *Die Bundesbank: Geschäfte mit der Macht*, Bertelsmann, München.

Mas, Ignacio (1995), 'Things Governments Do to Money: A Recent History of Currency Reform Schemes and Scams', *Kyklos*, Vol. 48, pp. 483–512.

Mastroberardino, Mónica Graciela (1994), *Kapitalflucht: Die Erfahrungen Argentiniens 1976–92*, Institut für Wirtschaftspolitik, Köln.

Mayer, Thomas (ed.) (1990) *The Political Economy of American Monetary Policy*, Cambridge University Press, Cambridge.

McCallum, Bennett T. (1995), 'Two Fallacies Concerning Central-bank Independence', *The American Economic Review, Papers and Proceedings*, Vol. 85, pp. 207–211.

McCallum, Bennett T. (1997), 'Crucial Issues Concerning Central Bank Independence', *Journal of Monetary Economics*, Vol. 39, pp. 99–112.

McCandless, George T. Jr. and Warren E. Weber (1995), 'Some Monetary Facts', *Federal Reserve Bank Minneapolis, Quarterly Review,* pp. 2–11.

Meier, Carsten-Patrick (1997), 'Assessing Convergence to Purchasing Power Parity: A Panel Study for Ten OECD Countries', *Weltwirtschaftliches Archiv*, Vol. 133, pp. 297–312.

Meltzer, Allan H. (1983), ' Monetary Reform in an Uncertain Environment', *Cato Journal*, Vo. 3, pp. 93–112.

Meyer, F.W. (1938), *Der Ausgleich der Zahlungsbilanz*, G. Fischer, Jena.

Moe, Therry M. (1990), 'Political Institutions: The Neglected Side of the Story', *Journal of Law, Economics, and Organization*, Vol. 6, pp. 213–253.

Moll, Robert (1994), *Ölreichtum, Unterentwicklung und Industrialisierungsanstrengungen: Venezuelas Erfahrungen mit der 'Holländischen Krankheit'*, Köln mimeo.

Monga, Célestin (1997), 'A Currency Reform Index for Western and Central Africa', *The World Economy*, Vol. 20, pp. 103–125.

Mueller, Dennis C. (1989), *Public Choice II*, Cambridge University Press, Cambridge.

Mundell, Robert A. (1969), 'The International Monetary Fund', *Journal of World Trade Law*, Vol. 3, pp. 455–456.

Murphy, Kevin M., Andrei Shleifer and Robert W. Vishny (1990), *The Allocation of Talent: Implications for Growth*, NBER Working Paper No. 3530, Cambridge, Mass.

Muth, John F. (1961), 'Rational Expectations and the Theory of Price Movements', *Econometrica*, Vol. 29, pp. 315–335.

Ndulu, Benno J. and Stephen A. O'Connell (1999), Governance and Growth in Sub-Saharan Africa, *The Journal of Economic Perspectives*, Vol. 13, No. 3, pp. 41–66.

Neumann, Manfred J.M. (1992), 'Seigniorage in the United States: How much does the U.S. Goverment make from Money Production?', *Federal Reserve Bank of St. Louis Review*, Vol. 74, pp. 29–40.

Neumann, Manfred J.M. (1996), 'A Comparative Study of Seigniorage: Japan and Germany, *Boj Monetary and Economic Studies*, Vol. 14, pp. 104–142.

Neumann, Manfred J.M. (1998), 'Geldwertstabilität: Bedrohung und Bewährung', in: Deutsche Bundesbank (ed.) *Fünfzig Jahre Deutsche Mark*, C.H. Beck, München, pp. 309–346.

Newlyn, W.T. (1962), *Theory of Money*, The Clarendon Press, Oxford.

New York University Law School (1999), Center for the Study of Central Banks, www.law.nyu.edu/centralbankscenter/.

North, Douglass C. (1993), 'Institutions and Credible Commitment', *Journal of Institutional Economics*, Vol. 149, pp. 11–23.

Nunnenkamp, Peter (1998), 'IMF Conditionality and Implications in Asia and Beyond', *Intereconomics*, Vol. 33, pp.64–72.

OECD (1998), *Poland*, Economic Surveys, Paris.

Parkin, Michael and Robin Bade (1977), *Central Bank Laws and Monetary Policies: A Preliminary Investigation*, University of Western Ontario, London, Ontario, mimeo.

Pedersen, Jørgen (1949), 'An Evaluation of Post-War Monetary Reforms', *Weltwirtschaftliches Archiv*, Vol. 62, pp. 198–213.

Persson, Torsten (1988), 'Credibility of Macroeconomic Policy: An Introduction and a Broad Survey', *European Economic Review*, Vol. 32, pp. 519–532.

Persson, Torsten and Guido Tabellini (1990), *Macroeconomic Policy, Credibility and Politics*, Harwood Publisher, London.

Pfleiderer, Otto (1979), 'Two Types of Inflation, Two Types of Currency Reform: The German Currency Miracles of 1923 and 1948', *Zeitschrift für die gesamte Staatswissenschaft*, Vol. 135, pp. 352–364.

Pick, Franz, *Pick's Currency Yearbook*, various issues, Pick Publishing Corporation, New York.

Pies, Ingo (1999), *Ordnungspolitik in der Demokratie – Ein ökonomischer Ansatz diskursiver Politikberatung*, Tübingen: Mohr Siebeck.

Polish Official Statistics (2001), http://www.stat.gov.pl./english/index.htm.

Posen, Adam S. (1993), 'Why Central Bank Independence Does Not Cause Low Inflation: There Is No Institutional Fix For Politics', in: Richard O'Brian (ed.) *Finance and the International Economy*, Vol. 7, Oxford University Press, Oxford, pp. 41–65.

Posen, Adam S. (1998), 'Central Bank Independence and Disinflationary Credibility: A Missing Link?', *Oxford Economic Papers*, Vol. 50, pp. 335–359.

Prast, Henriette M. (1996), 'Commitment Rather than Independence: An Institutional Design for Reducing the Inflationary Bias of Monetary Policy', *KYKLOS*, Vol. 49, pp. 377–405.

Radelet, Steven (1998), *Indonesia's Implosion*, mimeo, Harvard Institute for International Development, Harvard.

Raiser, Martin (1997), *Informal Institutions, Social Capital and Economic Transition: Reflections on a Neglected Dimension*, Working Paper No. 25, European Bank for Reconstruction and Development.

Randzio-Plath, Christa (1998), 'Die demokratische Rechenschaftspflichtigkeit der EZB muß erhöht werden', *Wirtschaftsdienst*, Vol. 78, pp. 269–276.

Richter, Rudolf (1996), 'Theorie der Notenbankverfassung aus Sicht der Neuen Institutionökonomik', in: Peter Bofinger and Karl-Heinz Ketterer (eds.) *Neuere Entwicklungen in der Geldtheorie und Geldpolitik*, Mohr (Siebeck), Tübingen, pp. 119-136.

Richter, Rudolf (1999), *Deutsche Geldpolitik 1948–1998*, Mohr (Siebeck), Tübingen.

Richter, Rudolf and Eirik Furubotn (1996), *Neue Institutionenökonomik: Eine Einführung und kritische Würdigung*, Mohr (Siebeck), Tübingen.

Rodrik, Dani (1996), 'Understanding Economic Policy Reform', *Journal of Economic Literature*, Vol. 34, pp. 9–41.

Rogoff, Kenneth (1985), 'The Optimal Degree of Commitment of an Intermediate Monetary Target', *Quarterly Journal of Economic*, Vol. 100, pp. 1169-1190.

Romer, David (1993), 'Openness and Inflation: Theory and Evidence', *Quarterly Journal of Economics*, Vol. 108, pp. 869–903.

Röpke, Wilhelm (1930), 'Zum Transferproblem bei internationalen Kapitalbewegungen', *Jahrbücher für Nationalökonomie und Statistik*, Vol. 139, reprinted in: Wilhem Röpke (1962), *Wirrnis und Wahrheit – Ausgewählte Aufsätze*, Eugen Rentsch Verlag: Zürich and Stuttgart.

Röpke, Wilhelm (1966), *Jenseits von Angebot und Nachfrage*, Eugen Rentsch Verlag, Erlenbach-Zürich, Stuttgart.

Röpke, Wilhelm (1979), *Internationale Ordnung – heute*, Wilhelm Röpke – Ausgewählte Werke, 3. Aufl., ed. by Friedrich August von Hayek, Hugo Sieber, Egon Tuchtfeldt and Hans Willgerodt, Karl Haupt, Bern.

Rülle, Thorsten and Ruz Knees (2000), 'Ecuador', *Perspektiven Spezial*, Dresdner Bank Lateinamerika, Hamburg.

Sachverständigenrat zur Begutachtung der gesamtwirtschaftlichen Entwicklung (1966), *Expansion und Stabilität*, Jahresgutachten 1966/67, W. Kohlhammer, Stuttgart and Mainz, quoted as SVR.

Sachverständigenrat zur Begutachtung der gesamtwirtschaftlichen Entwicklung (1998), *Vor Weitreichenden Entscheidungen*, Jahresgutachten 1998/99, Metzler-Poeschel, Stuttgart, quoted as SVR.

Samuelson Paul A. (1964), 'Theoretical Notes on Trade Problems', *Review of Economics and Statistics*, Vol. 46, pp. 145–154.

Samuelson Paul A. and William D. Nordhaus (1985) *Economics*, 12th edition, McGraw-Hill, Singapore.

Sargent, Thomas J. (1982), 'The Ends of Four Big Inflations', in: Robert E. Hall (ed.) *Inflations: Causes and Effects*, Chapter 2, Chicago: National Bureau of Economic Research and University of Chicago Press, pp. 41–97.

Sauermann, Heinz (1979), 'On the Economic and Financial Rehabilitation of Western Germany (1945–1949)', *Zeitschrift für die gesamte Staatswissenschaft*, Vol. 135, pp. 301–319.

Schadler, Susan and Rozwadowksi Franek et al. (1993), *Economic Adjustment in Low-income Countries*, IMF Occasional Paper 106, Washington D.C.

Schadler, Susan (1995), 'Can the IMF Help Low-income Countries: A Reply', *The World Economy*, Vol. 18, pp. 617–625.

Schadler, Susan et al. (1995), *IMF Conditionality: Experience under Stand-by and Extended Arrangements, Part I*, IMF Occasional Paper 128, Washington D.C.

Schadler, Susan (ed.) (1995), *IMF Conditionality: Experience under Stand-by and Extended Arrangements, Part II*, IMF Occasional Paper 129, Washington D.C.

Schaling, Eric (1995), *Institutions and Monetary Policy: Credibility, Flexibility and Central Bank Independence*, Edward Elgar, Aldershot.

Scheide, Joachim (1993), 'Preisniveaustabilität: Geldmengenregeln auch für unabhängige Notenbanken', *Zeitschrift für Wirtschaftspolitik*, Vol. 42, pp. 97–121.

Schneider, Friedrich and Alexander Wagner (1999), *The Role of International Monetary Institutions after the EMU and after the Asian Crisis: Some Preliminary Ideas Using Constitutional Economics*, Paper presented at the Annual Meeting of the Public Choice Society, New Orleans, March 13–15.

Schrader, Klaus and Claus-Friedrich Laaser (1994), *Die baltischen Staaten auf dem Weg nach Europa. Lehren aus der Süderweiterung der EG*, Mohr (Siebeck), Tübingen.

Schuler, Kurt (1992), *Currency Boards*, Ph.D. Thesis at the George Mason University, Fairfax, Virginia.

Schuler, Kurt (1996), *Should Developing Countries Have Central Banks? Currency Quality and Monetary Systems in 155 Countries*', Institute of Economic Affairs, Research Monograph No. 52, London.

Schuler, Kurt (1998), *Stabilizing the Indonesian Rupiah through a Currency Board*, http://www.users/erols.com/kurrency/indocybd.htm.

Schultz, T. Paul (1999), 'Health and Schooling Investment in Africa, *The Journal of Economic Perspectives*, Vol. 13, No. 3, pp. 67–88.

Schweickert, Rainer (2000), 'The Exchange Rate as a Nominal anchor in Mexico and Argentina: Old sins or New Insights? in: Federico Foders and Manfred Feldsieper (eds.) *The Transformation of Latin America. Economic Developments in the Early 1990s*, Edward Elgar, Cheltenham and Northampton, pp. 63–79.

Selgin, George A. (1988), 'A Free Banking Approach to Reforming Hong Kong's Monetary System', *Asian Monetary Monitor*, Vol. 12, No. 1, pp. 14–24.

Sepp, Urmas (1996), *The Economic Policy in Estonia*, Lohusalu, mimeo.

Sepp, Urmas and Martti Randveer (2001), *The Aspects of the Sustainability of the Estonian Currency Board Arrangement*, Paper prepared for the third workshop of the PHARE ACE project Alternatives of Exchange Rate Regime in Advanced Transition Countries in Vienna, September 21, 2001.

Sheffrin, Steven M. (1983), *Rational Expectations*, Cambrigde University Press, Cambridge.

Siebert, Horst (1999), *Improving the World's Financial Achitecture: The Role of IMF*, Institut für Weltwirtschaft, Kiel.

Sikken, Bernd Jan and Jakob de Haan (1998), 'Budget Deficits, Monetization, and Central Bank Independence in Developing Countries', *Oxford Economic Papers*, Vol. 50, pp. 493–511.

Smith, Vera C. (1936), *The Rationale of Central Banking and the Free Banking Alternative*, Liberty Press, Indianapolis.

Sörg, Mart (1999), 'Risks During the Restructuring of Banking: The Estonian Experience', *Eesti Pank Bulletin*, Vol. 45, pp. 23–39.

Sohmen, Egon (1969), *Flexible Exchange Rates*, Chicago and London.

Solveen, Ralph (1998), *Der Einfluß der Unabhängigkeit auf die Politik der Zentralbanken*, Mohr (Siebeck), Tübingen.

Statistisches Bundesamt (a) *Statistisches Jahrbuch für die Bundesrepublik Deutschland*, various issues, Kohlhammer, Stuttgart and Köln.

Statistisches Bundesamt (1994a), *Länderbericht Litauen*, Metzler-Poeschel, Stuttgart.

Statistisches Bundesamt (1994b), *Länderbericht Estland*, Metzler-Poeschel, Stuttgart.

Statistisches Bundesamt (1996), *Länderbericht Polen*, Metzler-Poeschel, Stuttgart.

Statistisches Reichsamt (a), *Statistisches Jahrbuch für das Deutsche Reich*, various issues, Verlag für Politik und Wirtschaft, Berlin.

Taylor, Charles and David A. Jodice (1983a), *World Handbook of Political and Social Indicators. Volume 1: Cross-national Attributes and Rates of Change*, Yale University Press, New Haven and London.

Taylor, Charles and David A. Jodice (1983b), *World Handbook of Political and Social Indicators. Volume 2: Political Protest and Government Change*, Yale University Press, New Haven and London.

The Economist (a), *The Economist*, various issues 1978–1999.

The Economist (1997), 'Fragile, Handle with Care. A Survey about Banking in Emerging Markets', *The Economist*, April 12, 1997.

The Economist (1998a), 'The Continent's Jubilant Left Breaks Free', *The Economist*, October 31, 1998, pp. 28–30.

The Economist (1998b), 'Central Banking', *The Economist*, November 14, 1998, pp. 21–28.

The Enzyclopedia Americana (1973), International Edition, Complete in Thirty Volumes, New York: Americana Corporation.

Tietmeyer, Hans and Caroline Willeke (1996), 'Zum Wechselverhältnis von Geldpolitik und Politik aus Sicht der Notenbank', in: Peter Bofinger and Karl-Heinz Ketterer (eds.) *Neuere Entwicklungen in der Geldtheorie und Geldpolitik*, Mohr (Siebeck), Tübingen pp. 43–69.

Tinbergen, Jan (1952), *On the Theory of Economic Policy*, North-Holland, Amsterdam.

Tkaczynski, Jan Wiktor and Klaus Mühlbauer (1998), 'Die Probleme des polnischen Geld- und Bankensystems in der Transformation', *Osteuropa-Wirtschaft*, Vol. 43, pp. 174–202.

Triffin, Robert (1946), *Monetary and Banking Reform in Paraguay*, Federal Reserve System, Washington D.C.

Tumlir, Jan (1983) 'International Economic Order and Democratic Constitutionalism', *ORDO*, 34, pp. 71–86.

Tumlir, Jan (1985), *Protectionism: Trade Policy in Democratic Societies*, American Enterprise Institute for Public Policy Research, Washington D.C.

Ugolini, Piero (1996), *National Bank of Poland: The Road to Indirekt Instruments*, IMF Occasional Paper 144, Washington D.C.

United Nations: *International Trade Statistics Yearbook*, various issues, New York.

Valavanis, Stefan (1959), *Econometrics: An Introduction to Maximum Likelihood Methods*, McGraw-Hill, New York, Toronto and London.

Vanberg, Viktor (1998), 'Freiburg School of Law and Economics', in: Peter Newman (ed.) *The New Palgrave Dictionary of Economics and the Law*, Vol. 2, Macmillan, London, pp. 172–179.

Vane, Howard R. and John L. Thompson (1992), *Current Controversies in Macroeconomics – an Intermediate Text*, Edward Elgar, Aldershot and Brookfield.

Vaubel, Roland (1983), *The German Stabilisation of 1923/4: Lessons for Liberalization Today*, Paper prepared for the conference on Tactics of Liberalization, Madrid, March 17–20.

Vaubel, Roland (1986), 'A Public Choice Approach to International Organization', *Public Choice*, Vol. 51, pp. 39–57.

Vaubel, Roland (1991a), 'A Public Choice View of International Organization', in: Roland Vaubel and Thomas D. Willett (eds.) *The Political Economy of International Organizations: A Public Choice Approach*, Westview Press, Boulder, San Francisco and Oxford, pp. 27–45.

Vaubel, Roland (1991b), 'The Political Economy of the International Monetary Fund: A Public Choice Analysis', in: Roland Vaubel and Thomas D. Willett (eds.) *The Political Economy of International Organization: A Public Choice Approach*, Boulder, San Francisco and Oxford, pp. 204–244.

Vaubel, Roland (2000), 'The Future of the Euro: A Public Choice Perspective', in: Forrest Capie and Geoffrey Wood (eds.) *Monetary Unions*, Macmillan, Houndsmill et al., forthcoming.

Végh, Carlos A. (1995), 'Stopping High Inflation: An Analytical Overview', in: Pierre L. Siklos (ed.) *Great Inflations of the 20th Century*, Edward Elgar, Aldershot and Brookfield, pp. 35–93.

Vickers, John (1986), 'Signalling in a Model of Monetary Policy with Incomplete Information', *Oxford Economic Papers*, Vol. 38, pp. 443–455.

Viñals, José and Javier Valles (1999), *On the Real Effects of Monetary Policy: A Central Banker's View*, Centre for Economic Policy Research, Discussion Paper Series No. 2241.

Wallich, Henry C. (1955), *Triebkräfte des deutschen Wiederaufstieges*, Frankfurt.

Walsh, Carl E. (1995), 'Optimal Contracts for Central Bankers', *The American Economic Review*, Vol. 85, pp. 151–167.

Wandel, Eckhard (1979), 'Historical Developments Prior to the German Currency Reform', *Zeitschrift für die gesamte Staatswissenschaft*, Vol. 135, pp. 320–331.

Weizsäcker, Carl Christian von (2000), 'Über die Schlusspassage der General Theory – Gedanken zum Einfluss ökonomischer Theorie auf die Politik', *Perspektiven der Wirtschaftspolitik*, Vol. 1, pp. 35–52.

Welfens, Paul (1998), 'Nur eine Scheintransformation', *Frankurter Allgemeine Zeitung* of September 19, 1998, p.15.

Welfens, Paul (1999), 'Die Russische Tranformationskrise: Monetäre und reale Aspekte sowie Politikoptionen', *Kredit und Kapital*, Vol. 32, pp. 331–368.

Wentzel, Dirk (1995), *Geldordnung und Systemtransformation: Ein Beitrag zur ökonomischen Theorie der Geldverfassung*, Fischer, Stuttgart, Jena, New York.

White, Halbert (1980), 'A Heteroscedasticity-consistent Covariance Matrix Estimator and a Direct Test for Heteroscedasticity', *Econometrica*, Vol. 48, pp. 817–838.

White, Lawrence H. (1999), *The Theory of Monetary Institutions*, Blackwell Publishers, Malden and Oxford.

Willgerodt, Hans (1978), 'Die "motivierte Zahlungsbilanztheorie" – Vom "schicksalhaften Zahlungsbilanzdefizit" und der Unsterblichkeit falscher Inflationslehren', in: Helmut Gröner and Alfred Schüller (eds.), *Internationale Wirtschaftsordnung*, Gustav Fischer Verlag, Stuttgart and New York, pp. 215–238.

Willgerodt, Hans (1990), 'Das Problem des politischen Geldes', *Hamburger Jahrbuch für Wirtschafts- undGesellschaftspolitik*, Vol. 35, pp. 129–147.

Williamson, John (ed.) (1994), *The Political Economy of Policy Reform*, Institute for International Economics, Washington D.C.

Williamson, John (1994), 'In Search of a Manual for Technopols', in: John Williamson (ed.) *The Political Economy of Policy Reform,* Institute for International Economics, Washington D.C., pp. 11–28.

Williamson, John and Stephan Haggard (1994), 'The Political Conditions for Economic Reform', in: John Williamson (ed.) *The Political Economy of Policy Reform*, Institute for International Economics, Washington D.C., pp. 527–596.

Wood, John H. (1997), '*Companies of Merchants: A Survey of the Theory and Practice of Central Banking*', Wake Forest University, mimeo.

World Bank (1996), *Trends in Developing Economies*, Washington D.C.

World Bank (1999), *Key Events of the Indonesian Crisis*, http://www.worldbank.org/html/extdr/offrep/eap/invents.htm.

Yeager, Leland B. et al. (1981) *Experiences with Stopping Inflation*, American Enterprise Institute, Washington D.C. and London.

Name Index

Subject Index